Statistics and Research Methods
Third Edition

PEARSON

We work with leading authors to develop the strongest educational materials bringing cutting-edge thinking and best learning practice to a global market.

Under a range of well-known imprints, including Financial Times/Prentice Hall, Addison Wesley and Longman, we craft high quality print and electronic publications which help readers to understand and apply their content, whether studying or at work.

Pearson Custom Publishing enables our customers to access a wide and expanding range of market-leading content from world-renowned authors and develop their own tailor-made book. You choose the content that meets your needs and Pearson Custom Publishing produces a high-quality printed book.

To find out more about custom publishing, visit www.pearsoncustom.co.uk

PEARSON CUSTOM PUBLISHING

Statistics and Research Methods
Third Edition

Compiled from:

Introduction to Research Methods and Data Analysis in Psychology
Second Edition
by Darren Langdridge and Gareth Hagger-Johnson

Introduction to Research Methods in Psychology
Third Edition
by Dennis Howitt and Duncan Cramer

Research Methods: A Practical Guide for The Social Sciences
by Bob Matthews and Liz Ross

Specially prepared material by Dr Paul Warren

ALWAYS LEARNING PEARSON

Harlow, England • London • New York • Boston • San Francisco • Toronto • Sydney • Auckland • Singapore • Hong Kong
Tokyo • Seoul • Taipei • New Delhi • Cape Town • Sao Paulo • Mexico City • Madrid • Amsterdam • Munich • Paris • Milan

Pearson Education Limited
Edinburgh Gate
Harlow
Essex CM20 2JE

And associated companies throughout the world

Visit us on the World Wide Web at:
www.pearsoned.co.uk

First Published 2011
This Custom Book Edition © Pearson Education Limited 2013

Compiled from:

Introduction to Research Methods and Data Analysis in Psychology
Second Edition
Darren Langdridge and Gareth Hagger-Johnson
ISBN 978 0 13 198203 1
© Pearson Education Limited 2009

Introduction to Research Methods in Psychology
Third Edition
Dennis Howitt and Duncan Cramer
ISBN 978 0 273 73499 4
© Pearson Education Limited 2005, 2011

Research Methods: A Practical Guide for The Social Sciences
Bob Matthews and Liz Ross
ISBN 978 1 4058 5850 2
© Pearson Education Limited 2010

Specially prepared material by Dr Paul Warren

All rights reserved. No part of this publication may be reproduced, stored in a retrieval system, or transmitted in any form or by any means, electronic, mechanical, photocopying, recording or otherwise, without either the prior written permission of the publisher or a licence permitting restricted copying in the United Kingdom issued by the Licensing Agency Ltd, Saffron House, 6–10 Kirby Street, London EC1N 8TS.

ISBN 978 1 78365 954 8

Printed and bound in Great Britain by Clays Ltd, Bungay, Suffolk

Contents

Starting out in research   1
Chapter 1 in *Introduction to Research Methods and Data Analysis in Psychology*
Second Edition
Darren Langdridge and Gareth Hagger-Johnson

Variables: definitions and measurement   38
Chapter 2 in *Introduction to Research Methods and Data Analysis in Psychology*
Second Edition
Darren Langdridge and Gareth Hagger-Johnson

Reliability, validity, sampling and groups   48
Chapter 3 in *Introduction to Research Methods and Data Analysis in Psychology*
Second Edition
Darren Langdridge and Gareth Hagger-Johnson

Collecting data 1: interviews and observation   59
Chapter 4 in *Introduction to Research Methods and Data Analysis in Psychology*
Second Edition
Darren Langdridge and Gareth Hagger-Johnson

Collecting data 2: questionnaires and psychometric tests   85
Chapter 5 in *Introduction to Research Methods and Data Analysis in Psychology*
Second Edition
Darren Langdridge and Gareth Hagger-Johnson

Fundamentals of qualitative research   111
Chapter 17 in *Introduction to Research Methods and Data Analysis in Psychology*
Second Edition
Darren Langdridge and Gareth Hagger-Johnson

Sampling   123
Chapter B5 in *Research Methods: A Practical Guide for The Social Sciences*
Bob Matthews and Liz Ross.

Transcribing, coding and organising textual data   145
Chapter 18 in *Introduction to Research Methods and Data Analysis in Psychology*
Second Edition
Darren Langdridge and Gareth Hagger-Johnson

The ethics and politics of psychological research   159
Chapter 25 in *Introduction to Research Methods and Data Analysis in Psychology*
Second Edition
Darren Langdridge and Gareth Hagger-Johnson

Evaluating and writing up qualitative research — 172

Chapter 25 in *Introduction to Research Methods in Psychology*
Third Edition
Dennis Howitt and Duncan Cramer

Tables — 185

Table A1:
z-scores and the proportion of the standard normal distribution falling above and below each score — 185

Dr Paul Warren

Table A2:
r to zr — 189

Dr Paul Warren

Table A3:
Critical values for student's t-distribution — 190

Dr Paul Warren

Table A4:
Critical values for the Pearson correlation coefficient — 191

Dr Paul Warren

Table A5:
Critical values for the chi-square distribution — 192

Dr Paul Warren

Table A6:
Critical values for the Mann-Whitney U-test: 5% level of significance — 193

Introduction to Research Methods and Data Analysis in Psychology
Second Edition
Darren Langdridge and Gareth Hagger-Johnson

Table A7:
Critical values for the Spearman correlation coefficient — 194

Introduction to Research Methods and Data Analysis in Psychology
Second Edition
Darren Langdridge and Gareth Hagger-Johnson

Table A8:
Critical values for the Wilcoxon Signed Rank Test — 195

Introduction to Research Methods and Data Analysis in Psychology
Second Edition
Darren Langdridge and Gareth Hagger-Johnson

1 Starting out in research

- This chapter explains why we need good quality research in psychology.
- It begins by introducing social science research and the philosophy underpinning it.
- It then covers the differences between quantitative and qualitative research methods.
- Finally, this chapter will introduce you to the nature of the research process itself, including the vital role of searching the literature.

INTRODUCTION

Let us start the journey. Research methods are the backbone of the social sciences and vital in the production of knowledge in psychology. They may not appear to be the most entertaining of topics to study but we promise to try to entertain you as long as you promise to read. If we had one wish as teachers of research methods it would be for all of our students to read about them. Like all good (although maybe our students should be the judge of that) teachers we provide up-to-date reading lists at the start of all our courses and talk our students through all the books on offer. But we are pretty sure a lot of our students do not read much about research methods and we cannot really blame them. Most research methods textbooks are not the sort of thing you want to sit down and read from cover to cover, especially when you have the allure of other more intrinsically interesting books (or the pub, of course). But we guarantee you will find your degree in psychology goes a lot smoother with a little reading about research methods, so stick with it and give it your best shot. You may even like what you read.

1.1 Why research?

We will start by explaining just what research methods are and why you need to complete several years of courses on research methods and data analysis during a degree in any social science, but most especially in psychology. In short, research is the systematic study of some topic in order to find answers to questions. In psychology these questions are invariably (though not exclusively) about people – while in chemistry, for example, they are about chemical things. The important issue at stake here is what evidence we can provide for the questions we ask and answers we give. So, if we want to know whether there is a difference between men and women in driving ability and, most particularly, whether women are safer drivers, we would want to provide evidence for any claims we make. Every day we see, hear and read things based on so-called 'common sense':

- Watching sex on television is harmful to children (or violence on television produces a more violent society).
- Children living with single parents do less well in school than children living with two parents.
- Women are more naturally caring and therefore make better parents than men.
- Men are better at mathematics than women.

However, these beliefs are often based on prejudice, speculation or just simply misinformation. Unless we have evidence, from good quality research (and it is very important that the research is good quality), we cannot make any reliable claims (for or against) these statements. As good psychological researchers we want better than that. Why else do we study this subject? We want to be able to contribute to debates such as these, understand more about human nature and provide evidence that either supports or challenges statements such as these. And this is why we need to know about methods of research and data analysis. Only through knowledge of research methods can we carry out good quality research that elevates our findings above the opinion and speculation that we encounter on an almost daily basis on TV, in the papers or in everyday conversation.

We need think only of some classic psychological findings to realise the value of good quality research. The studies by Solomon Asch (1951, 1952, 1956) on group conformity are a good example (see Box 1.1).

> **Box 1.1 Study box**
>
> Asch, S. E. (1956). Studies of independence and conformity: I. A minority of one against a unanimous majority. *Psychological Monographs*, **70** (9) (whole issue, no. 416).
>
> Asch recruited participants for a study on 'visual perception'. If you were a participant you would find yourself seated in the second to last row in a laboratory (with only one person behind you) and six to eight people in front of you. You would not realise that the other participants (who are all confederates, that is, people working with the experimenter) forced you into this seating position. You are asked to judge the lengths of vertical lines drawn on a board at the front of the room. There is one standard line and three comparison lines. All the people in the room are asked to call out which line is the same length as the standard line. The answer is very obvious as one line is the same length and the other two lines are either much shorter or longer than the standard line. Answers are called out person by person from front to back along the rows. In the first test everyone announces the correct answer and calls out the letter attached to the line that matches the length of the standard line shown on the board. Then the experimenter puts up a board with another standard line and three comparison lines (again with one obvious match). Once again, one by one, the participants (starting at the front) call out the correct answer. However, in the third round of the test with yet another board (once again with an obvious line match), the first participant calls out the wrong line letter, and so does the next person and the next (six people in total) until it is your turn. Of course you think you would give the correct answer regardless of what everyone else said as it was obvious what was the correct answer. Well, it is not that simple. Asch found that one in three people went along with the group and gave the wrong answer when it came to their turn to call out the letter of the matching line. Asch knew that the choice was obvious because he repeated the experiment with participants writing their answers privately on paper and the judgements were almost totally error free (less than 1 per cent of mistakes). It was obvious to Asch that the participant went along with the group because of the effect of group pressure and the desire to conform. This finding was found time and time again as Asch and others replicated the experiment and it has established itself as an extremely strong and stable psychological finding about human nature.

The Asch studies used an innovative experimental method to manipulate the participants and demonstrate a particular aspect of human behaviour. The thing to remember from this example is that the fascinating findings obtained about conformity and group pressure only happened through appropriate knowledge and use of research methods. Without an understanding of research methods we would not be able to carry out studies like this and make claims about human nature that are any better than 'common sense', and psychology would be a much more limited discipline.

1.2 A very brief history of science

First we must begin by stating that this will be a very (!) brief history of psychological research (if you want to explore the history of psychology and the social sciences in more detail look at the Further reading section at the end of the chapter for some suggested reading material). We will move rapidly (and superficially) through a great deal of history in order to show how current debates about particular approaches to research methods came about. We will also introduce you to several new ideas, which should enable you to understand more about the nature of psychological research today (and the structure of this book).

The beginnings of science

Social research as we know it today emerged out of a scientific age. Very early thinkers (before the sixteenth century) who wrote about human nature tended to speculate at a very general level about the nature of humanity and/or rely on their status as an 'authority' for justification of their arguments. Often these speculations were sophisticated and insightful but they were rarely based on evidence collected in a systematic manner. However, Francis Bacon (1561–1626) and Isaac Newton (1642–1727), working in the physical sciences (what we now tend to understand as biology, chemistry and physics), clearly and widely demonstrated the value of empirical work in making claims about the world. That is, work based on experience – invariably through observation of or experimentation with the natural world rather than theory or speculation. It is important to note that early scientists such as these still thought they were studying processes created by God, albeit in scientific ways. This scientific approach emerged as a force to be reckoned with, as it enabled technological innovations that had practical and beneficial impact on life at that time.

It is perhaps not surprising given the success of the physical sciences that many of the early figures in the social sciences wanted to position their work within the realm of science, for with science came credibility and respectability. So, for instance, Sigmund Freud (1856–1939) proclaimed his work to be the scientific study of human nature. At that time it was widely believed that the same scientific methods were applicable to both the physical and the social sciences and indeed this belief continues to this day among many psychologists. Freud, one of the early psychological theorists and founder of psychoanalytic theory, used clinical case studies based on therapeutic interviews with his patients to generate data and then theories (we talk more about these particular methods in Chapter 4). His theories about human nature came from close observation of his patients and led to an enormous body of work which still influences the discipline today. Psychoanalytic theory has, however, been subject to considerable criticism for not being scientific at all despite the claims of its founder to the contrary. The over-reliance on clinical case study to provide data has led to charges of bias in the data collected. But perhaps the most significant criticism that is levelled at psychoanalytic theory concerns the perceived lack of concrete testable statements about the theory. Instead, critics have argued that psychoanalytic theory is not scientific at all, for (1) there is little possibility of testing the imprecise statements that stem from theory, and (2) even when evidence provides a challenge to the statement it is not rejected but merely modified to fit the evidence. We will come back to some of these issues later when discussing the work of the philosopher Karl Popper, who strongly argued against psychoanalysis as a science (and also again in Chapter 17 when introducing qualitative methods).

Later psychological theorists have tended, often as a reaction against psychoanalysis, to embrace (what they believed to be) scientific methods more strongly (often more strongly than theorists in the natural sciences!). For instance, behaviourism emerged as the dominant approach to psychology in the middle of the twentieth century. Behaviourists concentrated on only that which was directly observable and dismissed research into the workings of the mind (like psychoanalysis and what we now call cognitive psychology) as unscientific. They believed that only through study of directly observable events could psychology be a truly scientific discipline. In their defence, this is not an untenable position. There are good philosophical arguments that lend support to this position. Needless to say, many others disagreed with this position. Cognitive psychologists believed that it was possible, and indeed scientific, to study the workings of the mind. This position became more and more influential and in the early 1980s cognitive psychology became the dominant theoretical approach in the discipline. At the same time, interest in behaviourism lessened. Although interest in behaviourism still continues to this day, it is no longer the dominant approach to psychological research that it once was. More recently, we can see other movements in the discipline that provide radical challenges to the dominant cognitivism. These approaches do not necessarily seek to be scientific at all and provide an alternative to more 'traditional' scientific psychological research. We will talk more about these recent developments later in this chapter and then again in Part 3 when we introduce the range of qualitative research methods within psychology that have assumed increasing importance in recent years.

So what is science?

This is not as simple a question as it seems. Although many people believe there is a single approach to method that we call science, the truth is that the criteria for scientific knowledge are controversial and subject to considerable debate. The desire to clearly explicate the scientific method exists because it is believed by many that only through use of the scientific method can we be confident in the quality of the knowledge we obtain about the world.

Perhaps the easiest way to answer the question posed at the start of this section is to contrast knowledge about the world obtained through science (or scientific investigation) with ordinary everyday (or 'common-sense') knowledge. Chalmers (1999: 1) starts his excellent discussion of the philosophy of science through an examination of the widely held 'common-sense' view of science:

When it is claimed that science is special because it is based on the facts, the facts are presumed to be claims about the world that can be directly established by a careful, unprejudiced use of the senses. Science is to be based on what we can see, hear and touch rather than personal opinions or speculative imaginings. If observation of the world is carried out in a careful, unprejudiced way then the facts established in this way will constitute a secure, objective basis for science.

This mistaken view still remains a widely held view about the nature of science. It is this understanding of science, in various guises, that has been taken up by many social scientists and most particularly psychologists. As you can see, the two factors that mark out science from everyday knowledge in this formulation are that we (1) acquire information about the world through experience and (2) that the information we acquire in this way is objective. The first claim, that science should be based on empirical evidence (evidence acquired through experience, observation, experimentation and so on), is less controversial for psychologists as many (but not all) would support this position. Without empirical data derived from good quality research many psychologists believe we would have no findings and therefore no evidence to enable us to make claims about human nature.[1] However, even this first issue is not as straightforward as it seems, for many 'mature sciences' such as physics do not simply rely on the collection of data for their advancement. Indeed, some of the most important and exciting work in physics is theoretical and not empirical at all. The second statement, that science (and therefore psychology if it claims to be a science) must be objective, is even more controversial. Many psychologists would support this claim and believe strongly that one of the central purposes of research methods is to enable us to collect empirical data that are objective and free from bias. These people believe that this approach enables psychologists to make stronger claims about human nature than those based on subjective information derived through everyday experience. While many, if not all, psychologists would wish for their research to be privileged above common sense, not all believe that we can claim the work we do is objective. Instead these psychologists argue that a more useful (and better/more accurate/realistic) understanding of the nature of the discipline comes about when we do in fact explicitly recognise the subjective nature of the research process. We will come

---

[1] It is important to clarify what we mean by empirical (and empiricist) here. In a very strict sense empiricism is based on the assumption that all knowledge claims about the world must be derived through direct experience of the world (through our five senses). Very few people would subscribe to this very strict definition today as it is generally believed that direct experience does not provide incontrovertible access to truths about the world. However, modern-day adherents of empiricism believe that gathering data (often through experimentation using instruments and tests rather than through direct experience) does move us closer to the truth than theoretical argument alone. Willig (2001) clearly and importantly marks out the difference between the terms **empiricism** and **empirical** as follows: 'While "empiricist" refers to the attitude that all knowledge claims must be grounded in data, "empirical" is a descriptive term referring to research involving the collection and analysis of data' (p. 4). And psychology is very much an empirical discipline.

back to these issues in more detail later when we discuss the differences between **quantitative** and **qualitative research** in the social sciences.

Induction

Induction is the process by which scientists decide on the basis of multiple observations or experiments that some theory is true or not. If we observe natural phenomena, such as the effect of a Bunsen burner flame on a chemical element like sodium, we can conclude, on the basis of multiple observations, a general principle: that all sodium glows orange when heated with a flame. The common nature of induction is that through a finite number of observations (or experiments) we generate a general conclusion for all such future observations (or experiments). A great deal of science relies on this principle. Drug efficacy and safety provide one obvious example. On the basis of repeated drug trials we learn which drugs are effective in treating which conditions and we also learn which drugs are safe for us to consume and which are not. Because we have repeatedly found a drug to work (and be safe) in these trials, we conclude that it will always act in this way in the future.

However, there is a problem with the method of induction that has challenged philosophers of science for many years. The problem is a simple one to pose but a very difficult one to answer (if it is possible to answer at all): how can a finite number of observations about some event in the past (such as the effect of a flame on sodium or a drug in treating some illness) *guarantee* that we will always see this same effect in the future? Firstly, we can never be certain that we have considered the full range of relevant conditions, and secondly, there is no certainty that the course of nature will not change. We cannot know with certainty that in the future sodium will always glow orange or the drug will work in the same way. Think of it like this. We set you the task of observing and describing the bird that we commonly know as the swan. You go out and about the lakes in the United Kingdom and observe a common pattern. The swan is a large white bird. Observation after observation demonstrates that the swan is always large and white when an adult. Therefore, you conclude, on the basis of your multiple observations, that *all* swans are large white birds. You have used induction from a finite number of cases to make a general theory (or in science, law) about the natural world. However, the next summer you go on holiday to Australia and discover a black swan on your first visit to a lake. This one observation immediately overturns your general theory of swans despite the very large number of observations you had in support of your theory. The problem is that we can never guarantee that our general conclusion formed from a number of observations (even if the number of observations is very large) will always follow in the future. This is, of course, a major problem for all scientific research that relies on an inductive approach to theory generation.

Popper and the need for falsifiability

Sir Karl Popper (1902–1994) responded to the problem of induction with what he believed to be the solution for scientific research. His arguments remain extremely influential in science and the philosophy of science today. Popper (1963) argued that science does not rely on induction in the first place. He thought that science started with theories (or in his words 'conjectures') which it sought to test. These initial theories were intuitive and lacking supporting evidence. Scientists seek to test their theories (or conjectures) through observation or experimentation to ascertain whether they stand up to the test. If they do not stand up to the test we must reject the theory or conjecture and start again with an alternative. If the theory or conjecture does work when tested then scientists are able to continue to uphold the theory (not as a statement of truth about the world but as an undefeated theory). In this form, Popper essentially argues that we learn from our mistakes. Science understood in this way does not therefore rely on induction. For Popper it is the *falsifiability* of conjectures that matters when making scientific inferences and not repeated positive tests of a conjecture. Evidence in support of a conjecture, from a finite number of observations – an inductive approach – is not important. What is important is that science forms clearly testable conjectures or theories which it then seeks to refute. Science is simply a series of 'conjectures and refutations' (the title of Popper's 1963 book on the topic).

But what separates science from non-science for Popper? If we do not search for evidence supporting a theory but only evidence designed to refute a theory, what makes physics a science and astrology a non-science? Popper termed this the 'problem of demarcation'. He believed that the key issue that separates science from non-science is that scientific conjectures are *at least falsifiable*. That is, they are always framed as clear and explicit statements that can be tested and refuted if the evidence from empirical research fails to support them. In contrast, disciplines that are not scientific, such as astrology, do not provide clear and explicit conjectures that can be refuted. Their conjectures are so imprecise that no evidence can ever serve to disprove the theory. Popper used the criterion of falsifiability to separate science from non-science and marked out psychoanalysis as a 'pseudo-science' despite its claims to be scientific (see Box 1.2).

Box 1.2

Activity box — **Science and pseudo-science**

- In pairs spend some time thinking of a couple of key conjectures (or theories) put forward by astrology or psychoanalysis. Write these down as clearly and explicitly as possible.
- Now plan a study to test the conjectures you have written.
    - Can these conjectures be falsified by your study? Does this differ from conjectures put forward in chemistry, physics or biology? Why?
    - How do you think astrologers or psychoanalysts would respond to and explain your findings if the conjectures were falsified? Do you think chemists, physicists or biologists would react differently? Why?

The failings of falsification and Bayesianism

Although Popper's ideas remain influential in science today, they have been subjected to considerable criticism. The principal criticism is an obvious one. While Popper has produced a sophisticated understanding of science that enables us to separate science from pseudo-science, he has not actually dealt with the problem of induction at all. He has not given us a way of understanding *positive* scientific knowledge, only *negative* scientific knowledge. And for most scientists it is *positive* scientific knowledge that is the most important. Popper shows us that a single negative example can disprove a theory but provides no mechanism for judging whether a theory is right or not. We treat and cure illnesses because we know that certain causes (such as a drug) always (as far as we can tell) have certain effects (such as a cure for illness). We need to know why we should prefer one theory to another and for that we need some criteria for judging the quality of theories on the basis of how much evidence we have in support of them. Popper seems to have ignored what is arguably most important for science.

So, how are we going to resolve the problem of induction? For if we believe in positive science and the benefits of past observations (or experiments) in predicting future effects we need to deal with the problem of induction. One possible (although not perfect) solution has been proposed by the Bayesians (named after Thomas Bayes, 1701–1761). Bayesians are philosophers who argue that our beliefs (including scientific beliefs) come in degrees. So, for example, we may believe that there is a 50 per cent chance (or 0.5 degree likelihood) of rain tomorrow and only a 10 per cent chance (or 0.1 degree likelihood) of snow. That is, we express the likelihood of future events on the basis of past knowledge. These degrees of belief are the extent to which events are subjectively probable (and we will talk about probability much more in later chapters on statistics).

The essence of Bayesianism is that it does not matter what degree of probability you assign to some event in the first place (for instance, when you propose a conjecture or theory) as long as you revise your probability prediction in a rational way when faced with evidence in support of or against your conjecture. With this principle in mind we can see a way through the problem of induction. For, although we still cannot state with absolute certainty that sodium will always glow orange when subjected to a flame or a particular drug will always cure an illness, we can state that it is very likely that they will act in these ways in the future because we have so much evidence in support of these conjectures from past observations. It is highly probable that sodium will burn orange and we would be very surprised if it did not. The Bayesian approach to probability enables us to revise our conjectures on the basis of empirical evidence and be confident (or not) to different degrees in the strength of our conjectures on the basis of past evidence. This clearly enables us to say something about our knowledge of the world on the basis of positive evidence supporting our theories.

Like all philosophical principles the Bayesian approach has been the subject of considerable criticism. In essence, the criticism concerns the subjective nature of the judgements being made about probability and inherent difficulties in deciding between two competing positions. However, even accepting this difficulty, we think it serves as a useful way of understanding the nature of particular approaches to the generation of social scientific knowledge. If you want to read more about this approach and the debates surrounding it, see Chalmers (1999).

The hypothetico-deductive method

The approach most commonly understood as the principal scientific method within the social sciences is known as the **hypothetico-deductive** method. This is often, mistakenly, contrasted with the method of induction. In fact this approach must be seen in relation to an inductive approach rather than in opposition to it. The hypothetico-deductive approach first entails the researcher producing **hypotheses** (or specific predictions) to be tested. These predictions are subject to some empirical test and deductions made from the results of the test. Most often the hypotheses to be tested stem from **theories** about the object of study. Theories are systems of ideas or statements that explain some phenomena. They are generally derived from previous inductive research (series of observations for instance) or through intuition and reasoning. Through empirical tests of the hypotheses we can find evidence that supports or challenges our theory. If there is evidence to challenge the hypothesis it is rejected and the theory must be abandoned or amended to account for the data. If the test produces evidence in support of our hypothesis we can say we have support for our hypothesis and therefore our theory (see Fig. 1.1).

The hypothetico-deductive approach continues in a cyclical fashion, with hypotheses generated from theories being tested empirically and this evidence providing support for or challenges to the theory that generated the hypotheses. On this basis, increasing knowledge is gathered about the object of study and theories are developed and modified to account for the empirical data we have about the world. Much, though not all, research in psychology follows this hypothetico-deductive approach. This has prompted criticism from some

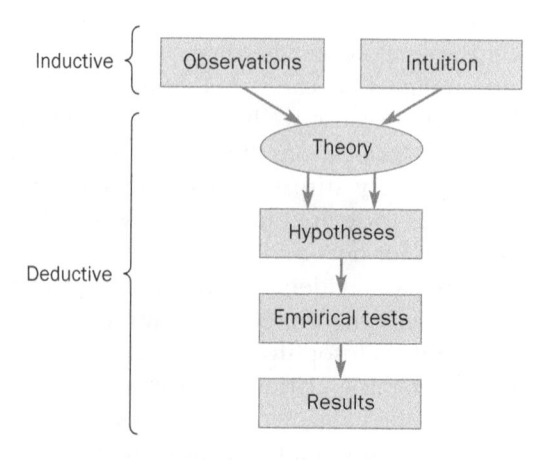

Figure 1.1 The hypothetico-deductive approach

people who believe that psychology has moved too quickly to model itself on a particular, rather restricted, view of the natural sciences. This move is considered a problem, for many people believe that the discipline has not yet built a sufficiently strong base of knowledge discerned from inductive research to produce generally accepted systems of ideas, or **paradigms**, that can be tested (Kuhn, 1970). It is, arguably though probably, the case that psychology needs both inductive and deductive approaches to research.

1.3 Quantitative versus qualitative?

Although the preceding discussion of philosophy was necessary and important, the distinction between types of research that you will most often encounter on a regular basis in psychology is that between **quantitative** and **qualitative** research. The reason for needing to engage with the difficult philosophy so early on is because it provides the backdrop necessary for understanding the essential differences between quantitative and qualitative research and it is vital for psychologists to understand the differences between these two types of research. At a very simple level, quantitative research is that which involves numbers and qualitative research is that which does not. However, there is more to this important distinction than these simple principles and we address this in more detail below.

Quantitative research

Quantitative research (and therefore quantitative research methods) is research that concerns the quantity or measurement of some phenomenon. What this means is that quantitative research is concerned with quantifying (measuring and counting) phenomena. This is still the dominant analytic approach used in psychology in the United Kingdom, continental Europe, Australasia and the United States today. As stated in the previous section, quantitative research tends to subscribe to a particular empirical approach to knowledge, believing that if we measure things accurately enough we can make claims, with some degree of certainty, about the object of study. Quantitative research also tends to use the hypothetico-deductive approach to knowledge acquisition. See Box 1.3 for a good example of quantitative research.

> **Box 1.3** Study box
>
> Loftus, E. F. & Palmer, J. C. (1973). Reconstruction of automobile destruction: An example of the interaction between language and memory. *Journal of Verbal Learning and Verbal Behavior*, 13, 585-9.
>
> Elizabeth Loftus and colleagues have conducted numerous experiments on eyewitness testimony over the years. In this study Loftus & Palmer showed their participants a short film of a traffic accident in the laboratory. Participants were given questionnaires about what they had just witnessed. Unknown to the participants the questionnaires they completed were worded differently depending on which condition they were assigned to (all watched the same film). In one condition participants were asked the question 'How fast were the cars going when they *hit* each other?' and in the other condition they were asked the question 'How fast were the cars going when they *smashed* into each other?'
>
> Those asked the latter question (with the prime word 'smashed') gave consistently higher speed estimates for the cars than those asked the former question (with the prime word 'hit'). Furthermore, when participants were questioned one week later about whether they remembered seeing any broken glass in the film those asked the question with 'smashed' were twice as likely to recall broken glass as those asked the question with 'hit'. In fact, the film showed no broken glass. This, and many later studies, demonstrate the effect of what we now call 'leading questions' on memory and recall and has had very important implications for the way people are questioned in the criminal justice system.

Quantitative research also tends to be characterised by a number of other qualities. Firstly, quantitative research is often conducted in controlled settings, such as psychology laboratories, in an attempt to produce findings that are as objective and unaffected by external influences as possible. Quantitative research also tends to focus more on behaviour than qualitative research (which tends to focus more on meanings). Quantitative research also tends to be concerned with prediction rather than 'mere' description (the remit of much qualitative research). Finally, quantitative research tends to involve the use of experimental methods and/or the use of structured questionnaires or observation, often conducted with large numbers of participants. As we are sure you will have noticed, we have avoided saying that quantitative research *always* subscribes to one particular philosophical

Advantages	Disadvantages
■ Precise (in terms of measurement) ■ Controlled (in terms of design) ■ Makes claims about causation ■ Has predictive power (can generalise to other settings on the basis of some finding in a particular setting) ■ Is the dominant approach in psychology	■ May grossly oversimplify the complexity of human nature ■ May fail to recognise or be explicit about the subjective nature of social science research ■ May fail to recognise the individuality and autonomous nature of human beings

position or method. Like much in life, and certainly like much in the social sciences, things are not so clear-cut. For there will always be research that crosses and challenges these traditional divisions (see Chapter 24 on mixed methods).

Qualitative research

Qualitative research (and therefore qualitative research methods) is research that is concerned with the quality or qualities of some phenomenon. Unlike quantitative research, qualitative research is principally concerned with text and meaning. Unlike many quantitative researchers, qualitative researchers predominantly reject the idea that there is a simple relationship between our perception of the world and the world itself. There is also a greater focus on an inductive,[2] rather than hypothetico-deductive, approach to research. However, much qualitative research in psychology is still empirical though often based on the collection of data from a relatively small number of individuals. In general, then, qualitative researchers do not believe that there exist 'definable and quantifiable "social facts"' (Rist, 1975: 18). That is, there are not truths about the world that are waiting to be discovered through more and more sophisticated methods of investigation and measurement. Qualitative research often involves the collection of text-based data through, for instance, small numbers of semi-structured or unstructured interviews. This text then forms the basis of the material for analysis. We will talk about the nature of qualitative research much more in Part 3 where we will also introduce some of the (many) different approaches to this increasingly important type of research.

Advantages	Disadvantages
■ Recognises the subjective experience of participants	■ Cannot apply traditional notions of validity and reliability (see Chapter 3) on the data
■ Often produces unexpected insights about human nature through an open-ended approach to research	■ It is often not appropriate or even possible to make generalisations or predictions
■ Enables an 'insider' perspective on different social worlds	■ Needs justification for it is still not a widely and consistently accepted approach to psychological research
■ Generally does not impose a particular way of 'seeing' on the participants	■ Lack of replicability

---

[2] Strictly speaking, no approach can be purely inductive for we always set out to study *something*. So, for instance, if we set out to study the qualities of dogs we must first find a number of dogs to study. There is always a theoretical backdrop to the questions we ask, no matter how much we try to approach the objects of study without preconceptions. However, qualitative researchers would argue that their approaches attempt to be inductive through explicitly recognising this issue and attempting to understand the qualities of phenomena 'in their appearing' rather than from a particular theoretical perspective (with all sorts of assumptions and expectations that that entails).

1.4 A brief introduction to methods in the social sciences

Now that we have covered the important background to social science research through a quick excursion into philosophy, we will briefly give you a taste of the variety of research methods and forms of data analysis available to researchers in psychology. As you probably know already, psychology is an extremely broad and disparate discipline. In reality there are many 'psychologies' rather than one psychology. At their heart all forms of psychology are interested in understanding more about people and human nature and sometimes animals and animal nature, but tackle this question in radically different ways. So, in biological psychology we see a concern with understanding the biological processes (most often, within the brain) underpinning human behaviour. In social psychology we see a concern with understanding the person (or groups of people) in relation to other people and the wider world more generally. Not surprisingly, these different forms of psychology require quite different methods of research and data analysis.

We have already outlined the basic distinction between quantitative and qualitative research methods (and previously explained the philosophical principles upon which this distinction is based). Quantitative methods of data collection include experiments, structured interviewing, structured observation and the use of structured questionnaires. Interviews, observations and questionnaires are structured, as opposed to unstructured or semi-structured, in that they consist of a predetermined structure (so a set list of questions in an interview or questionnaire or a predetermined list of things to observe). We talk more about these methods in Chapters 4, 5 and 6. Qualitative methods of data collection include unstructured and semi-structured interviews, participant observation (where you observe while taking part in the setting you are observing) and occasionally use of semi-structured questionnaires. Quantitative methods of analysis are principally concerned with the analysis of numerical data and this is where the use of statistics is encountered (Chapters 8 to 16). Qualitative methods are quite varied but principally concerned with the analysis of text and include approaches such as phenomenological/thematic analysis, grounded theory and discourse analysis (Chapters 17–22).

1.5 Planning research

At last we can move on to a little more about the practicalities of carrying out research and tackle a few of the key aspects of psychological research. The sooner you can carry out your own research the better, for it is only through doing this that you can truly understand what the excitement of research is all about. Some of what is written below, with the notable exception of the material on searching and reviewing the literature below, relates to *quantitative* research rather than *qualitative* research. We will cover the planning and process of qualitative research specifically in Part 3.

The 'explosion' of psychological literature

A new psychology article is now published, on average, every 15 minutes (Adair & Vohra, 2003)! The increasingly fast pace of research in psychology means that we cannot possibly read all of the relevant articles, even within specific topic areas. With the best will in the world, we have to make a conscious decision *not* to read a good proportion of the available literature. Four problems have been created, which apply to academics and students alike:

1 How can we access the growing literature?
2 How can we stay up to date with the literature?
3 How can we read all of the relevant literature?
4 How can we cite literature appropriately and selectively?

We cannot control which literature our institutions have access to, but we can develop some practical strategies for finding, reading and citing research effectively. By effective, we mean methods that are the best use of your time. That is, to find a manageable number of relevant articles quickly, read them, and summarise their content. By relevant, we mean relevant *to* your research question (see below). Some of the more traditional strategies are increasingly less effective. For example, we could only read textbooks, but these provide second-hand accounts of a field, and tend to date quickly. Psychology research moves fast. We could read **narrative review** articles. These are written accounts of the literature, similar to an essay, but without a systematic strategy for deciding which research articles should be included (**systematic reviews** are described below). Narrative reviews would not provide the substantive detail that research papers offer. Narrative reviews can be biased by what the author of the review decided was important to include. In the two sections that follow, we provide some practical strategies for searching the literature in two scenarios. The first part of this section describes how to search the literature (**searching for reading**). The second describes how to write about the literature in the form of a literature review (**searching for writing**), which is also mentioned again in Chapter 26.

Searching for reading

The term 'literature review' can sometimes refer to the broad and 'light' reading of a wide body of literature(s) in a fairly general topic area. This is a worthwhile activity, but is better described as browsing or skimming. Browsing and skimming are valuable activities that have their place in the student toolbox, but have their limits. They do not provide a summary of the body of work that surrounds a specific topic or research question. We need to read existing work before starting our own research, and that means selecting relevant articles to read. A literature review can be formally defined as 'the comprehensive study and interpretation of literature that relates to a particular topic' (Aveyard, 2007: 5). The term 'comprehensive' may seem at odds with the term 'particular'. Reading comprehensively requires a deep approach, whereas focusing on one topic may seem like a surface approach. This is not the case. By focusing on one topic, it is possible to read comprehensively *within* that topic. There are at least seven reasons why this kind of literature review is an important part of the research process. It will enable you to:

- improve your knowledge and understanding;
- keep abreast of new developments;
- find out what research has been conducted before;
- identify gaps in the literature;
- find validated and reliable scales or tests;
- find examples of appropriate research designs;
- avoid committing a jingle or jangle fallacy (discussed below), and to clarify terminology.

It is not sufficient simply to browse the literature in order to understand a topic. There is simply too much information. If you are planning your own research, you will normally want to find relevant existing research before you begin. To do that, you need to design a research question, before searching the literature with that question in mind. This will help you find out what has been done before.

Jingles and jangles

You may think that there is no existing psychological literature for a topic you have decided to study. This is highly unlikely. Psychological terms tend to suffer from the **jingle** and **jangle** fallacies. Terms which are different, but given the same name, are jingles (e.g. some researchers use the term **short term memory** instead of **working memory**). Jangles are terms that are the same, but are given new words (e.g. **sociability** is more or less the same as **extraversion**). A plethora of different terms to describe personality traits appeared in the literature during the twentieth century. It took several decades for researchers to agree on a common language to describe them (see Chapter 5): the big five model. Eventually, this made the literature much easier to read! When embarking on new research, you are most likely to commit a jangle fallacy. It is all too easy to assume that your topic is a new one, and proceed straight into research without a thorough review of the literature. Researchers frequently declare that they have discovered a new construct or psychological mechanism that is simply old wine in new bottles. It often turns out that there is already a great deal of research in the published literature, described using different names.

Narrow your focus

Searching the literature depends on having a focus for the search. Usually this is in the form of a research question (or questions) that is guiding your investigation. You may have been assigned a topic, or a choice of topics, as part of your course. If you are lucky, you will have the freedom to choose what topic you study. You may have been inspired to conduct a project through reading an article or book on the topic. This is very often the starting point for any search of the literature as you can identify the sources given in the study in the reference list (the list at the end of a journal article, book or book chapter) listing the exact source of information being used in support of an argument (see Chapter 26 on report writing for more on the practicalities of referencing sources). Simply by looking at the sources listed in the reference list you may begin to gather a body of evidence. However, this is not a systematic strategy for searching the literature. You may miss newer research, and relying on other researchers' reference lists can provide a biased picture of the literature. Once you have chosen a topic, or been assigned a topic, we recommend designing a research question and then searching electronic databases. These methods are both described below.

Designing a research question

It is worth spending some time designing a good research question before you approach the literature. This is easier said than done. You may find that you struggle to design a research question because you don't know enough about the literature. This can leave you in a 'catch 22' situation. You may be able to get guidance from a supervisor, or use a pre-specified list of ideas (see Box 1.4). If not, there is no easy solution, but remember that you can modify your search question. The trick is not to spend too long reading the literature without a specific aim. Learning what *not* to read is an important skill. In the health sciences, and frequently in psychology, the PICO model can be used to create a clearly defined research question (adapted from Lewis & Roberts, 2008):

- Patient/Population/Problem. This will determine the sampling frame (described in Chapter 2). For example, we might restrict the search to elderly people, or to adolescents.
- Intervention. The treatment or condition which participants were assigned to.
- Comparison/Control. This is usually a control group, or a group not receiving a treatment. In psychology, it is usually another 'level' of the condition which participants were assigned to (the other level of the independent variable, a term defined in Chapter 8).
- Outcome. This is the dependent variable. We want to know if the independent variable (the treatment) influences the dependent variable (the outcome).

PICO can be modified for psychology research by replacing 'intervention' with the independent variable (e.g. the effect of the manipulation in the experiment) in a study design. In Chapter 6, we will describe the various kinds of experimental designs and the terms 'independent' and 'dependent' variable more fully. Part 3 of this book describes how to generate qualitative research questions.

As an example, we were interested in what research had been published into the effect of jogging on depression in adults. Using the PICO model, the research question can be defined in the following way:

- Population: adults.
- Intervention: jogging.
- Control: no jogging.
- Outcome: depression.

The research question is, therefore, 'In adults, does jogging reduce depression?' Because the intervention is not being compared with a different kind of treatment, in this example we can ignore the 'control' part of the PICO model. It is likely that many studies will include a control condition, 'no jogging', but we will need to read the literature before making assumptions about what kinds of studies have been conducted (see below).

Selecting databases

There are specialist databases for psychology which will enable you to identify appropriate material to read and then if it is relevant include in your review (e.g. PsycINFO). By learning to use these databases you will have a vast amount of information at your fingertips. We strongly recommend searching more than one database for relevant articles. It is not sufficient to rely on PsycINFO, because it does not provide coverage of many journals that could be relevant. A considerable amount of qualitative research is published in sociology journals, many of which are not included in PsycINFO. No single database provides complete coverage of all relevant journals. One of the strengths of psychology as a discipline is that none of its topics are studied exclusively by psychologists. Important research can be found in sociological, medical and biological journals, for example. Normally, at least three databases should be searched. For example, you may search PsycINFO, then Medline, then EMBASE. There will almost certainly be duplicates (articles that appear in more than one database), but you are less likely to exclude important articles.

Databases should not be confused with interfaces. Interfaces are software that allow you to search databases, using an Internet browser. The interfaces and databases available to you will depend on what is available at your library. This table shows some of the most popular interfaces and the databases they cover. The interfaces available to you may vary, and so may the databases available

	Interfaces		
	Ovid	Web of Knowledge	PubMed
Databases			
PsycINFO	Y	N	N
Medline	Y	Y	Y
EMBASE	Y	N	N
Science Citation Index	N	Y	N
Social Science Citation Index	N	Y	N
Arts & Humanities Citation Index	N	Y	N

within each interface. For advice, contact your library or information services support team. The table on page 20 provides an approximate guide to which databases are indexed by three popular interfaces. It illustrates the importance of using more than one interface and database. Psychology research can be found in any of the 18 boxes that follow! To get a good picture of the literature, you need to look through more than one 'window'.

Designing search terms

Search terms are the words you will use when searching databases. It is important that you include synonyms (different words for the same concept), especially if there are lots of jangles for the phenomenon you are interested in. If you have a supervisor who is familiar with the subject area, they may be able to help you identify appropriate search terms. For example, if you are interested in the relationship between emotion and the stress hormone cortisol, a psychologist familiar with the area would know that the term 'HPA axis' should also be included. If your research is in the area of health, the PubMed and Ovid interfaces can help you identify synonyms and related terms (see below).

Controlled vocabulary

Some databases, such as Medline, require a **controlled vocabulary** approach. When several different terms are available that describe a similar thing, it will encourage you to select a single heading for these terms. This helps keep the medical literature controlled, avoiding terms that are jingles and jangles of each other. **MeSH headings** (**Me**dical **S**ubject **H**eadings) are useful if your research involves health, but are not available in all databases. We find PubMed's MeSH facility quite useful as a starting point (see **www.ncbi.nlm.nih.gov/sites/entrez?db=mesh**). For example, we looked for synonyms for 'fish oils' and found the terms 'cod liver oil', 'fatty acids, omega-3', 'docosahexaenoic acids' and 'eicosapentaenoic acid'. These are all included by the MeSH heading 'Fish Oils' [Mesh]. It even provided a definition: 'Oils high in unsaturated fats extracted from the bodies of fish or fish parts, especially the livers. Those from the liver are usually high in vitamin A. The oils are used as dietary supplements, in soaps and detergents, as protective coatings, and as a base for other food products such as vegetable shortenings.' When we entered 'working memory', we learned that this term is covered by 'Memory, Short-Term' [Mesh]. In PsycINFO, the 'Map Term' feature can be used in a similar way (see Box 1.5).

Link key words together

Key words and phrases should be linked together into a **search string**. Phrases are often identified using inverted commas (e.g. 'working memory'). This means that the terms 'working' and 'memory' will not be treated as separate terms, but as a single term. Different databases have different methods for linking key terms together. Some interfaces (e.g. Web of Knowledge) use **Boolean operators**: the words **AND**, **NOT** and **OR**. When combined to form a search string, they tell the database how to combine your key words. **AND** will narrow a search, reducing the number of articles retrieved. This is a good way to focus your search, and shows that you have a well-designed research question (e.g. fish oil **AND** working memory. The keyword **NOT** will also narrow your search, by excluding irrelevant papers (e.g. cows **NOT** beef). The **NOT** operator should be used carefully, because it can exclude many articles that could be relevant. The keyword **OR** will expand your search, by including either of the terms (e.g. fish oil **OR** omega-3). Some interfaces (e.g. Ovid) link key words and phrases in a different way. In Ovid, each search string is stored separately and then combined using **AND** or **OR**. (see Box 1.5 for an example).

Truncation symbols and wildcards

Truncation symbols are used when the suffix of the word is allowed to vary. For example, 'memor*' would retrieve the terms 'memory', 'memorize', 'memorization'. These vary, depending on the database and interface. Usually the symbol is an asterisk (*) but sometimes an exclamation mark (!), question mark (?) or dollar symbol ($) is used.

Wildcards are symbols that represent *any* letter. There are two types of wildcard. A question mark can be used to identify *one or more* letters. For example, behavi?r would retrieve behavior (sic) and behaviour. A hash can be used to identify *one letter only*. For example, organi#e would retrieve organize and organise.

Box 1.4

Activity box — Searching the literature

The purpose of this literature review protocol (Lewis & Roberts, 2008) is to illustrate how you can search the literature in an organised way. The table below can be modified to suit your needs. A blank version is available to download from the book website. You can print this and use a separate copy for each search that you perform. Remember to pick a topic for review that is neither too broad nor too narrow (approximately 10–15 articles maximum). If your topic is too broad:

- focus on a narrower population;
- focus on a more specific intervention;
- focus on a more specific outcome;
- consider using the NOT operator to make your search string more precise.

We have not provided instructions on how to use every database. However, you may find the instructions for using PsycINFO useful (see Box 1.5). If you are new to literature searching, don't worry about the level of detail

Box 1.4 *Continued*

included here. Focus on steps 1 to 5. We have included later steps so that you are aware of the need to look at different sources in your future study.

1.	My research question is:						
	Population or Problem		Intervention or Independent variable		Control (if relevant)		Outcome or Dependent variable
2.	adults	AND	jogging	AND	[keyword]	AND	depression
3.	OR		OR		OR		OR
4.	[keyword]		running		[keyword]		major depression
		Date:	Search string used:	Enter number of articles:	Comments:		
5.	PsycINFO						
6.	Medline						
7.	EMBASE						
8.	Science Citation Index						
9.	Social Science Citation Index						
10.	Arts & Humanities Citation Index						
11.	Other databases?						
12.	Unpublished research?						
13.	Grey literature?						
14.	Other strategies?						
15.	Create single list		Filename: (e.g. Endnote or Reference Manager)				
16.	How many duplicate articles?						
17.	Create final list (duplicates removed)		Filename:				

For each article from your final list, make notes under the following headlines:

	Unique ID number	Available?	Retrieved?	Where stored?	Have I read it yet?	My thoughts and comments
e.g.	ID1	Yes	Yes	In my cognitive psychology folder	Yes	Enjoyed this one. Lots of strengths to mention in my literature review

Note: The numbered steps in the table correspond to the numbered steps in the text that follows

Box 1.4 *Continued*

1. Design a specific research question. Use the PICO model if appropriate. Express this clearly at the top of the literature search table. A poorly designed research question will make it much more difficult to search the literature. The PICO model will not be appropriate for qualitative searches where it is necessary to work more flexibly to identify appropriate sources.

2. Enter the keywords for each part of the research question, combining the terms using AND.

3. Use the controlled vocabulary feature (e.g. in MeSH or PsycINFO) to identify synonyms or other appropriate search terms.

4. Under each keyword, enter synonyms or other appropriate keywords for each part of the research question, combining them with the search terms above using OR. You have now created a search string.

5. to 10. For each database, starting with PsycINFO, modify the search string as appropriate for that database. Most databases will contain help files or instructions, and your library website may contain useful resources to help you. Make a note under each heading for:

    a the date of the search;
    b the exact search string you used;
    c the number of articles;
    d any comments about the search (e.g. ways in which the search string needed to be modified for this database).

    This may seem like a lot of detail, but it can be extremely useful later in the research process. It is likely to save time in the long run. If you are writing a literature review, it is essential to report your search strategy in detail. Readers should be able to reproduce the search that you performed.

11. Decide what other databases you want to include, if any. For example:

    - Cochrane Database of Systematic Reviews (produced by the Cochrane collaboration: www.cochrange.org/reviews);
    - CINAHL – Cumulative Index to Nursing Allied Health (www.wales.nhs.uk/sites3/docmetadata.cfm?orgid=520&id=96462);
    - Biological Abstracts (may be available to you using Ovid).

12. Decide what unpublished sources you want to include. For example:

    - ISI Conference Proceedings (http://wok.mimas.as.uk/)
    - ProQuest Digital Dissertations (http://proquest.umi.com/login)
    - Zetoc Conference Proceedings (http://zetoc.mimas.ac.uk/)
    - UK Clinical Research Portfolio Database (http://public.ukcrn.org.uk/search/)

Box 1.4 *Continued*

13. Grey literature refers to work that is published, but has not been peer reviewed for an academic journal. For example, it may include government policy documents or a research report produced by the voluntary or community sector. Small-scale evaluations and audits can be classed as grey literature.

    - Grey Net (www.greynet.org)
    - Open-SIGLE (http://opensigle.inist.fr/)

    Do not assume that grey literature has a lower quality than academic research published in journals. Research can be produced outside the academic sector and be high in quality.

14. Other strategies can be useful for finding relevant literature. Try the following:

    - Hand search in journals that are appropriate for your topic. For example, if you are interested in the effect of emotions on memory, then flicking through the journal *Cognition and Emotion* could help you find relevant articles. This can often be particularly helpful when searching for qualitative articles as they are often (though by no means always) published in specialist journals (such as *Qualitative Research in Psychology*; *Discourse & Society*; *Journal of Phenomenological Psychology*; and so on).
    - Asking fellow students or colleagues what they have read. Very often, the best articles that we have read are those recommended to us by colleagues. These articles are not always detected by an electronic literature search. Word of mouth is a valuable search tool.
    - Exploring a social bookmarking tool, such as *CiteULike* (www.citeulike.org).
    - Asking an expert in the field. Consider asking someone in your department who is knowledgeable in the topic area what key readings they would recommend. Do not, however, send e-mails to academics asking for help with your literature review. It is fair to ask for a pointer in the right direction, but not to ask for help with search strategies. If you do, you are very unlikely to receive a reply!

15. Compile your results into a single list, and save this. Many interfaces will let you export the results from searches into bibliographic software, such as *Endnote* or *Reference Manager*, which help you organise your references.

16. Identify which articles are duplicates (the same article retrieved by more than one database) and remove them.

17. Create a final list, with duplicate articles removed. This is the list you will use. Make sure that each article has a unique number that you can use to identify it.

Box 1.4 *Continued*

Decide which articles you want to retrieve for reading. Carefully make notes that tell you whether you have retrieved an article, and where it is. Some articles may not be available because your library does not have access to the journal. Interlibrary loans can be useful, but you may be charged for this service. Seek advice from your library or information support team for guidance. Consider excluding the article from your review if you cannot get access to it.

Consider using social bookmarking to store and share your references (e.g. on CiteULike, **www.citeulike.org**).

Make a **mind map** of the literature you have selected. Mind maps are creative diagrams where you organise your thoughts and ideas by association, rather than logic. You can draw arrows, make connections between concepts, and learn about which areas you need to consider in more detail. Mind mapping can help you connect the themes, findings, strengths and weaknesses of each article. All you need is a blank sheet of paper, but you may want to consider downloading a free mind mapping tool, such as Freemind (**www.freemind.org**).

Searching the World Wide Web (WWW)

You may also find it useful to look for information on the Web but you will need to be very careful about the quality of the material you find there. It is (mostly) not **peer reviewed**, meaning that the quality of the research has not been approved by other academics as suitable for publication in a journal. Whilst there is clearly well researched and documented information on the Web, there is also a lot of rubbish. Deciding what is sound and what is not is no easy task and you would be well advised to focus your search – initially at least – on academic books and journals that can be found through university libraries. There is a stronger likelihood that the information in these sources will be the result of good quality research and theorising, though it is by no means certain even here. One of the key transferable skills that all psychologists should be able to demonstrate is a critical scepticism about knowledge claims. Your training in research methods – and this book – will help you develop that invaluable skill.

Box 1.5

Command box | **Searching PsychINFO using the OVID interface**

This box illustrates how to perform a basic search of the PsychINFO database, using the Ovid interface. The databases and interfaces available to you may vary.

1. Open the Ovid interface. Seek advice from your library or information support team on whether this interface is available to you (if not, there may be other interfaces available).

Box 1.5 *Continued*

2. Select **PsycINFO** for the range of dates you would like to restrict your search to (we have selected the year 2002 onwards for this example, see Fig. 1.2). Click on the **Open selected resources** button (Fig. 1.3) to open the database interface.

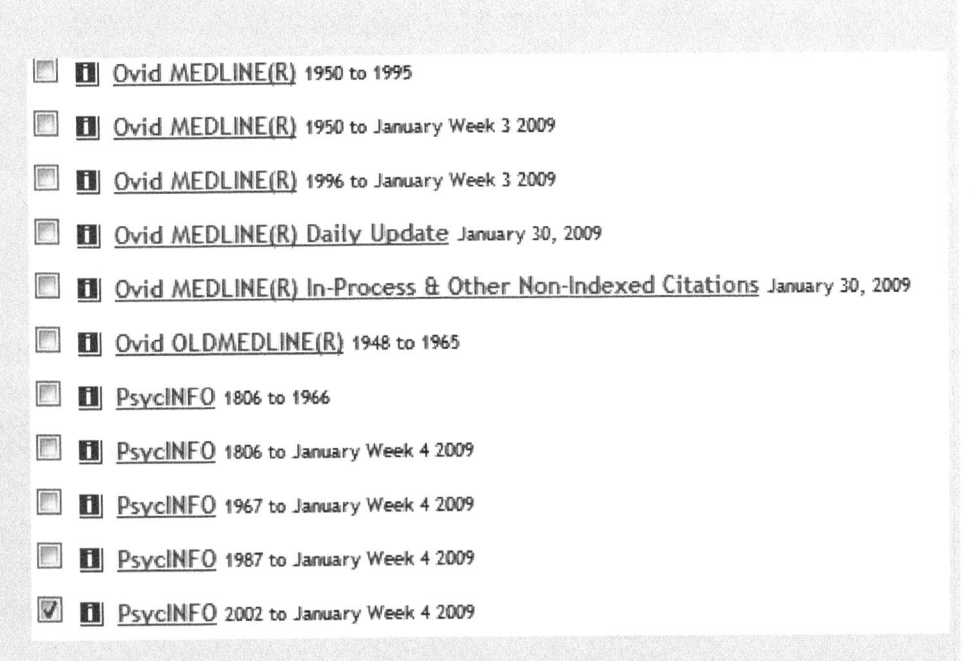

- Ovid MEDLINE(R) 1950 to 1995
- Ovid MEDLINE(R) 1950 to January Week 3 2009
- Ovid MEDLINE(R) 1996 to January Week 3 2009
- Ovid MEDLINE(R) Daily Update January 30, 2009
- Ovid MEDLINE(R) In-Process & Other Non-Indexed Citations January 30, 2009
- Ovid OLDMEDLINE(R) 1948 to 1965
- PsycINFO 1806 to 1966
- PsycINFO 1806 to January Week 4 2009
- PsycINFO 1967 to January Week 4 2009
- PsycINFO 1987 to January Week 4 2009
- ☑ PsycINFO 2002 to January Week 4 2009

Figure 1.2 Location of the PsycINFO database in Ovid*

Open selected resources »

Figure 1.3 Open selected resources button*

3. Click on the **Search Tools** tab (see Fig 1.4) which will switch to the **Search tools** function. The **Map Term** option is selected by default. Enter the keyword you would like to map (e.g. jogging) and then click on **Search** (see Fig. 1.5).

Search Tools

Figure 1.4 Search Tools tab*

---

* Screenshots courtesy of Ovid Technologies, Inc.

Box 1.5 *Continued*

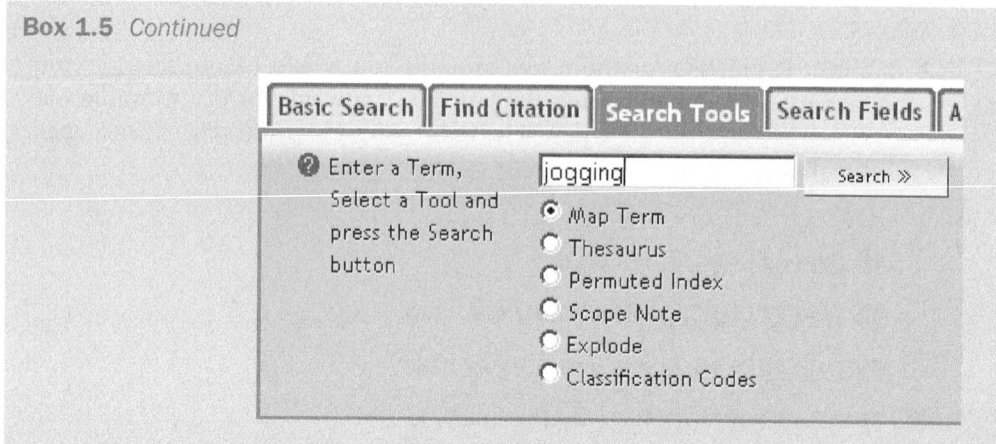

Figure 1.5 Map Term dialogue box*

4   A list of mapped terms is displayed. In our example, we have chosen a *specific* search strategy, and want to focus on jogging (not general terms such as **Exercise**). The appropriate term for this database has been identified as **Running**. Tick this box and then click on **Continue** (see Fig. 1.6). The **Explode** option should be ticked by default. Explode means that any subheadings under the heading you have selected will be included in the search.

Figure 1.6 Mapping Display*

5   The appropriate search string (set of search terms) has been sent to the **Search History** box (see Fig. 1.7). We can see that the string **/exp Running** has retrieved 255 articles. '/exp' means that the term has been explored. If you repeat this search, you may find that more articles have been published on this topic since we performed our search.

* Screenshots courtesy of Ovid Technologies, Inc

Box 1.5 *Continued*

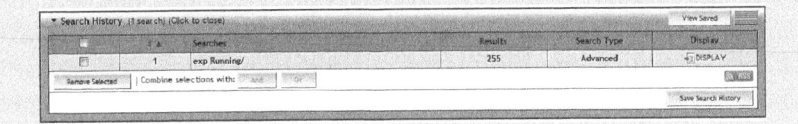

Figure 1.7 Search History*

6. Repeat steps 3 to 5 for the outcome variable we are interested in (depression). Here, several different kinds of depression are listed. We decided to focus our search on the subject heading **Major Depression**. This retrieved 26,845 articles.

7. If necessary, repeat steps 3 to 5 for other keywords (e.g. the population group you are interested in, any other variables which are relevant). In our example, it would not be appropriate to specify such a broad population group as adults. We can always exclude articles that do not describe adults, later on.

8. Combine the two separate searches using the Boolean operator AND. In Ovid, this can be performed automatically. Tick the two boxes for each search you have performed. Next to **Combine searches with:**, click on **And** (see Fig. 1.8).

Figure 1.8 Two search histories*

9. The two strings have been combined (exp Running/ AND exp MAJOR DEPRESSION/), and three articles have been retrieved (see Fig. 1.9). Click on **DISPLAY** to see their details.

Figure 1.9 Combining two search histories*

---

* Screenshots courtesy of Ovid Technologies, Inc

> **Box 1.5** *Continued*
>
> 10. The list you have created is displayed in a new window (see Fig. 1.10). You can store your list by clicking on **Email** or **Save**. Consult your library or information support team if you want to use software to store your results. Some universities make **Endnote** or **Reference Manager** available for students.
>
> Figure 1.10 Search results display*

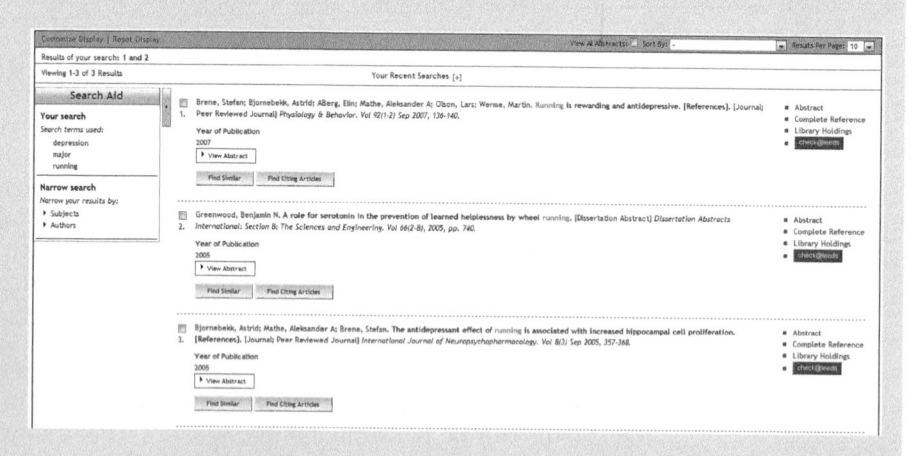

Reading review articles

Review articles are secondary accounts of the existing literature on a topic. Obviously, it is a good idea to read review articles if you want to find out more about an area. Using the word 'review' in a search can identify review articles. Finding review articles is a useful scoping exercise, performed before you conduct your own search of the literature. Review articles come in two forms: narrative and systematic.

Reading narrative reviews

These are verbal descriptions of the literature, as interpreted by a researcher. Their length can vary – anything from 2,500 words to 10,000 words. As such, a narrative review is a secondary account of the available research. Narrative reviews are a good way to sensitise yourself to recent developments in a particular area. However, they may date quickly. Many journals now exist that are devoted to the publication of review articles: for example, *Annual Review of Psychology* is a very good place to start. The *Trends* journals are useful summaries

---

* Screenshot courtesy of Ovid Technologies, Inc

of recent developments in a field (e.g. *Trends in Cognitive Sciences*). Other journals carry reviews alongside original research articles. For example, *Personality and Individual Differences* publishes a small number of review articles.

Reading systematic reviews

Systematic reviews are reviews where the authors declare a pre-specified search strategy. Inclusion and exclusion criteria are agreed in advance, to avoid possible bias that may occur in a narrative review. Without a search strategy, the danger of narrative reviews is that the author can present their personal interpretation of the literature. This can be a good thing, but it means that studies with particular findings or views can be excluded. Some authors begin with a systematic review, and then switch to a narrative review if the strategy does not produce enough results (e.g. Shenkin, Starr & Deary, 2004). Narrative reviews and systematic reviews can both be considered pieces of research in their own right. The discussion section at the end will often provide clues about hot topics for future research in the area – perfect when deciding what research question you can ask in your own research.

Meta analysis

It is sometimes useful to combine the results from several different research studies. This can be used to produce a single estimate of the findings across the whole literature. The results of different research studies can vary, so it is important to consider the totality of evidence, rather than looking at individual studies. Meta analysis is often a supplement to systematic reviews. Usually, the meta analysis will be performed on a selection of studies which were included within a systematic review. Not all systematic reviews are suitable for meta analysis, because the studies may be too different to make meaningful comparisons. This is called the **apples and oranges problem**. Despite this weakness, meta analyses are an efficient way to learn about the existing research in your topic area, if one has been conducted.

Overviews

Believe it or not, there are now systematic reviews of systematic reviews! In the Cochrane collaboration (see http://thecochranelibrary.com), these are called **overviews**. There aren't too many at the moment, but if the current rate of 'explosion' continues in psychology, we will increasingly rely on systematic reviews and on overviews to critically appraise the literature. You may find one or two relevant overviews in your area.

Writing your review

Many psychology students are asked to *write* a literature review. This is a written account of many of the processes described above. As such, it requires more than reading. You have to evaluate, or critically appraise, the literature. A written literature review can take several different forms:

- a separate piece of work, assessed separately;
- a preliminary exercise that will form the basis of a research project;
- a section of a larger piece of written work, such as a report or dissertation.

The section below outlines the processes involved in writing a literature review, which are similar in all three cases. The level of detail you are expected to include will vary, depending on your task. But what is a written literature review exactly? Well, a written literature review critically summarises and evaluates existing research findings (see Box 1.6). Reviews should highlight relationships between different material in the form of similarities and differences. It should also show how previous material relates to original research. It is useful to ask the following questions when writing a review:

- What do we already know?
- What are the main concepts?
- What are the relationships between these concepts?
- What are the existing theories?
- Where are the gaps in existing understanding?
- What views need to be tested further?
- What evidence is lacking?
- Why study the research problem?
- What contribution will the present study make?
- What research designs or methods are appropriate/inappropriate and why?

The purpose of writing a review is usually to demonstrate that you can evaluate, not simply re-describe, the literature. The person reading your review will want to see that you can:

- identify a clear research question (e.g. in the PICO format), not too broad and not too narrow;
- search several databases;
- select relevant readings;
- critically appraise evidence;
- balance conflicting evidence;
- focus on a specific topic;
- cite references appropriately;
- identify gaps in existing research and hot topics for future research.

If a review has already been conducted, this does not mean that you cannot produce one yourself. In fact, you may find that you interpret the literature in a different way. However, it does mean that you have to read the literature yourself. You cannot rely on existing reviews if you are writing about primary research.

Many students assume that they cannot criticise published work, because if it has been published, it has nothing wrong with it. This is not the case. You may be surprised at the range in quality of published research. Put simply, some articles are better than others. This is why we have to appraise the literature, rather than simply absorb and describe it. In the chapter on ethics and politics of research, we alert you to some of the reasons that research does and does not get published. Bad papers can be published and good papers can go unpublished! Systematic reviews (described previously) try to include unpublished research, for this reason. Further tips on writing a good literature review are given in Box 1.7.

Box 1.6

Information box

Critical appraisal

What does it mean to critically appraise the literature? It involves giving considered and justified examination of the methods, findings and interpretations of the data. When critically evaluating a piece of research you need to go beyond description by giving opinions (based on psychological knowledge and not your own personal opinions) and evaluations. It is important that you do not take everything at face value and instead you must question and explore the literature. This can be done by relating different types of material to each other, looking for similarities, differences and contradictions. You should also be explicit about underlying theories and values in the work you are reviewing.

- Give considered justified examination of the methods, findings and interpretation.
- Go beyond description by giving opinions (based on psychological knowledge and not your own opinions) and evaluations.
- Do not take everything at face value – question and explore the literature.
- Relate different types of material to each other – look for similarities, differences and contradictions.
- Be explicit about underlying theories and values in the work you are reviewing.

Choosing a topic to write about

You may have been assigned a research topic or research question to review. If not, and you have a choice, pick a topic that interests you or one which you think is important. Start with a general area. For example:

- mental health;
- cognition;
- emotion;
- development.

Next, narrow the topic. You cannot conduct a literature review of the areas listed above, because they are too broad. Refine your topic by specifying the constructs you are interested in, within the topic area. For example:

- depression;
- attention;
- sadness;
- stress.

These constructs are still too broad to conduct a literature review. Using the PICO model (if appropriate), you can combine these constructs with an intervention to create a research question. For example, 'in adults, does running reduce depression?' Alternatively, you can narrow the focus by combining two or more constructs together:

- depression and personality traits;
- attention and mood;
- sadness and lifestyle choices;
- stress and social phobia.

To refine even further, you may want to restrict the topic to a particular population:

- depression and theory of mind in children;
- attention and mood in adolescents;
- sadness and lifestyle choices in adults;
- stress and social phobia in the elderly.

Use the literature searching techniques described above to find out how many articles you are likely to find. If it is the first literature review you have conducted, aim for a maximum of 10 to 20 articles. You need to be able to read the articles in depth, without going too narrow. Some topics will not have enough published articles to justify a review (e.g. 'Synaesthesia in people with Down's syndrome', 'Extraversion in tree lizards'). If you are conducting a review for a large piece of work (e.g. a dissertation), you will need to read more.

Box 1.7

Information box

Writing a good review

If you are required to write a literature review as a form of assessment, please consult the guidelines you have been given. The form of a written literature review can vary. Some may require specific features, such as an abstract, word count, structured headings, and particular styles of referencing.

Remember the purpose

- What questions are you trying to answer?

Read with a purpose

- What sort of literature is appropriate?
- What ideas or information is important?
- Do not try to read everything.
- Read critically.
- Keep organised notes and bibliographic information.
- Draw a mind map.

Write with a purpose

- Start writing as soon as you can.
- Look at previous reviews for ideas about structure and style.
- Write a plan.
- Decide what you are going to say before you decide how to say it.
- Write critically.
- Do not use other researchers' reference lists when making citations. If you need to, you must cite these appropriately as secondary sources (e.g. Smith, 1990, cited in MacDonald, 2000).

Organising ideas

- Structure in a logical way – generally *not* by author – tell a story as you would in an essay.
- Group similar information together.
- Show the relationship between the work of different researchers, highlighting similarities and differences.
- Indicate the position of the work in the history of the research area.
- Start general and move to more specific issues.
- Include enough description to let the reader know what you are talking about.
- Describe your search strategy in detail.

Theory

Following a review of the literature you will encounter theories or ideas designed to explain or further understand the topic you are interested in. This is the starting point for the hypothetico-deductive research process (although you may occasionally start with an unsupported conjecture instead) and much quantitative research in psychology. In general, a theory may be characterised as *abstract* or *specific*. Abstract theories are general theories that may be applied to a number of particular topics or settings, while specific theories are, as the name suggests, specific to a particular setting or topic. The theory being investigated in a particular study informs the formation of the hypothesis (or hypotheses) to be tested.

Variables

Variables are identified events that change in value. We devote all of the next chapter to defining and measuring variables in quantitative research so we will not dwell on it too long here. In brief, variables are the things that vary (or alter) so we can make comparisons. So, we might want to look at whether women are better drivers than men. But how do we define the concept of 'a better driver'? We need to specify what our variable is here – is it fewer crashes? Or fewer people injured or killed? Or some other measure of being a good driver? As we are sure you can imagine, there are very many different ways of measuring the concept of 'being a good driver'. It is vital that we are clear and explicit about what we mean when carrying out studies in psychology, for other researchers must be able to see exactly what we have done when we report our findings (so they know what we have done and can try to replicate our study if they wish). In addition, it is only through explicit definitions of variables and accurate measurement that we can be sure we are all measuring the same thing.

Hypotheses

A hypothesis is a specific statement concerning a limited element of a theory. It needs to be highly specific and unambiguous so that it can be appropriately tested and either supported or refuted (e.g. Alcohol consumption is the strongest predictor of condom non-use among young people). We talk more about hypotheses in the following chapters. We say we **operationalise** concepts when we develop specific ways of measuring something. This essentially entails the translation of psychological concepts into specific variables that can then be incorporated into hypotheses to be tested empirically. For instance, how do we measure alcohol consumption and condom non-use among young people? In order to answer this question we need to operationalise the concepts of alcohol consumption and condom use such that we could produce a hypothesis to test.

Sampling

A sample is very simply the group of people we are studying in our research. It is rare to be able to study everyone in the population of interest to us. It would not really be feasible to survey every man and woman driver in the country to find out who has fewest crashes or the best attitude towards driving. What we need to do instead is take a smaller number of people from our population of interest (in this case male and female drivers) and study them. In quantitative research we will then tend to make claims about the whole population on the basis of what we find out from our sample (you would rarely do this in qualitative research). Just think of opinion polls (or surveys) to get a good grasp of the idea here. The researchers in the opinion poll agency send out questionnaires (or more often these days use the telephone or e-mail) to question a number of people believed to be representative of some population (Labour Party members or young people, for instance). Then, on the basis of the responses given by the people in the sample, claims are made about the views of the whole population. The danger, of course, is that we may have a sample that is *not* **representative** of the population as a whole and whose responses therefore are very different from the majority of people in the population. We need an appropriate sample that is representative in some way of our population, and there are a number of techniques to help us do this (this is covered in detail in Chapter 3).

Design

The design of a study is the overall structure of the research. So, do we need to conduct a survey using a questionnaire or carry out an experiment? Is it best to carry out an observation or use a case study method? The decision about which design we use is dependent on a number of factors but most importantly on the type of question we wish to seek answers to. If we want to understand what being a single parent means to young women it is probably a bad idea to choose an experimental design. Instead, we should seek to use a design that emphasises meaning and the subjective experiences of our participants (such as a phenomenological investigation – a qualitative approach). Conversely, we may want to know very simply whether women believe they are better drivers than men. In this case we might be advised to use a questionnaire survey and ask the opinions of a large number of women so that we can make claims about women in general. While the design of any study should be principally informed by the research questions (or hypotheses), this is not the only consideration that impacts on design. Another factor that is important is the researcher's belief about research (and also their ability to use different methods). Some qualitative psychologists believe that quantitative (positivist) research using, for instance, experiments or questionnaire surveys is fundamentally flawed and therefore pointless. Similarly, some quantitative psychologists believe that qualitative research with small numbers of participants is fruitless. These debates are ongoing and are unlikely to be resolved in the very near future. We will discuss such debates a little more in Part 3 when we cover qualitative methods in more detail. Another constraint on the design you may use concerns your available resources. If you do not have access to the population of interest or cannot afford to survey 10,000 people then you will have to adapt your design accordingly. We do not live in a world of infinite resources and research must be 'real world' (Robson, 2002).

Analysis

Your chosen design will affect the type of analysis that is appropriate. If you have a qualitative case study design you will want to analyse your data using an appropriate qualitative method. Conversely a large-scale survey or experiment may call for the use of statistical analysis. A quick word of warning for when you conduct your own research: remember to think about the method of analysis early on when planning your research. Do not leave this to the end after you have collected your data, for you may find yourself in the unenviable position of being unable to analyse your data in the way you wished. We have had to 'rescue' a number of research projects where students had not thought carefully about the particular statistics that they wished to use in advance of distributing their questionnaires. You can carry out some forms of analysis only if you have collected the right sort of data in the right way (this is covered in relation to quantitative research in the next chapter and in relation to qualitative research in Part 3).

Findings

Once you have analysed your data you will produce findings based on your interpretation of your data and results. Your findings will feed back to your theory by providing support for or evidence against the theory. This may lead to a rejection of or, more likely, reformulation of the theory. What is often important in making this judgement is whether your findings can be replicated. **Replication** is very important in all scientific enquiry as we can only be confident in our findings if they are found again when another person repeats the study (exactly) with another sample of participants.

Further reading

Butler, G. & McManus, F. (2000). *Psychology: A Very Short Introduction*. Oxford: Oxford University Press.

> As you might expect from its title, this book is very short. However, it provides concise accounts of the history of psychology and its current sub-disciplines. There are several other books in the *Very Short Introduction* series that you may find relevant.

Chalmers, A. F. (1999). *What Is This Thing Called Science?* 3rd edn. Milton Keynes: OU Press.

> A classic text with good coverage of all the major debates in the philosophy of science.

Hart, C. (2001). *Doing a Literature Review: Releasing the Social Science Research Imagination.* London: SAGE.

> This is a popular text for students who have been asked to conduct their first literature review.

Hart, C. (2007). *Doing a Literature Search: A Comprehensive Guide for the Social Sciences.* London: SAGE.

> This book is an excellent accompaniment to Hart's older book on literature reviewing.

Richards, G. (2002). *Putting Psychology in its Place: A Critical Historical Overview*, 2nd edn. London: Routledge.

> Superb coverage of the history of psychology from the earliest days of the discipline through to the present day.

Sternberg, R.J. (2003). *The Psychologist's Companion: A Guide to Scientific Writing for Students and Researchers*, 4th edn. Cambridge: Cambridge University Press.

> This book is aimed at psychologists who want to write about their research, but is worth the investment if you plan to become a psychologist. It covers everything from planning a study to writing it up and submitting it for publication. See chapter two for literature searching advice.

Williams, M. & May, T. (1996). *Introduction to the Philosophy of Social Research.* London: UCL Press.

> The name says it all – an excellent introduction to the philosophy of social research which will take you much further than you need in the first year of a psychology degree. In fact this one should last you all the way to your third year and beyond.

2 Variables: definitions and measurement

- This chapter explains why we need to define variables explicitly in psychology.
- It begins by introducing the varieties of variables that you may encounter.
- It then covers differences between independent and dependent variables.
- Finally, this chapter will introduce you to important issues in the measurement of variables.

INTRODUCTION

As mentioned in Chapter 1, a variable is simply something that *varies* (hence **variable**) in some way that we seek to measure. In psychology (and particularly quantitative research in psychology) we need to be very explicit about what it is we are measuring. Woolly definitions are no good here as they result in poor quality research with inconsistency about the exact focus of the investigation. We want to produce high quality research and so we need to make sure that we are very clear about what it is that we are measuring.

Variables can be any number of things, such as a person's height or weight, attitudes towards fox-hunting or the latest 'boyband', self-esteem or anxiety and so on. As stated earlier, really anything that varies that we choose to measure can be a variable. You will already be familiar with measuring many variables such as height, weight and age. There are standard units of measurement for these variables (metres, kilograms and years respectively) and we all understand how to measure these variables and what the results mean. However, some other variables (such as self-esteem and anxiety) that you are very likely to encounter in psychology are much harder to measure accurately, and furthermore there is often considerable disagreement over the best way to measure them. Measures that are not easily measured are called **constructs**. Constructs are unobservable variables, and therefore variables that have to be measured indirectly.

2.1 Operationalising variables

When we try to explicitly define and then measure variables, or constructs, we say that we are **operationalising** variables. Try to define some of your own variables and see how you get on – it is not as easy as it seems (Box 2.1).

> **Box 2.1**
>
> **Activity box — Operationalising variables**
>
> - Try to write your own definitions of the following constructs:
>   1. Self-esteem
>   2. Anxiety
>   3. Love
> - How did you find it? The last one, in particular, is not easy. Now try to think through how you could measure these constructs. What variables do you need to explicitly define and how would you measure them?
> - Yes, that was even harder. We guarantee that by the end of this book, if you stick with it, you will be considerably better at being able to define and measure constructs.

We all have common-sense understandings of self-esteem, anxiety and love so there must be some mutual understanding of these constructs. What we need to do in psychology is draw out these common understandings (and also quite possibly elements that are not commonly understood) and make them explicit so we can measure them. So, how would we measure self-esteem? Well, there are a number of standardised tests (such as the Rosenberg Self-Esteem Inventory) for self-esteem that are in widespread use in psychological research. The most commonly used version of the Rosenberg Self-Esteem Inventory consists of ten statements (including statements such as 'I like myself'). Responses to these statements are measured using a four-point scale (a **Likert scale**) recording how much you agree or disagree with the statement (1 = I disagree very much, 2 = I disagree, 3 = I agree and 4 = I agree very much). This test is considered to be a **valid** and **reliable** measure of self-esteem (these concepts are discussed in detail in the next chapter) and has been tested on a wide variety of populations. It is these qualities that enable us to state that the test has been **standardised**. Tests of these kinds are available to measure many psychological constructs and are widely used in psychological research (and clinical settings). However, sometimes we have to create our own scales (see Chapter 5), and we do this by defining our variables and operationalising their measurement. The important point, however, is that we need to be clear, unambiguous and explicit about what it is we are measuring.

2.2 Independent and dependent variables

When we carry out experiments (and often in survey research as well) we need to distinguish between two kinds of variables: **independent** and **dependent variables**. Very simply, the independent variable (or **IV** for short) is that which we (the experimenters) manipulate in order to measure an effect in the dependent variable (or **DV**). The IV is completely under our control while the DV is not under our control (in fact it is the data). Let us suppose we have an experiment designed to investigate children's memory for numbers. We design the experiment so the children are assigned to two **conditions** ('conditions' is simply the technical term used in experimental design for the groups that participants are assigned to where they experience different manipulations by the experimenter). In the first condition, children are simply left alone for ten minutes to remember a list of ten five-digit numbers (let us call this the 'unassisted learning condition'). In the second condition, children are taught the numbers (by a teacher) in the same ten-minute period with a particular memory technique of story-telling association (let us call this the 'assisted learning condition'). After the ten minutes children are tested (using a pencil and paper test) on their recall of the numbers. In this study the IV is the learning method (whether children are in the assisted or unassisted conditions) and the DV is the children's recall of the numbers (our data on their success).

In experimental design (and indeed in most scientific research) the central process is to ascertain the relationship between the IV (or IVs – plural – we often have multiple independent variables) and the DV (or occasionally multiple DVs). Traditionally, we would try to keep all other relevant variables constant while we manipulate the IV (or IVs) in order to measure the effect on the DV. This is why we frequently carry out experiments in a laboratory setting (see Chapter 6 on experimental design). Have a go at distinguishing between the independent and dependent variables in Box 2.2.

Box 2.2

Activity box — **IVs and DVs**

Which are the independent variables (IVs) and dependent variables (DVs) in each of the statements below?

- Attitudes to condom use are influenced by health promotion campaigns.
- As your age increases your IQ decreases.
- Women are better drivers than men.
- John's behaviour when at a football match is much more violent than when at home with his family.
- People with a 'type A' personality are more likely to smoke.

Talk to your tutor if you struggle to identify the IVs and DVs in the statements above.

2.3 The problem of error and confounding variables

Constant versus random error

As we stated above, when we conduct experiments in psychology we try to measure the effect of our IV (or IVs) on our DV. However, there are a number of other factors (or **extraneous variables** – sometimes called **nuisance variables**) that may get in the way of us accurately measuring the relationship. These other variables may be categorised as producing either **constant error** or **random error** according to the effect that they have on the findings. Constant error occurs when we have a systematic effect of some extraneous variable on one (or more) of our experimental conditions. That is, the extraneous variable is affecting the relationship between our IV and DV in one (or more) condition more than the other (or others) in a constant manner. Obviously, constant error seriously damages what we can say about our results, because we may actually be measuring an effect that is not really present (and is really simply the result of constant error from an extraneous variable).

One of the key issues in experimental design is how we minimise (and if at all possible, eliminate) constant error. Let us imagine a natural experiment concerned with measuring the effect of lecturing style on student learning. The IV is style of lecture (traditional versus interactive) and the DV is success in a multiple-choice test about the material presented in the lecture. Students are selected for one or the other condition on the basis of where they sit in the lecture theatre. So, students who sit at the front of the lecture theatre are given the interactive lecture, while the other students who sat at the back are taken to another room and given the traditional lecture. There is a danger here of constant error from an extraneous variable. It is quite likely that where students sit in a lecture theatre is not random. For instance, we might suspect that students who elect to sit at the front of a lecture theatre are more motivated to learn than those who sit at the back. This may therefore mean that any effect we find on account of the IV is directly affected by a constant error (motivation for learning among the students). If we were trying to minimise the effect of error in this piece of research we might want to allocate students to experimental conditions in a more random manner than where they elect to sit. Indeed, **randomisation** of participants is a key technique used in experimental design to minimise the effect of constant error on an experiment.

Random error presents the researcher with quite a different problem to constant error. Although in many cases we can eliminate (or at the very least, minimise) constant error through good experimental design, it is often not possible to eliminate random error despite our best efforts. This does not mean that we should not try to eliminate random error; just that we should be realistic about what we can control in an experiment. Random error is, very simply, where we have an effect from an extraneous variable on our measurement of the relationship between the IV and DV that is random (and therefore, unlike constant error, *not* constant towards one condition more than another). If we study the performance of mice in solving mazes we might encounter the problem of random error. In animal studies of this kind psychologists frequently use food to reinforce correct behaviour. Mice are therefore kept hungry before the maze-solving exercise and receive a food reward for successful completion (the food acts as the motivation to complete the task as quickly as possible). However, even with mice randomly assigned to experimental conditions (such as maze in darkness versus maze in daylight – the IV – to investigate the effect of visual perception on maze-solving ability), we might still have some mice who are more strongly motivated by food than others. This is an individual difference that we cannot control for. However, this random error should contribute to unpredictable error in our measurement of the DV (the success of mice in completing the mazes) because we have randomly assigned mice to the two conditions. We would expect a roughly equal mix of hungry and not-so-hungry mice in the two conditions because they were randomly assigned.

As you can see above, random error *obscures the effect* we are interested in identifying in our experiment whereas constant error *biases (or distorts)* our results. Ideally we would have neither type of error but research can never be perfectly controlled. We must try to minimise both and be particularly alert to the possibility of constant error, which may produce findings that are biased and unreliable.

Confounding variables

When we have a biased result due to constant error from an extraneous variable we say that our findings have been **confounded**. Confounding occurs when a real effect between the IV (or IVs) and the DV is biased or distorted (and sometimes obscured completely) by another (often unexpected) variable. If we had expected an effect from this variable then we would have either included it in our study as another IV or controlled for its effect through the careful design of our study. However, no matter how careful we are, we may sometimes discover the effect of a **confounding variable** during the course of our research.

Confounding variables can act on the relationship between an IV (or IVs) and a DV in a number of different ways. They can result in (1) an effect being observed in the DV apparently on the basis of the IV when in fact there was no effect produced by the IV at all, or (2) their action can obscure a real effect between an IV (or IVs) and DV. Imagine that we are interested in consumer behaviour and particularly ice cream consumption. We, being very naive psychologists, search for variables that seem to have an effect on ice cream consumption and discover a very strong effect for shorts-wearing in men. That is, as the wearing of shorts (among men and to a lesser extent women) (our IV) increases so does the consumption of ice cream (our DV). We have found an effect – Eureka! We contact the major ice cream manufacturers immediately and state with certainty that if they want to increase ice cream consumption they must try to increase the number of people wearing shorts. But as we are sure you know, we would be mistaken if we thought that the wearing of shorts increased the amount of ice cream consumption, and very stupid in contacting the ice cream manufacturers on the basis of this very poor quality research. The relationship we have measured between the IV and DV is in this case caused by a third (**confounding**) variable – hot weather! Although this is an obvious example that shows the effect of a confounding variable, the history of psychology is littered with examples of people getting it wrong because of the effect of confounding variables. So, beware – the solution to this problem is careful planning of your study, good design and vigilance when conducting your analysis.

2.4 Levels of measurement

Accuracy of measurement, very generally, is an important issue in all quantitative social science research. However, the specific topic of measurement *scales* (or levels of measurement) is thought to be crucial by some writers. It is worth being familiar with the basic issues and aware of why some consider an understanding of measurement levels crucial to psychological research.

Four measurement levels (that all psychological phenomena can be measured on – from a quantitative perspective at least) have been identified in the literature on statistics. The distinction between these four types of scales is considered important for what they enable us to do with our data when conducting statistical analyses. The argument is that we can use certain statistics only with certain types of data (that is, data measured at a particular level – **nominal**, **ordinal**, **interval** or **ratio**). In essence, higher levels of measurement (interval and ratio) give greater amounts of information about our data and therefore whatever it is that we have tried to measure. This in turn enables us to use a wider variety of statistical tests (tests that rely on this extra information to work correctly) than if we had used lower levels of measurement (such as the nominal and ordinal levels).

Nominal

Nominal-level scales are really best understood not as scales but as a way of labelling categories of data. Variables such as 'sex' or 'ethnicity' are nominal-level variables. In fact, categorical data (see Section 2.5 below) are often measured at the nominal level for we merely assign category labels at this level of measurement. At this level of measurement we assign numbers to meaningful categories (that are *mutually exclusive* – items in categories cannot be placed in more than one category) in order to count membership of that category. So, for instance, we may give the value of 1 to women in our study and 2 to men when collecting data. This does not mean that women are half men – just that when we have a value of 1 it represents a woman and a value of 2 represents a man in our study. Other examples of nominal-level data are:

- Number of voters supporting each political party in a general election campaign:

Labour	Conservative	Liberal Democrat
10,236	2333	7667

  or

- Number of people in our study subscribing to different religious beliefs:

Protestant	Muslim	Atheist
122	56	47

Ordinal

Ordinal-level scales are the simplest true scale in which phenomena (people, objects or events of some kind) are ordered along some continuum. At this level of measurement phenomena are ranked or ordered along some dimension of meaning. We will know who came first, second or third in a test but not how much higher the score was of the person in first place over the person in second place. That is, we do not gather information at this level of measurement about the distances between positions. The ordinal level of measurement gives us more information about our data than the nominal level for it tells us about the order of the individual values. An example of the ordinal level of measurement would be as follows:

- results of a 100 m run (position only and not times):

1st place	2nd place	3rd place
Jane	Jenny	Joanna

Interval

With an interval-level scale we have a measurement scale where the differences between items on the scale really mean something. When we measure temperature (in Celsius or Fahrenheit) we measure it at the interval level. A difference between 10 degrees and 20 degrees Celsius in terms of its value is the same in quantity as the difference between 70 and 80 degrees. That is, a ten-point difference has the same meaning anywhere along the scale. As you can see, interval scales have intervals equal in amount across the entire scale. We do need to be a little bit careful here. While the measuring system we use is interval (that is, the mercury in the thermometer changes by an equal amount for each equal unit of change in temperature), we cannot say that 20 degrees Celsius is twice as hot as 10 degrees Celsius. For us to make this claim about the level of measurement we would need to be measuring the phenomenon at the ratio level where we have a true zero point.

This is the most common form of measurement used in psychological research, although it is worth noting that many people argue that much of what psychologists treat as interval-level data is in fact ordinal data. Many of the scales used in psychological research, such as scales of self-esteem, anxiety, depression and so on, or five-point (or seven-point) Likert scales (more about these later) of a person's attitude to fox-hunting (how much they agree or disagree with it), are assumed to be interval. That is, we assume that the difference between scores on the scale is equal. So, when we have one person who marks that they 'strongly agree' with fox-hunting (and score 1 on our scale) and another who marks that they 'agree' (and score 2 on our scale) we assume their scores are the same distance apart as the two people who mark that they 'strongly disagree' (and score 4 on our scale) and 'disagree' (and score 3 on our scale) with fox-hunting. In truth we cannot know this from our simple five-point scale of attitudes towards fox-hunting, and the criticism of psychological research of this kind is valid. However, psychologists respond very simply by stating that the scales they use consist of, at least, approximately equal intervals and are meaningful measures of the phenomenon being studied. Another distinction has been proposed at this level of measurement to help deal with this problem – the **plastic interval** level of measurement (Wright, 1976, cited in Coolican, 1994). However, we do not believe that this approach really solves the problem of measurement for psychological scales but merely serves to introduce another category of measurement, which is not in widespread use and has no implications for the method of statistical analysis employed by psychologists. There are no tests employed by psychologists that are specifically appropriate for a plastic interval level of measurement (only tests at the nominal, ordinal or interval level). It is generally considered acceptable in psychology to treat ordinal data as interval; if there are at least five (Johnson & Creech, 1993), and preferably at least seven, points on the scale (Miles & Banyard, 2007).

Ratio

Ratio scales, like interval scales, have intervals of equal amounts but also, unlike the interval level, have a *true* zero point. This results in a scale where the relative proportions on the scale make sense when compared with each other. This is, not surprisingly, the 'gold standard' of levels of measurement and also, rather ironically, very rarely found in psychological measurement. Time is perhaps the best example of ratio-level measurement. With time there is the possibility of a zero point – where we have no time to measure (unlike temperature measured in Celsius or Fahrenheit where zero does not mean that there is no temperature to measure). The distinction between interval and ratio levels of measurement will rarely be of concern to you as a student of psychology (or indeed later on as a professional psychologist or researcher). When choosing statistical tests it is generally considered appropriate to treat both interval and ratio levels of measurement in the same way. However, the distinctions between nominal, ordinal and interval levels of measurement are believed by some to have important implications for the statistical tests you are able to conduct on your data (although see our discussion of levels of measurement below).

The need for common sense in psychological research

Why do we (rather controversially) believe that a concern with measurement levels is overstated among some (though not all – Howell, 2001, is a notable exception) writers on research methods in psychology? Indeed, some authors structure their books on research methods entirely around levels of measurement and position all other material on method and statistics in relation to this. We think this is missing the point about why measurement levels matter. It would be very easy for us to be very prescriptive about levels of measurement and issue reams of rules to follow. But this is not the answer to the problem of measurement in the social sciences (and would merely complicate issues for students wanting to learn how to be good researchers). What we need (when measuring variables) is common sense and understanding and not lists of rules about which test is needed in which circumstance.

The central issue we need to understand when considering measurement in the social sciences is the meaning of the numbers that we collect. It is useful to draw a distinction (in our minds) between the numbers themselves, which we collect in the course of some investigation and then subject to statistical tests, and the objects to which they refer. We can pretty much quantify and count anything we wish but that does not guarantee that it means very much psychologically speaking. Statistical tests enable us to carry out mathematical manipulations of numbers but they do not have any consideration of the meaning of these numbers built into their procedures. This is where we (as psychologists) come in when we interpret what the numbers mean when the tests are carried out. Without our interpretations the statistics we end up with are meaningless. What we need to do when we carry out a statistical test is ascertain whether the results are related in any meaningful way to the phenomena we have investigated. So, when we claim to have measured self-esteem using a questionnaire containing seven-point Likert scales (see Chapter 5), we need to acknowledge that the numbers are only surrogates for the underlying construct we are trying to measure. As noted by Miles & Banyard (2007), 'almost no data in psychology are *really* measured on a *truly* continuous scale' (p. 138). We can treat the data as interval (continuous) and perform statistical procedures, because we have a substantive theory that self-esteem exists as a continuous quantity. The greater the number of points on the scale, the greater the correspondence between the data and the construct (Johnson & Creech, 1993). It is important to perform tests that are appropriate for the level of measurement of the data, but you should consider the role of substantive psychological theory in deciding what that level is.

2.5 Categorical and continuous variables

Variables can be distinguished from each other in a number of ways (one of the most important was given above – the distinction between independent and dependent variables). We can also discriminate between **discrete** (or **categorical**)

variables, such as sex or social class, and **continuous variables**, such as age or anxiety score. Discrete variables are those that take on only a limited (or discrete) number of values (sex is male or female, social class may be A, B, etc.). This is in contrast to continuous variables which can have (in theory at least) any value between the lowest and highest points on the scale. That is, there is no limit to the subdivision of the scale. Age can be measured to the nearest year (most commonly) but also (to a finer level) in years and months or (finer still) years, months and days or years, months, days, hours. You get the idea – we can keep subdividing a continuous scale into finer and finer units of measurement.

All the scales mentioned above (and also all IVs and DVs) can be divided into two categories according to whether they are discrete or continuous variables. Nominal-level data, as stated above, can only be discrete whereas ordinal may be discrete or continuous (although strictly speaking it cannot be truly continuous as ordinal scales will usually have 0.5 as the smallest unit of measurement). As you might expect, interval and ratio scales can be either discrete or continuous. This distinction becomes particularly important when we want to carry out statistical analyses on our data, for some tests are appropriate for discrete variables while others are appropriate for continuous variables. We will return to this distinction again in Part 2 when we explore the statistical analysis of quantitative research data.

Further reading

We would not recommend a great deal of further reading on the topics raised in this chapter. For most students there is a real danger in getting bogged down in detail that may obscure the bigger (and much more important) picture. However, there are a couple of texts that include comprehensive coverage of, for instance, the measurement of data.

Black, T. R. (1999). *Doing Quantitative Research in the Social Sciences: An Integrated Approach to Research Design, Measurement and Statistics*. London: Sage.

> This book also provides comprehensive coverage of the definition and measurement of variables.

Pashler, H., Yantis, S., Medin, D., Gallistel, R. & Wixted, J. (2002). *Stevens' Handbook of Experimental Psychology*, 3rd edn. New York: John Wiley & Sons.

> A classic book on experimental psychology with considerable information on the issues raised in this chapter.

3 Reliability, validity, sampling and groups

- This chapter begins by explaining the concepts of reliability and validity.
- It then covers sampling, sampling bias and methods of sampling.
- Finally, this chapter will introduce you to the use of control and placebo groups in experimental research.

INTRODUCTION

As you saw in the previous chapter, psychological research requires us to be very precise in the ways we measure variables. Without precision we cannot guarantee the quality of the findings we produce. This chapter introduces you to some more technical issues in research. Two concepts that are central to any understanding of whether our findings are of worth or not are **reliability** and **validity**. These two watchwords are first introduced in this chapter, but covered in greater depth in Chapter 5 because they are central to the topic of questionnaire design. This chapter then covers the important, but sadly often neglected, topic of **replication**. We then move on to look at how we select participants for our studies, that is, how we **sample**. Finally, in this chapter we look at the benefits that can be gained through the use of **control** and **placebo groups**.

3.1 Reliability

Reliability concerns the stability of what we are measuring. That is, do we get the same result from our test (or study) on more than one occasion or was the result a freak instance (and therefore fairly meaningless if we are trying to say something general about human nature)? We want our results to be rigorous and this can be partly achieved through us gathering data that are reliable. So, for example, imagine we wish to produce a test of attitudes towards animal welfare. We give this test to our 'guinea pig', John, and he scores high (positive) on attitudes towards animal welfare. We then give John the same test on another occasion (several weeks later) and find he scores very low (negative) on attitudes towards animal welfare. So, what happened here? Well, very simply, our test is probably not reliable. We have tested it with the same person (so a comparable situation) on two occasions (this is a way of measuring **test–retest reliability**, which is discussed in Chapter 5) and found the test produced different results. This is not good enough if we are trying to produce a rigorous test of attitudes towards animal welfare. We want our measures to be reliable and provide similar results on different but comparable occasions.

3.2 Validity

Validity is another key element that should concern us when we are trying to carry out rigorous research. In short, validity is about whether a test (or measure of any kind) is really measuring the thing we intended it to measure. In chemistry or physics it is often the case that the item being measured exists in the world in a simple physical way (even if we need very sophisticated devices to see or measure it). However, psychological phenomena are not like these physical phenomena. Psychologists *assume* that people have 'attitudes' or 'personality traits' on the basis of our theories and evidence from studies of the way people behave in the world. However, we cannot ever really know if we are *really* measuring an attitude or personality trait in the same way as we know we are measuring wind speed or an electrical current since we cannot gather direct physical evidence for attitudes or personality traits.[1] In spite of this obvious limitation, psychologists have attempted to develop measures of psychological phenomena that are as valid as possible. Like reliability, there are several forms of validity that we should take into account when developing or testing measures of psychological phenomena. All types of validity have limitations, of course, and should be considered as ways of *increasing*, not proving, the *validity* of our measures. No measure is perfect, and there are no guarantees. These

---

[1] We will discuss this much more in Part 3 on qualitative approaches to data analysis. However, many qualitative approaches are not modelled on the natural sciences at all for the simple reason that (they argue) people's psychology is not like molecules or atoms in that it is not a measurable object extended in the world that is perpetually unchanging. Instead researchers from these perspectives argue that we can know about people (and their psychology) only in interactions between people or through language as that is the only information about our psychology that is publicly available to us all. We can never 'go inside' people's heads to find an attitude or personality trait (we could, of course, go inside to find some neurochemical pathways or anatomical structure). The other major factor that makes some researchers question an approach based on the natural sciences concerns human agency (the capacity, that we appear to have at least, to act in the world). Molecules and atoms do not make decisions and do not therefore have the potential to be different when placed in identical situations: human beings do and are often contradictory. We only need to observe other people to see this element of human nature in action.

issues are discussed in more detail in Chapter 5, in relation to questionnaires and psychometric tests. One type of validity is worth mentioning here, because it is relevant to psychological studies in general: ecological validity.

Ecological validity

Ecological validity is being increasingly examined in psychological studies. This is because a great deal of psychological research has been modelled on the natural sciences and therefore conducted in laboratories. Psychologists carry out rigorous studies in laboratories in an attempt to minimise the effect of extraneous variables. The worry with this approach is that these studies may lack ecological validity. That is, we may question whether the results gathered in a laboratory about some psychological phenomenon will generalise to other settings or places. Would our participants behave in the same way outside the laboratory as they do when subjected to a study within a laboratory setting? There is increasing concern that many of the findings produced through laboratory studies may lack ecological validity and therefore not reflect the natural behaviour of human beings at all. So, for instance, Asch's study of conformity, which we referred to in Chapter 1, was a laboratory-based study, which may have some limitations on account of its ecological validity. The participants were all strangers and were not given the opportunity to discuss their thoughts about the line lengths with each other. How often are you in a situation like that? We may seek to replicate Asch's study among an established group (such as friends in a lecture theatre) and allow people the possibility of discussion in an attempt to improve the ecological validity. What effect do you think this would have on the findings of the study? However, while many laboratory studies do suffer problems on account of a lack of ecological validity, it is important to be both realistic and thoughtful about the implications of this problem for research from this perspective. It is all too easy to criticise laboratory studies in this way but we do not think that this means all findings from laboratory-based research are just plain wrong! We have gained (and will continue to gain) considerable knowledge about human nature from laboratory-based research in spite of the limitations to this kind of work. All research in the social sciences suffers from some problems. What we need, if we wish to be good, effective and rigorous psychologists, is an awareness of these limitations and knowledge of how best to minimise their effects.

3.3 The role of replication in the social sciences

Replication is an important aspect of a traditional scientific approach to research in the social sciences. It is, however, often neglected because of the demand to produce new and novel findings. However, replication is important and worthy of attention. In order to establish the reliability and validity of research findings we need to be able to repeat a study exactly and find the same results as the original researcher. This is why you are instructed to produce research reports in a particular format (with all that detail). Other researchers need to be able to read a research report and carry out the same study themselves (that is, replicate it). As well as establishing whether findings are reliable and, to some extent, valid, replication also protects the discipline against fake (or fraudulent) findings. While this is uncommon, there are some notorious cases of psychologists inventing their results!

3.4 Populations and samples

Within a traditional scientific approach to psychology we often wish to generalise findings from a **sample** of people (a smaller subset) to the **population** from which they came. It is obviously impractical (if not impossible) in many cases to carry out research on every person within a particular population. We therefore need to be able to select a smaller number of participants for our research who are representative of the population as a whole. So, if we wish to carry out research on the phenomenon of the 'white van man' we cannot send a questionnaire (or interview) to every man who drives a white van in the United Kingdom (let alone every man who drives a white van in the rest of the world). What we need to do is select a smaller number of men who drive white vans as our sample. If our sample is a good one we would expect it to be representative of the population as a whole (all 'white van men'). The findings from our study of 'white van men' should tell us something about the whole population of 'white van men'. This is not as easy as it seems for we are always at risk of generating biased (or inaccurate) findings if our sample is not truly representative.

3.5 The problem of sampling bias

As mentioned above, we need our sample to be representative of the population from which it was drawn. If we studied only student samples in psychology we might well end up believing that most people stay up late, enjoy drinking and study hard. We need to be aware of the possibility of sampling bias when choosing who we are going to select from our population to study in our research. A great deal of research in the social sciences has been conducted with **convenience** samples (more on these below) which often comprise students. People who volunteer for social science research (and students in particular) have been found, in many ways, to be unrepresentative of the wider population. This is clearly a worry if we attempt to generalise our findings beyond our sample to the population. The principal way of minimising sampling bias is to employ one of the many sampling strategies recognised in the social sciences.

3.6 Methods of sampling

The first thing that is needed for all sampling to be effective is to clearly define the population of interest. All key variables that are used to define and mark the population of interest must be known and clearly defined. Once the population is clearly defined we then use an appropriate sampling strategy to draw our sample participants from the population of interest. Most of the strategies below (with the notable exception of convenience sampling) are ideals which are very difficult (if not impossible in some cases) to achieve in day-to-day real world research.

Random

This is generally considered to be the 'gold standard' for sampling. With **random sampling** each member of the population being studied has an equal chance of being selected for the sample. Furthermore, the selection of each participant from the population is independent of the selection of any other participant. There are a number of different methods for carrying out random sampling but it often involves potential participants being given a number (1 to N, where N is the total number of participants in the population). Then random number tables (or some other method of random number generation – e.g. through a calculator or computer) are used to generate numbers between 1 and N and those numbers selected become our sample participants. Random sampling is a particularly effective and unbiased method of sampling but, like all methods, cannot completely eliminate the sampling error that always occurs when we take a sample from a population (more of this in Chapter 6). Furthermore, random sampling is often an impossible ideal when we do not have access to the total population of interest.

Systematic

Systematic sampling is often used as a substitute for random sampling whereby we draw the sample from the population at fixed intervals from the list. So, if we had a list of addresses from the electoral roll for Sheffield we might decide to select every tenth address to make up our sample (which will receive our questionnaire). This approach is much simpler and easier to achieve than true random sampling. The main disadvantage of this approach is that there may exist some periodic function of our sample. If we decided to select the first ten members of a class of schoolchildren from a range of schools we might find that boys' names are always listed first. If this were the case our sample would probably consist of boys. Similarly, if we selected the first people to respond to a request for help with our research we might be selecting people who demonstrate particularly high levels of sociability or compliance. We must be careful with this approach to sampling that we do not accidentally introduce bias into our study (and it is easily done, for it is difficult to think of every possible factor that may influence our findings in advance of carrying out a study).

Stratified

Stratified sampling may be random or systematic and introduces an extra element into the process of sampling by ensuring that groups (or strata) within the population are each sampled randomly or to a particular level. We might, for instance, wish to carry out a survey of all first year students at the University of Imaginarytown about attitudes to a new university-wide compulsory course in IT and study skills. We cannot afford (in terms of time or money) to send a questionnaire to all first year students so we decide to randomly sample from the population (to a total of 10 per cent). However, we realise that simple random sampling may result in biased findings if, for instance, more students respond from the faculties of arts and humanities than from the faculties of science and engineering. This is where we might choose to use random stratified sampling. With this sampling technique we randomly sample from each faculty in the university until we have a final sample that reflects the proportions of students that we have in each faculty in the university. So, for instance, if we have 1000 students in the faculty of science and 500 in engineering we would want (if we were sampling 10 per cent of all university students) to randomly sample 100 students from the science faculty and 50 from the engineering faculty. This would mean that our final sample would be randomly generated in proportion to the number of students in each university faculty. Of course, university faculty is just one example of how we might stratify a sample. We might choose to stratify according to sex or age, social class and so on (the list is endless).

Cluster

There are times when we may wish to sample entire groups of people rather than individuals for our research. One common example of this is when psychologists carry out research in educational settings (especially schools). It is often most appropriate to sample entire classes from schools (for a variety of practical and ethical reasons). Sampling of natural groups (such as classes of students or schoolchildren) rather than individuals is called **cluster sampling**. Like the previous methods of sampling, care needs to be taken when sampling clusters to make sure those clusters are representative of the population. At the simplest level a researcher may just sample one cluster (a class of schoolchildren from one school). Here there is considerable danger in generalising from one's results to other classes and schools in the area and beyond. At the other extreme a researcher may randomly sample classes across age ranges and stratified by geographical region from the entire population of schools in the United Kingdom.

Stage

Stage sampling entails breaking down the sampling process into a number of stages. So, for instance, we may (in stage one) randomly sample a number of classes of children from schools in the United Kingdom. Then (in stage two) we may randomly sample a number of children from those classes that we have sampled. This approach would be called multi-stage cluster sampling (and you could even throw in a 'random' there if you liked and have 'multi-stage random cluster sampling'). Multi-stage designs are often particularly useful in very large studies. It is often (practically) impossible to randomly sample individuals from very large populations (for instance, all children from all schools in the United Kingdom). But if we wish to have a large sample that is representative of a very large population (such as all children in school in the United Kingdom) then multi-stage sampling may be the answer. So, for instance, if we wish to generate a sample of children that is representative of all children in school in the United Kingdom (a very ambitious thing to do!) we could begin by getting lists of all schools in the United Kingdom. We could then randomly sample from this list of schools (stage one), taking care to stratify our sample appropriately (e.g. by geographical region). Then we could contact those schools and get lists of all classes and randomly sample from those class lists (stage two) – again using appropriate stratification techniques. And finally in stage three we could get lists of children who belong to those classes and randomly sample from them. This would provide us with a random sample that (to a certain extent at least) would be representative of the total population of schoolchildren in the United Kingdom. We should point out that this particular example is not terribly realistic (as various aspects of the research process would intervene along the way to make things much more difficult and messy). Furthermore, this grand random multi-stage sampling strategy would be enormously expensive in terms of both time and resources.

Opportunity (or convenience)

This is, unfortunately, one of the commonest sampling strategies used by researchers in the social sciences today. Very simply, it entails us recruiting participants in any way possible (or convenient). So, we may recruit students in lecture theatres or people from the office block across the road. We may advertise and take all those that volunteer. This approach is clearly not ideal as we have little idea about whether our sample is representative of the population of interest to us in our research. However, **opportunity** sampling may be the only approach possible in some circumstances and we may have to tolerate the potential biases that ensue from this strategy. A lot of research in the social sciences is poorly funded (if funded at all) and conducted under extreme time pressure and may therefore necessitate a simple recruitment strategy. We might only have the resources available to recruit students in lecture theatres to our research. This may still be acceptable if we believe this strategy will introduce minimal (or irrelevant) bias to our findings. What we need to do if we use this approach is be sceptical of our findings and keep a careful watch on whether they seem to be valid and reliable.

Snowball

Snowball sampling is a very common sampling strategy that is often no more than convenience sampling under another name. However, there are times when snowball sampling is an appropriate (sometimes necessary) and strategic form of sampling. With this sampling technique the researcher will make contact with a small number of potential participants whom they wish to recruit to the research study. They will then use these initial contacts to recruit further participants (by recruiting friends and then friends of friends until the sample is sufficiently large). This strategy may be the most appropriate sampling strategy with some research studies. For instance, if you wish to study street gangs or drug users, access to these populations will be particularly difficult unless you are already a member of the group, and it is highly unlikely that you will be able to recruit many participants using the usual sampling strategies. However, if you can establish contact with just one or two gang members (or drug users) you can then use snowball sampling to recruit a sufficiently large sample. You would ask your initial participant to recruit fellow gang members (or drug users) to the study on your behalf. You can then ask this second set of participants to recruit some of their friends and so on until you have a large enough sample for your study.

The obvious problem with snowball sampling is that members of the sample are unlikely to be representative of the population. However, this depends on what we consider the population in our study. If we are interested only in the experience of a particular gang or members within this gang then it may be appropriate to recruit using a snowball strategy. This is more often the case with qualitative research concerned with understanding the experience of a (often small) number of people.

3.7 Sample sizes

So, the sixty-four million dollar question – does size really matter? Well, in general yes, the larger the sample size the better. This is simply because larger samples have less sampling error (we will return to sampling error in Part 2 – for now, take it on trust that the larger the sample size, the greater the precision of the sample in representing the population from which it was drawn). However, with all research there is a trade-off between size of sample and time and cost. With small sample sizes (50, 100, 150) precision increases significantly as the sample size increases and it is worth making every attempt to recruit as many participants as practically possible. However, once a sample gets above 1000 or so then there is less to be gained from significant increases in size. Sample error (and therefore precision) will continue to increase above 1000 but at a less rapid rate than below this figure. It is also important to remember that it is *absolute*, rather than *relative*, sample size that is important. Therefore, a national sample of 1000 children in the United Kingdom is as valid a sample as a national sample of 1000 children in the United States, despite the much larger population of children in the United States.

There are a number of additional factors that should be borne in mind when attempting to decide on the most appropriate sample size for your study. Firstly, it is important to consider the *kind of analysis* that will be conducted on your data, for this will have an impact on the size of sample needed. Students commonly forget to consider this factor in calculating their sample size and then run into problems when the time comes for them to analyse their data. Very simply, you need larger samples the larger the number of variables you plan to include in your study. This is sometimes referred to as the ratio of cases to IVs. There is no simple figure we can give you, for the ratio of cases to IVs will vary depending on which statistical technique you use to analyse your data. Various writers have provided formulae for calculating these ratios and the minimum sample size needed for different forms of analysis. This is beyond the scope of this text but worth checking out if you are carrying out your own research and need to know the minimum sample size for particular forms of statistical analysis (see the Further reading at the end of this chapter for more details).

Another factor that needs to be taken into consideration when calculating what sample size is needed is the likely response rate for the study. You will often see or hear mention of response rates in social survey research. In any research you will find people deciding not to respond to your request for them to participate. So, whether you send out 1000 unsolicited questionnaires or stand on a street corner asking every passer-by to come into the laboratory, a number of people will not complete the questionnaire or will refuse to take part in your experiment. It is important to know how many people have refused to take part, for a very high refusal rate may produce concerns about the **representativeness** of your sample. Are you recruiting only a particular type of person? How can you trust your findings if you do not have data on 90 per cent of those you sent the questionnaire to or asked to take part? We therefore try to maximise the response rate (the proportion of those contacted that agreed to take part). However, not everyone we contact may be suitable for our study or able to take part, so we tend to calculate the percentage response rate as follows:

$$\frac{\text{Number of questionnaires completed and returned (or people agreeing to take part)}}{\text{Number of questionnaires sent (or people approached) – unsuitable or uncontactable members of the sample}} \times 100$$

So, for instance, if we sent out 1000 questionnaires and had 100 returned correctly completed, 10 returned but not completed correctly and 10 returned because the addressee was not known then we have a response rate of $[100/(1000-10-10)] \times 100$, or 10.2 per cent. This is obviously a very low response rate but it is not uncommon to have low response rates (around 25 per cent) with unsolicited self-completion questionnaires sent by post. As well as trying to maximise our response rate (more on this in Chapter 5) we may need to try to predict the response rate if we wish to recruit a particular number of participants to our study. So, if we are sending out an unsolicited self-completion questionnaire and we need a sample size of 500 for our analysis, then, if we expect a return rate of 25 per cent, we need to distribute 2000 questionnaires.

The final factor that will be briefly mentioned here that may impact on the size of sample needed concerns the heterogeneity of the population from which we draw our sample. When a population is very heterogeneous, such as a national population of schoolchildren, then we are going to need a larger sample from this population than if the population is fairly homogeneous. Conversely, if our sample is very similar and demonstrates little variation (homogeneous across a number of characteristics of interest) then we will have less need to recruit a larger sample. It is also worth adding a note of caution about very large samples. Very large samples increase the likelihood of getting significant results (for a variety of statistical reasons). Good, you may think. Well, not necessarily, as the results may be significant but of no importance or practical consequence. This issue is discussed further in Chapter 11. So, while size does matter, it is not everything!

3.8 Control and placebo groups

In experimental (and some quasi-experimental) research we may need to recruit participants and assign them to one of two groups: **experimental** or **control**. We do this so that we can make comparisons between two (or more) groups of participants. The **experimental group** would be that which was given some intervention or programme (whether a new drug, education programme or psychological intervention) while the **control group** would be a matched (on appropriate characteristics, such as age, social class, etc.) group who did not receive the intervention. It is important to predict accurately which variables are likely to be important when matching participants. These variables are often demographic characteristics (such as age, sex, ethnicity and social class) but may also be psychological variables (such as attitudes or personality traits). When we sample for experimental research of this kind we often recruit matched pairs of participants so that we can then randomly allocate them to either the experimental or control groups.

A variation on the control group is the placebo group. We may employ a placebo group if we are worried about the possibility of a **placebo effect**. This is where a person (or group of people) responds to some stimulus as if it were having an expected effect when in fact it should have no effect at all. The classic example of this, which is tried and tested, is when we assign participants to two groups and give one group alcohol and another group (the placebo group) a liquid that we tell them is alcohol (but in fact contains no alcohol at all). What you find is that the placebo group who received a pretend alcoholic drink act as if they have consumed alcohol. So, we employ placebo groups in many situations (such as trials for new drugs) in order to minimise the expectation effects. We will address the issue of experimental and control groups further in Chapter 6.

Further reading

Robson, C. (2002). *Real World Research*, 2nd edn. Oxford: Blackwell.

Contains further information on reliability and validity and, most notably, sampling strategies not covered here that are rarely, but occasionally, used in the social sciences.

Tabachnik, B. G. & Fidell, L. S. (2006). *Using Multivariate Statistics*, 5th edn. New York: HarperCollins.

This is an advanced text! We do not recommend it at the introductory level of your studies. We have included it here because it contains useful information on how to calculate the minimum sample sizes for statistical tests.

4 Collecting data 1: interviews and observation

- This chapter introduces two of the main methods of data collection in psychology.
- It begins by introducing types of interviews, techniques and purposes. This includes coverage of group discussion and repertory grid techniques.
- The chapter then moves on to cover types and methods of observation.

INTRODUCTION

Psychology is a discipline reliant upon empirical evidence. Without empirical evidence to support our ideas we have no reason to believe our arguments about people any more than those of any man or woman in the street. It is through the use of empirical data that psychology strives to achieve the status of a science. However, it requires real skill to collect data and this chapter will sensitise you to some of the issues you must address when you seek to collect data about some topic. Without knowledge of the appropriate techniques of data collection the quality of your results may be questioned. This chapter focuses on the use of interviews and observation to collect data. The following chapter is devoted to questionnaire design and psychometrics and the next chapter experimental (and quasi-experimental) design – the other main approaches to collecting data in psychology. It should be noted that these chapters address only issues of data collection and not analysis (which is dealt with in Parts 2 and 3).

4.1 Interviewing

With the increasing use of qualitative approaches in psychology the use of interviews to collect data has grown. Interviews have always been a valuable method of data collection in psychology, particularly social psychology. They are a flexible method that enables researchers to collect detailed conversational material for analysis. Most of us have some experience of interviewing through, for instance, job applications (see Box 4.1). However, while interviews appear straightforward, there are particular issues to bear in mind when using them to collect data for psychological research. The following two sections will examine some of the most important factors in research interviewing.

Box 4.1

Activity box — Experiences of interviews

- Spend some time thinking about the possible places where interviews may be used (we have already mentioned job applications).
- How do the different types of interview differ?
  - Was the interviewer very formal or informal?
  - Did they follow a set list of questions or make them up as they went along?
  - How much control over the interview did the interviewee have?
- Finally, list some reasons why you think different types of interview are used in different settings.
  - For instance, you could argue that an interview using a set list of questions means that everyone gets the same chance (in a job interview, for instance).

4.2 Types, purposes and structures of interviews

Types and purposes of interviews

Only a few types of interview are commonly used for psychological research, including clinical/therapeutic interviews and face-to-face or telephone research interviews (and, recently, Internet/e-mail interviews).

Research interviews

Research interviews are the most common type of interview that you will encounter as a student of psychology. Their main function is to gather data (generally in the form of audio-recorded speech) from the participants about a topic that you, the interviewer, decide to study. You will talk to your interviewee face to face or on the telephone and use a series of questions to try to gather information about the thoughts, feelings and beliefs that the interviewee has about a particular topic. Box 4.2 gives an example of a typical study using semi-structured interviews. It highlights the usefulness of semi-structured interviews to generate text-based data where participants are attempting to understand or construct meaning about an experience they have had.

> **Box 4.2** **Study box**
>
> Reavey, P. & Gough, B. (2000) Dis/locating blame: Survivor's constructions of self and sexual abuse. *Sexualities*, **3** (3), 325-46.
>
> This study used semi-structured interviews with women who self-identified as survivors of sexual abuse to explore the way in which the participants made meaning out of their experience. The study interviewed only five women but generated a large amount of textual data that was then analysed using discourse analysis (see Chapter 21). This study found that women drew on several different discourses (think of them as stories for now), including discourses concerning the participant's past as blameworthy and present as 'survivors'. The participants made sense of their differing (present) situations through the use of these discourses. The authors argue that the work has implications for therapeutic practice through an examination of the ways in which talk of 'psychological problems' can be integrated into therapeutic narratives.

Therapeutic interviews

Therapeutic interviews (unlike research interviews) do not have data collection as their main function. This type of interview is generally conducted by a clinical professional with training in counselling or psychotherapy. Their primary function is (not surprisingly) concerned with the effective psychotherapeutic treatment of the client (interviewee or participant) rather than with data collection. Professionals in these settings may, however, audio record (or even video record) sessions to generate data for analysis at a later date.

Recording data

There are obviously a variety of methods of recording data from interviews, including note taking, audio recording and video recording. Each is dealt with briefly below:

- *Note taking.* This approach to recording data in an interview is difficult, slow and highly selective. It is generally only used in psychology where the use of audio recorders is too distracting or where recording equipment is unavailable (for instance, if you were interviewing in the field with people who find modern technology disturbing).

- *Audio recording.* This is the most commonly used method of data collection in interviews. Good quality audio recording equipment is readily available and familiar to most people you are likely to interview. There is a danger that the use of audio recording equipment may inhibit responses but this is generally compensated for by the fact that you have a permanent record of all verbal information exchanged. Now, for some practical advice about audio-recording interviews. Firstly, make sure you are familiar with the operation of the equipment you are using. While you do not need to be a rocket scientist to operate a tape recorder or digital recorder, many of us have been in the embarrassing situation of not knowing which socket to plug the microphone into or where to find the eject button. Secondly, make sure your equipment is up to the task at hand. You will have to go through the recording many, many times when transcribing the data (that is, making a written record of exactly what was said – see Chapter 18) and this is not a pleasant task when you are straining to hear what is being said. Thirdly, take along spare tapes (unwrapped!) if using a tape recorder, batteries and if possible another microphone (it is always best to be prepared). Finally, do not switch the recorder off immediately you finish the interview. The number of times you finish an interview, switch the recorder off and then find people telling you the most fascinating stories is amazing. So, leave the recorder going until the very last moment! Trust us, it will be worth it.
- *Video recording.* If we ask a group of students which is the best method of recording data they will inevitably say video recording. While we are increasingly living in a visual world, with video recording equipment readily available, more often than not it is *not* the best method of recording data in an interview. Video recording is likely to dominate the setting and disturb your participants, and although it records all information, much of this is excessive and irrelevant. However, video recording can be particularly useful where you are conducting a group interview. Trying to work out who said what can be very difficult with just an audio recording.

Interview structures

Interviews used to collect data in psychological research are generally categorised as one of three types: unstructured, semi-structured and structured.

Unstructured interviewing

Unstructured interviews are characterised by their lack of a predetermined interview schedule. They are usually exploratory and most useful where little is known about the topic. They may be particularly appropriate for certain theoretical perspectives (such as ethnography or life-story research) or in a clinical setting (such as a therapy session).

Advantages	Disadvantages
■ Flexible ■ Rich data ■ Relaxes interviewee ■ Should produce valid (meaningful) data	■ Unsystematic ■ Difficult to analyse data ■ Strongly influenced by interpersonal variables ■ Not reliable

Semi-structured interviewing

Semi-structured interviews, unlike unstructured interviews, use a standardised interview schedule. The interview schedule consists of a number of pre-set questions in a mostly determined order. However, this type of interview is not completely reliant on the rigorous application of the schedule. If the interviewee wanders off the question then the interviewer would generally go with it rather than try to return immediately to the next question in the schedule. In addition, the questions that make up the schedule are usually open-ended to encourage the respondents to elaborate their views about the topic (see the section on creating a good interview schedule below). And to further focus attention on the interviewee and their views the interviewer generally says very little. This is the most common type of interview used in psychological research.

Advantages	Disadvantages
■ Can compare responses and analyse data more easily ■ No topics missed ■ Reduction of interpersonal bias ■ Respondents not constrained by fixed answers	■ Some loss of flexibility for interviewer ■ Question wording may reduce richness ■ Less natural ■ Coding responses still subject to bias ■ Limits to generalisation

Structured interviewing

Structured interviews rely on the application of a fixed and ordered set of questions. The interviewer sticks to the precise schedule rigorously and will (politely!) keep the interviewee concentrated on the task at hand. There is also a set pattern provided for responses. In many ways this type of interview is more like a guided

Advantages	Disadvantages
■ Easy to administer ■ Easily replicated ■ Generalisable results (if the sample is adequate) ■ Simple data analysis ■ Reduced bias ■ Lower influence for interpersonal variables ■ High reliability	■ Respondent constrained ■ Reduced richness ■ Information may be distorted through poor question wording ■ Suffers from difficulties associated with questionnaires

questionnaire. This type of interview is often used when you have a very complex questionnaire to administer or where your participants are unable to complete a questionnaire on their own (for instance, very young children).

4.3 Interview techniques

For an interview to be successful (i.e. enable you to collect the data you want) it is vital that the interviewer has knowledge of (and sensitivity to) the effect of interpersonal variables, knowledge of techniques needed for successful interviewing, a good interview schedule and plenty of practice.

Effect of interpersonal variables

It is important to be aware of the possible effects of interpersonal variables on an interview and the data you collect. Because interviews are generally conducted face to face, people being interviewed are particularly susceptible to the influence that your sex, ethnicity, use of language or formal role (as a researcher/academic/expert) may have on them. Furthermore, people often feel the need to present themselves to others who are perceived to be in positions of power (such as an academic) in as good a way as possible (the **social desirability effect**). This can be particularly problematic with some topics where you want to hear about the failures or difficulties people have experienced rather than just their successes.

The effect of interpersonal variables and social desirability can be minimised in a number of ways. For instance, the type of language you use will affect the way the interviewee responds to you. If you use unfamiliar language (for instance, formal academic terms) people may feel alienated and try to present themselves in a similarly formal manner. So, always try to use appropriate language in a research interview. Obviously, rapport is also vital for effective interviewing. It can address the impact of social desirability and other interpersonal effects.

While it is important to make efforts to minimise the effects of interpersonal factors when interviewing, they will always be present in some form. However, this is not as big a problem as it seems as most analysis of interview material relies on an awareness of the effect of the interviewer on the interviewee. When carrying out qualitative analyses particular attention is paid to the influence of the interviewer on the production of the data.

Techniques needed for successful interviewing

As mentioned above, it is important to make your respondents comfortable and attempt to generate rapport with them if you are to stand any chance of carrying out a successful research interview. The best interviews are those where you develop a relationship with the interviewee such that they feel comfortable, relaxed and able to tell you about even the most intimate aspects of their lives. But how do you achieve rapport in an interview?

- *Use of appropriate language.* It is important that your participants feel comfortable if you are to establish rapport, and the use of appropriate language is an important factor in doing this. For instance, if you use very formal language and technical terms your participants may feel even more anxious and uncomfortable. It is often advisable to try to use the language that your interviewee would normally use (but do not fall into the trap of trying to speak in a way that is not natural for you as well – you will only look stupid and lose any credibility you may have had).

- *Neutrality.* As in counselling, you should appear neutral in a research interview. This means that you do not judge an interviewee or look shocked (not even a raised eyebrow) – no matter what! This is easier said than done, and worth practising in role-play.

- *Confidentiality.* Most of the time you will be able to assure your participants of confidentiality and you should tell them this. This should help generate a feeling of safety for your interviewee. However, do remember that if you guarantee your participants confidentiality then you must really maintain confidentiality – so keep that data safe and remove any identifying features from your written report/s (this is discussed in more detail in Chapter 25).

Successful interviewing also requires the use of effective listening skills. Many lessons can be learnt from client-centred counselling where the focus of attention is always on the client receiving therapy. Through the use of a variety of listening skills you will be able to communicate to the interviewee that you want them to talk and keep talking. A number of key skills are listed in Box 4.3.

Box 4.3

Information box

Key skills for successful interviewing

Give your respondent permission to speak

One of the first things many experienced interviewers do is share information (with the interviewee) at the start of the interview about the purpose and importance of the research and why the information they will receive from the interviewee is of value. However, it is also worth telling the interviewee about the process of the interview as well. That is, that you will not be saying much (because you are interested in hearing what your respondent has to say) and that you want them to tell you as much as they can, even if they do not think it is important or of value. In other words, you encourage them to elaborate stories from the outset by giving them permission to speak.

▶

Box 4.3 *Continued*

Learn when not to talk

It is important to leave gaps so that an interviewee is able to find space to think, compose their response and talk. This is easier said than done and another technique worth practising in role-play. One more thing – try not to make too much noise when encouraging your participant to keep talking; a nod of the head will generally have the same effect without producing incessant grunts (that you have to transcribe later – see Chapter 18) on your audio recording.

Be comfortable with silence

When people first start interviewing (and for that matter counselling) they often find it difficult to step outside the normal conversational rules that are vital for effective communication in everyday life. One of those unwritten rules for many people is to fill silent pauses (have you ever wondered why we have so many conversations about the weather?). However, when you are interviewing you need to allow silence (as long as the interviewee is comfortable with it) so that people have sufficient time to think about their responses (remember you are familiar with your interview schedule but your respondents are not).

Do not trivialise responses

Another important lesson from counselling here. It is important that all responses are treated with respect. If you look like you could not care less (or shocked and disgusted) this will be picked up by your interviewee. You must listen to everything that is said and treat everything said with appropriate respect. This is important for both ethical and practical reasons.

Do not dominate

Some people can appear a little forceful in conversation. It is important that you recognise these aspects of your personality and try to lessen their effect in an interview. So, when we interview we may need to think about slowing down and talking more softly so that we do not dominate the interview and inhibit the interviewee. Of course, if you are very quiet and softly spoken you may have to learn to speak up. And one more thing – try not to let the setting (including the recording device) intimidate your participants. Many people feel intimidated by universities (especially laboratory rooms in a university) and surprising numbers of people are anxious when there is a tape or digital recorder present. So, try to interview people in a setting where they feel comfortable and keep the audio recorder out of the way so people forget about it.

Box 4.3 *Continued*

Look interested!

There are a number of ways of looking interested even if you are not! Firstly, appropriate listening and responding demonstrate interest. Secondly, the use of appropriate non-verbal communication (leaning forward and nodding) also helps. However, there is no substitute for genuine interest, so always try to interview people about things you care about.

A good interview schedule

A good interview schedule is a key factor for successful interviewing. At its most basic it is nothing more than a list of questions that you will ask your participants. However, a well-constructed schedule will enable you to gather much more detailed information about a topic than a hastily constructed list of questions. Semi-structured interviews (the most common form used in psychology) rely on a good schedule. Unstructured interviews generally require a list of questions or topics but not really a schedule that you follow in the interview. Conversely, you cannot conduct a structured interview without a formal list of questions and responses to communicate to your participants (often looking more like a complicated questionnaire than an interview schedule).

The way questions are worded in an interview schedule is important (although less so than with a questionnaire as you are present to clarify issues if they arise). However, the rules for wording appropriate questions for an interview are pretty much the same as those for questionnaires (see the advice given in Chapter 5 for questionnaires). There are a few issues of particular importance for writing good interview questions in Box 4.4.

Box 4.4

Information box

Writing interview schedules

Avoid jargon

Use language your respondent (and you) will feel comfortable with. Try to avoid jargon or technical terms that are not widely used and understood.

Try to use open rather than closed questions

Open-ended questions enable the respondent to open up about their thoughts and feelings.

- Bad: Should the president resign?
- Good: What do you think the president should do now?

Box 4.4 *Continued*

Minimal encouragers/probes

These are single words or short phrases that encourage or reinforce the interviewee. They are very helpful in demonstrating that you are listening and encouraging your participant to keep talking.

- Examples include: 'I see', 'Go on', 'Yes', 'Hmm', 'Can you tell me more?', 'What happened next?'

Probes can also be used to encourage the elicitation of specific types of information.

- For example, *affect*: 'How did that make you feel?'
- Or to focus on *awareness*: 'What do you think about that?'

Funnelling

Start by eliciting the respondent's general views and then move on to more specific concerns. The respondent may answer the later questions when answering the first (in which case you move on) but listing the more detailed questions enables you to check out all possible responses. This approach enables you to gather the most detailed information possible in a way that is led by the interviewee.

- For example:
    1. What do you think of current government policies?
        (a) On health issues?
        (b) On welfare issues?
    2. Is there anything you would like to see changed?
    3. Are there any new health or welfare policies you think should be introduced?
        (a) Integrated service delivery?
        (b) New national service framework?

Practice

There is no substitute for plenty of practice if you wish to become proficient at interviewing. Although the advice given in this chapter will help you write a good schedule and teach you the basics of interviewing, you will only develop the key skills you need through practice (see Box 4.5).

Box 4.5

Activity box — Developing interview skills

- In a group of three, role-play some interviews. One of you should be the interviewer, one the interviewee and one an observer. Each of you should write a short interview schedule about a particular topic. Once you have done this, swap schedules and offer constructive criticism (about more questions, question-wording, etc.) to each other.

- Now it is time to practise interviewing (three in total) with each of you in a different role in each interview. All three of you should concentrate on the skills and techniques outlined in this chapter and identify any problems you encounter (for instance, the strengths and weaknesses of the schedule, what do you need to practise and improve, etc.).

- Following this role-play you should next try out your skills on a friend (who is not a psychologist) or (better still) a member of your family. Pick a topic that your friend or family member could talk about (for instance, talk to a grandparent about their wartime experiences) and write an appropriate schedule. Find a time when you will not be disturbed and carry out the interview (you should ideally audio-record this so you can listen to how it went later). Try to avoid sensitive topics until you have had more practice and – most importantly – support from an experienced researcher.

4.4 Group discussions

Group discussions have become an increasingly popular and important method of data collection in psychology in recent years. There has been a long tradition of *focus group* research, most often conducted within a broadly positivist tradition and used primarily in market research. In focus group research the primary aim is normally to survey public opinion about products or services using both quantitative and qualitative analysis of group member responses to prompts and questions. Focus groups offer a number of advantages, the primary one being the collection of large amounts of data in a relatively short space of time. More recently, there has also been growth in the use of group discussions to collect data within more critical qualitative perspectives. This latter approach employs group discussions to collect data which may be more naturalistic than that from individual interviews and one in which interactions can be foregrounded. Whilst the growth of this alternative use of group discussions has been relatively recent, the focus on interaction and – in particular – group dynamics has a long history, primarily within psychoanalytically informed analyses. Effectively, we see a split here between a concern with focus groups on content (e.g. attitudes or beliefs about a product) and process (e.g. the way in which people take turns in conversation or how power is employed between people). Of course, this is a crude split as many researchers will be interested in both aspects when using group discussions to collect data. Indeed, an additional benefit from using group discussions is the ability to collect data which better reflects shared meanings – that is, collective or socially constructed understandings – rather than simply garnering data from individuals necessarily reflecting their individual viewpoints. As a result, group discussions have proved to be a particularly important method of data collection (along with the collection of truly naturally occurring talk) in discursive methodologies (see Chapter 21).

There are a number of issues to be considered when using group discussions to collect data which are distinct from those issues common to both individual interviews and group data collection and we will outline a few of these below.

Selecting participants

The choice of participants for a group discussion will of course be dependent on the research question but there are additional concerns. A group could be selected from a naturally occurring group, such as a group of work colleagues or family unit. In contrast, a researcher might decide to recruit participants who are unknown to each other but have some connection to the research topic (for instance, by constructing a group of people who have never met but who all have experience of living with a medical condition). Regardless, it is important to make sure that the focus of the group discussion has been planned in advance and the group facilitator well placed to ensure that the group members feel comfortable and able to contribute to the discussion that takes place. When using pre-existing groups it is important to be mindful of existing group relationships and the impact that these will have on the discussion that takes place. Families, for instance, will invariably have well-established modes of communication, which – if the focus is on understanding naturally occurring discussion in families – may be part of the aim of the research but if this is not the primary concern may lead to some members dominating whilst others are silenced. Conversely, groups of strangers may feel distinctly uncomfortable in a group discussion setting unless the facilitator acts to ensure that any tension is dealt with early on. There are a variety of methods for dealing with this, including the use of warm-up exercises and by outlining group rules.

Warm-up exercises and group rules

A useful technique for establishing a sense of rapport within groups is to use some simple warm-up exercises. This can also form part of the data collection process. For instance, it might be useful to have some index cards with statements about the topic being studied on them for people to sort into groups or order of importance. As they do this they can be asked to explain their reasoning to fellow members of the group. When using such exercises it is important to keep them brief so there is plenty of time for the discussion proper and also to ensure the recording device is turned on as they often generate valuable verbal data.

Establishing group rules is vital when conducting group discussion research and is likely to involve a balance between providing a set of rules and negotiating particular issues. At the most basic it would be usual to make clear to all participants that it is crucial to respect each other and ensure that all information will be kept confidential. This can sometimes create problems when working with established groups or with people who are likely to encounter each other in settings outside the research group. Consent must also be established and this needs to be done on both an individual basis as well as a group basis. A researcher should talk through the research aims with each individual group member before they participate in the group and then also address this with the group as a whole. There should also be an opportunity for individual debriefing should participants want it and here they should be given the opportunity to withdraw their consent. A further issue that warrants some discussion is the level of participation and disclosure of individual members as participants need to be advised to ensure that they feel comfortable sharing information with others.

The role of the group facilitator

Facilitating a group is quite a different process from conducting an individual interview, although there are similarities with regard to the need to keep the focus on the participants and their views and ensure they feel comfortable to articulate whatever they wish. Like interviews, it will be necessary at times to ask questions but with groups these may be either to individuals, to encourage them to speak, or to the group to keep them on topic or to develop their arguments further. A facilitator might ask if people agree or disagree with something someone has stated but, regardless, it is important to try to be inclusive and supportive when posing questions. A group setting can feel quite threatening and it is therefore particularly important that a facilitator ensures no one feels isolated or threatened by any questions asked. Occasionally one or more people may dominate and it may be appropriate to intervene to enable others to speak. This needs to be done tactfully by, for instance, thanking the person for their views and then asking others about their views on what has been said. Alternatively, it might be appropriate to target questions to individuals but here it is often best to do this to a number of people rather than just one person to avoid them feeling exposed. Finally, it is worth being aware of the tendency for people to direct their responses to the facilitator rather than each other and inadvertently produce what is in effect a series of public individual interviews. Turning the response towards others is a useful technique to encourage people to talk with each other in such situations.

Recording the group discussion

Group discussion will invariably be recorded like individual interviews but they pose additional problems which should be considered. First, it is important to limit the numbers of participants to a relatively small number (four or five is usual) as it can become difficult not only to deal with managing a larger group but also transcribing the voices of so many people. Another tip is to try if at all possible to ensure that people have different-sounding voices. This is not of course possible all the time but it can make transcription an awful lot easier! Finally, it is important to think through – in advance – how such data will be analysed. A number of methods rely primarily on individual interviews and it can be difficult to use or adapt these methods for group data. As in all research, think through the whole process before embarking on any data collection to ensure you are not left with data that you do not know how to analyse.

4.5 Repertory grid techniques

Repertory grid methods (often known as rep grids) developed within personal construct theory (see Butt & Burr, 2004, for an introduction), a theory developed by personality theorist George Kelly. They have become an important method independent of personal construct theory, and are used in a wide variety of applied situations from clinical settings to business. Rep grids are used idiographically (focusing on one person's outlook) and also nomothetically (concerned with finding patterns amongst people). Their idiographic use has been particularly valuable in clinical settings. The essence of rep grids is how people understand the meanings that define their perception of relationships to others (a person's repertory of role constructs). At the simplest level, a person would be asked to compare and contrast sets of three people (for instance, themselves, their mother, their father) on dimensions of meaning. This is done by asking people how they think two of the figures are alike and different from the third. A person might, for instance, describe themselves and their mother as loving and their father as distant and thus produce a dimension of meaning of loving versus distant. This dimension would then be considered a significant construct for the person in how they understand their social world. By asking participants to compare a number of triads (self, mother, father, sibling, liked other, disliked other, ideal self, etc.) it becomes possible to elicit a broad range of constructs that describe a person's outlook on life. These constructs can then be examined to form the basis of further interviewing (or indeed, psychotherapeutic interventions) or subject to quantitative analysis using SPSS or a variety of dedicated computer programs to identify patterns and/or categories of meaning.

A further step that is commonly used is to ask participants to rate or rank each element (e.g. people) on the constructs that have been elicited. This results in a grid in which the elements constitute the columns and the constructs the rows. Participants then rate each element (for instance, using a seven-point scale with 1 equivalent to one end of a construct and 7 the opposite end) against each construct. So, for instance, self might be one of the elements which the participant rates as 1 on the construct loving versus distant to indicate that they perceive themself to be a very loving person. Rep grids of this form can be almost any size, from a minimum of six constructs to hundreds. Most researchers would expect to have reached saturation point with about 15 to 20 constructs, however. Grids (matrices of elements against constructs) can then be subject to a number of quantitative analyses to discern patterns in individual grids and also across a number of grids. It is also possible to use some of the specialist grid software to elicit constructs directly rather than use paper and pen. Analyses may involve correlating particular elements (such as self and ideal self) to reveal valuable information for use in, for instance, psychotherapy or personal development programmes. In many research applications researchers will often employ complex statistical methods such as factor analysis or multi-dimensional scaling, which are beyond the scope of this text, to determine patterns within the data. Interested readers should be able to find more on this by reading the sources listed in the Further reading section below.

4.6 Observation

Observation has a long tradition within psychology, particularly developmental psychology where for many years researchers have observed children in order to (for instance) identify developmental milestones. However, observation is not the exclusive preserve of developmental psychology. Studies of human interaction, animal behaviour and so on have relied upon observation for the collection of their data. Furthermore, participant observation (which is discussed in detail below), where the observer participates in the setting being observed, has played an important part in sociological (and to a lesser extent psychological) research. This section will introduce you to the various types of observational method in common usage, from structured observation in a laboratory setting to full participant observation. You will also be exposed to the particular uses of observation and some of its strengths and weaknesses. Observation can be of great use in gathering descriptive information about some behaviour (such as children's play). However, it is often difficult to ascertain a causal relationship between variables (e.g. the effect of number of toys on amount of play engaged in) with observational studies. This is because naturalistic observation does not allow you to manipulate independent variables (e.g. the number of toys available in a nursery) and measure the effect on the dependent variable (amount of play). However, there have been some innovative studies that have addressed this issue. For instance, there have been studies where independent variables are manipulated (number of toys or space available for play) in an ecologically valid way (e.g. in a nursery attached to a psychology department).

Choosing what to observe

One of the first issues that you will encounter when deciding on observation as a method is the decision about what to observe. It is all too easy to decide to observe some children playing but you will quickly encounter problems without a little more thought about what you will focus your observation on. Are you going to observe one child or several children? Are you going to record their speech and non-verbal behaviour? How will you know when they are playing? Are all types of play the same? These are just a few of the issues that you would need to address before starting an observation of children's play. Many people find they have observed much of what was going on but found to their cost that none of it was relevant to the research question they wanted to address. You need to know what it is that you want to get from your observation and what you need to observe to do that. Good observation is often theoretically informed so you have some principles guiding the focus of your research.

4.7 Structured and non-participant observation

Structure

Observations, like interviews, vary in the degree of structure that is imposed. They range from the fully structured with formal observation schedules to the relatively unstructured form that is participant observation.

Fully structured laboratory (controlled) observation

Fully structured observation involves the collection of data in a systematic, structured manner. You would generally use some method of data collection and coding to maximise the reliability of material collected. Observers may use grid recording systems where they make a note of how often a particular behaviour occurs. This obviously requires the use of a coding system, which enables you to decide to which category a particular behaviour should belong (coding is discussed in more detail below). These methods can be complex and often require training so that an observer can appropriately categorise behaviour and use the coding system reliably. A classic example of structured observation comes from Ainsworth's (1979) studies of attachment and separation amongst children. In these studies Mary Ainsworth video recorded children when their mothers left and a stranger entered. From these video recordings Ainsworth was able to understand more about the attachment needs and styles of children. Very often these types of study are conducted in a laboratory setting.

When attempting to collect data systematically and reliably we often want to control the effect of extraneous variables on the behaviour or setting. Obviously this is much easier in a laboratory than out in the field. Furthermore, the reliability of our observations will be improved through the use of, for instance, video recording equipment. It is much easier to observe (and then code) a situation using video recording in a laboratory. A great deal of structured observation is conducted in a laboratory for these reasons.

Advantages	Disadvantages
■ Systematic collection of data ■ Permanent record of data kept (if using recording equipment) ■ Extraneous variables controlled ■ Setting can be kept constant ■ Replication possible ■ Observer bias should be minimised	■ May lack ecological validity (see below) ■ Behaviour may not be spontaneous or realistic ■ May not be possible (where participants would not cooperate) or ethical in some situations

Naturalistic field (uncontrolled) observation

Unlike laboratory-based observation, **naturalistic observation** involves the observer studying people in their natural environment. This type of 'field' research has a number of benefits over laboratory-based observation, including, for instance, greater **ecological validity**, but not without some costs! This type of observation involves the observer recording data through video recording or, more often, note taking while trying to remain unobtrusive.

One of the main problems with naturalistic observation is the danger of your presence affecting the (naturally occurring) behaviour of the participants. We all know what it is like when someone produces a camera – some play up to it while others run for the hills, but no one acts naturally again until the camera is put away! This is especially true of children. However, given enough time children (and adults) tend to forget the camera is present and return to behaving naturally. This is very important for naturalistic observation. The best observational studies repeatedly observe the participants so that they get used to the presence of the observer and observing equipment. It is hoped that over time people will forget about the presence of the observer and act naturally. One other method for limiting your effect on the people being observed is by assuming a role where observation (in some form) is expected. So, for instance, we expect people sitting in a street-side coffee bar to watch the world go by. By assuming a role of this kind you can blend into the background and limit the influence you have on the setting.

Advantages	Disadvantages
■ Greater ecological validity (see below) ■ Realistic, spontaneously occurring behaviour ■ Useful where it is not possible to observe participants in a laboratory ■ Behaviour should be less subject to the demand characteristics of the setting	■ More difficult to conduct ■ Difficult for observer to be unobtrusive ■ Extraneous variables poorly controlled ■ Greater potential for observer bias ■ Replication may be difficult ■ Use of recording equipment may be difficult

Ecological validity

One of the key distinctions between laboratory and non-laboratory (or naturalistic) settings is the degree of **ecological validity**. Ecological validity concerns the meaningfulness of data collected in settings where it would naturally (and spontaneously) occur. Obviously, most observation in a laboratory is low in ecological validity because the behaviour would not occur naturally or spontaneously. Most of us are unfamiliar with laboratory settings and tend to produce very little behaviour spontaneously without some manipulation by the experimenter. However, if we are observed playing sport or drinking with friends (naturalistic observation) we tend to act as we always do in that setting – naturally and spontaneously (unless influenced by the presence of the observer, of course).

So, why conduct observations in laboratories at all if your data lack ecological validity? Well, there are lots of good reasons. Firstly, although ecological validity is important and is undoubtedly reduced in a laboratory, it does not mean that the data have no validity at all. We always have to compromise when conducting research in psychology and it may be worth sacrificing some degree of ecological validity for the benefits of a laboratory setting. These benefits include the following.

The practicality of observing complex behaviour

It may not be possible to observe some types of behaviour in a setting other than the laboratory. Laboratories may have equipment available that is necessary for the study in question. Observation laboratories typically include two-way mirrors (where you can observe your participants without them knowing you are there – all they see is a mirror), which are particularly useful for observing children (adults tend to guess what is going on very quickly), and high quality audio and video recording equipment. There may also be other equipment available (such as experiment generator software and/or psychophysiological measuring equipment – discussed in Chapter 6, on experimental design) that you want to use in conjunction with observation.

Control over the setting

There are many benefits to recording natural spontaneously occurring behaviour but we invariably have no control over the person or people we are observing and their environment. It is important to remember that we do not just collect descriptive data through observation. Sometimes we want to test a theory about human behaviour where observation is the most appropriate form of data collection. Without the ability to manipulate the setting (as is often the case with field observation) it may prove impossible to test our theory (see Smith & Cowie, 1988, for examples of experimental observations of children).

Recording data

Note taking

Taking notes is the most traditional way of recording observational data but it is a difficult and highly subjective method. There are, of course, times when it is not possible (or desirable) to use video recording and here note taking comes into its own. For instance, participant observation (where you are immersed and active in the setting) generally requires the use of note taking to record data. Audio or video recording would often prove too intrusive when collecting data in this way.

Video recording

It is perhaps not surprising to find that video recording is most often the method of choice for observational studies. Certainly observations of large numbers of participants are not really practical without video recording. In addition, when the observation is based in a laboratory it may be convenient (and no more obtrusive) to use video recording.

Coding

As discussed above, **coding** may be a useful and necessary technique for data collection when carrying out systematic structured observations. If we wish to collect data in a systematic way we need some predetermined framework to impose on the setting we are observing. Without a framework of this kind it would not be possible to collect complex data in a reliable, systematic way. Generally a coding frame consists of a number of predetermined codes (symbols or shorthand codes) which should be comprehensive enough to cover most behaviours you are interested in observing (but not so many that you are unable to apply them reliably). Observers then indicate (on a coding sheet) every time some type of behaviour occurs (codes enable observers to cluster similar types of behaviour together). Some systems are more elaborate and involve rating scales for each behaviour (so, for example, the severity of some violent encounter may be rated 1 (minimal violence) to 7 (maximum violence)). An example of a coding frame is given in Box 4.6.

> **Box 4.6**
>
> **Information box**
>
> **Coding frame for structured observation**
>
> An example (part) of a coding frame designed for observing play in children.
>
> | Verbal behaviour | | Non-verbal behaviour | |
> |---|---|---|---|
> | ATT | – Demands attention | HAN | – Holds hand |
> | WINF | – Wants information | SMI | – Smiles |
> | GINF | – Gives information | LOOK | – Looks around |
> | IMT | – Imitates other child | REA | – Reaches out hand |
>
> - And so on until you have enough categories to cover all elements of the behaviour you wish to observe (and there are many more categories needed to observe children's play).
> - These codes could then be arranged in an observation grid so that you can place a mark in a box every time the behaviour occurs during the observation period. The data can then be analysed statistically.

In addition to a coding frame, structured observation often needs some method of data sampling. When it is not possible to record a setting, 'live' coding is necessary. Obviously this is much more difficult than coding data in your own time from video after the event (for one thing, you do not have a rewind button when coding 'live'). When coding 'live' it may not be possible for you to observe some event or behaviour continuously for several hours as you wish. In these cases you may find a sampling strategy useful where you observe only the setting when some behaviour occurs (such as a playground fight starting) or for repeated (short) periods of time. If you ever try 'live' coding you will quickly appreciate the need for a sampling strategy. Two of the commonest sampling strategies are discussed below.

Event sampling

Event sampling is where you observe only when a particular event (such as a playground fight) occurs. This is generally over a sustained period of time and may be particularly useful if you are interested in observing some specific behaviour or event. For example, you may be interested in observing the ways in which playground fights dissipate. Choosing to observe the playground when a fight breaks out (the event of interest) should enable you to do this effectively. However, if you are interested in how fights start event sampling may be problematic, as the fight will invariably have started before you begin observing it! In this case you may need to use time sampling instead.

Time sampling

Time sampling involves repeated observations (for short periods of time) over a longer period of time. So, for instance, you may observe a setting (making detailed observations) for 15 seconds every five minutes over a two-hour period. This would result in 360 seconds (or six minutes) of observation in total, produced from a series of 'snapshots' of the setting. If the behaviour is complex then this may be all you can manage in one sitting. Further two-hour observations can then be undertaken until you feel you have collected sufficient data. Time sampling is best used where you can expect the behaviour of interest to occur repeatedly (such as playground fights). However, it is important to be aware of the possible limitations of this method of sampling. It is possible to produce a very unrepresentative picture of a setting if the time period chosen for the observation is not appropriate (for instance, too short or infrequent).

Multiple observers and reliability

When observing 'live' it is often advisable to have at least two observers. With particularly complex behaviour or many people being observed, you may need very large numbers of observers (at least two people per person being observed). All observers should be trained to use the coding framework so that it is applied consistently to the setting. When you have a record of observation from at least two observers it becomes possible to check the inter-rater (or inter-observer) reliability of your observations.

Inter-rater reliability

Inter-rater reliability is a measure of the degree of agreement (or disagreement) between two observers of an event (it can also be used for judging agreement in areas other than observation). Obviously, if your observation is reliable (and the coding system is working well) you should find that both observers record pretty much the same information (that is, when we recorded a fight in the playground of moderate severity, so did you). If a structured observation has produced reliable data there should be high inter-rater reliability. Inter-rater reliability is measured by correlating the scores (see Chapter 12) recorded by both observers. Values of inter-rater reliability range from 0 to 1 (or between 0 and 100 per cent), where 0 indicates no agreement and 1 total agreement, with good inter-rater reliability generally above 0.8 (80 per cent). However, the level of agreement deemed satisfactory is dependent on what is being observed. There are some situations where relatively modest levels of reliability may be acceptable (but there must be good reasons). Inter-rater reliability may be low for many reasons, including observer bias (where observers are evaluating behaviour rather than simply recording when it occurs). Training is often useful for minimising observer bias. Through role-play and practice observers can be taught to avoid evaluating the events they are observing and instead concentrate on producing as accurate a written record of the situation as possible.

However, human beings are always likely to miss the odd thing even when it may appear obvious to others. How often have we shouted our dismay (and much more!) at a soccer referee when they appear to be blind to what is happening straight in front of them?

4.8 Participant observation

Participant observation is a method very familiar to sociologists and social anthropologists but somewhat less so to psychologists. However, psychologists have used participant observation as a particularly insightful form of observation. Social psychologists have found the method useful for gaining insights into the way people understand and operate in their own environments. Participant observation produces highly subjective but very meaningful data that often cannot be collected in any other way. So what is participant observation? Well, when carrying out most forms of observation the observer tries to be unobtrusive. Participant observation accepts that in many cases this may not be possible or desirable and encourages the observer to participate in whatever is being observed (see Box 4.7).

Box 4.7
Activity box — Participant observation

This activity is designed to sensitise you to some of the difficulties involved in participant observation. Upon first inspection, participant observation seems a relatively easy method of data collection. However, as you should discover when you carry out your own observation, it can be surprisingly difficult.

- Decide on a setting to observe involving your friends or family. This could be an evening out in the pub with friends or a family mealtime; it does not matter as long as you are in a familiar (and safe) setting where you can observe for an hour or two.

- Observe the goings on – who said what, when and to whom, in other words what interactions took place. Try to find discreet moments to make some notes on a pad throughout the observation period. And at the end of the observation session write down as much as you can remember.

- Debrief the people who were the focus of your study fully about your activities once you have finished. You will need to explain what you were doing and why. Furthermore, you need to allow people to withdraw from the study at this time if they so wish. This should be unlikely when observing friends and family. See the discussion on ethics at the end of this section and Chapter 25.

Box 4.7 *Continued*

- When you have some spare time, write up your notes with a commentary where you should attempt some analysis of what went on. Finally, reflect on the process of carrying out the observation, the effect you had on the setting, how easy or (more likely) difficult it was and what you think of the quality of your notes, analysis and write-up.

One of the biggest difficulties with participant observation is recording the data. How can you make notes when participating in a setting? Furthermore, if you are pretending to be a member of the group (rather than a researcher), as is sometimes the case with participant observation, then you may not want to risk being found out by making notes. What often happens is that notes are made at the end of the day (in private). Obviously this produces highly subjective data. However, this is less of a problem than it first seems. Firstly, many people using this method are working within the qualitative tradition of research (as discussed in Chapter 1). Qualitative approaches recognise and accept the subjective nature of data and work with it rather than trying to reduce it. Secondly, most participant observation studies involve the immersion of the observer in a setting for long periods of time so that individual observations are not crucial to the findings. Instead, experience gained through participation (over time) leads to personal insight into the lives of the people being observed.

However, there are different types of participant observation. In some situations participant observation is barely different from naturalistic observation with only limited involvement of the observer. However, participant observation may also involve the complete immersion of an observer into a setting (often for extended periods of time) where they become more of a participant than an observer.

Types of participant observation – full participant observation to full observation

Patton (1980) describes several types of participant observation with varying degrees of participation.

Full participant observation

With full participant observation the researcher does not disclose their identity but instead pretends to be a full member of the group being observed. The aim is for the people being observed to take the researcher as a full and authentic member of the group. It is thought that the trust that comes from the belief that the researcher is 'one of us' should lead to greater disclosure and greater ecological validity. Obviously, the deception involved in full participant observation raises serious ethical concerns (discussed below).

Participant as observer

With this type of participant observation the researcher's identity is not secret but simply kept quiet. The main reason given for the researcher being present is not their role as observer but some role salient to the group. This type of observation may be useful for research about a setting where you are already a participant (e.g. your workplace) or where you can easily become a temporary member of that group (for instance, as a relief teacher in a school). Box 4.8 describes a participant observation similar to this where the researcher lives in the city they observe (there are also some similarities to the 'observer as participant' approach described below).

Box 4.8 Study box

Beattie, G. (1986). *Survivors of Steel City – A Portrait of Sheffield*. London: Chatto & Windus Ltd.

This book presents a predominantly observational study of the lives of people living in Sheffield in the 1980s. It consists of observation of people in their natural settings supplemented by informal interviews. The data generated are rich and alive with the experiences of the men and women of Sheffield struggling to survive in a city suffering from years of unemployment, poverty and neglect. However, what emerges are the ways in which people have creatively carved out valuable and worthwhile roles in their particular communities. The researcher is often a participant in the settings he chooses to observe. However, he keeps his distance and tries to present an account that prioritises the experiences of the people he meets. There are no simple results or conclusions with work of this kind but instead a graphic insight into a community, and the people within it, fighting for its survival.

Observer as participant

This approach recognises the central importance of the observer role but relies on group members accepting this and over time learning to trust the researcher. It is this development of trust that is thought to facilitate the sharing of intimate information. The researcher needs to manage their role carefully in this situation. It is important to engender trust and not interfere in the natural actions of the setting being observed.

Full observer

This is not really participant observation at all but naturalistic observation as described previously in this section.

The table below outlines some of the advantages and disadvantages of participant observation.

Advantages	Disadvantages
■ High ecological validity ■ Detailed, insightful data ■ Highly contextual data ■ Development of trust may produce information inaccessible by other means	■ Researcher needs to rely on memory ■ Highly subjective ■ May be unreplicable ■ May be difficult to generalise results ■ There may be problems and even dangers in maintaining cover if full participant

Ethics

As mentioned above, participant observation raises a number of important ethical issues that need to be addressed (these are also dealt with in more detail in Chapter 25). The most important concern with full participant observation is the use of **deception**. Wherever possible, psychological research tries to minimise deception and maximise **informed consent** (that is, where the participants are *fully* aware of the nature of the study and still choose to participate in it). Obviously full participant observation involves deception and does not involve informed consent. It is therefore vital that there are very strong grounds for using this particular method. Unless there are, it would be unethical to proceed. Another concern with this method is the effect that disclosing your identity will have on the people you have been observing. What harmful effects might this betrayal have on those involved? Some previous studies have demonstrated the utility of this approach in ways that might be argued to justify its use. Holdaway (1982) studied 'canteen cultures' in the police force and revealed the deeply entrenched racist attitudes there. This important information might not have been revealed through any other method. However, despite studies of this kind there are still some who argue that there is never a good enough reason for this level of deception and betrayal (Banister, 1994). Certainly, before you contemplate using undisclosed participant observation you should think very carefully about whether there are less invasive ways of gathering the data and always seek advice from more experienced researchers.

Further reading

Arksey, H. & Knight, P. (1999). *Interviewing for Social Scientists*. London: Sage.

Bakeman, R. & Gottman, J. M. (1997). *Observing Interaction*. Cambridge: Cambridge University Press.

Jorgensen, D. L. (1989). *Participant Observation – A Methodology for Human Studies*. Sage Applied Social Research Methods Series Vol. 15. London: Sage.

Kvale, S. (2007). *Doing Interviews*. London: Sage.

Neimeyer, R.A. & Neimeyer, G.J. (Eds.)(2002). *Advances in Personal Construct Psychology*. New York: Praeger.

http://www.pcp-net.org/

Further information on personal construct psychology and repertory grid methods (along with several other methods that have been derived from personal construct theory) can be found in this book and website.

Wengraf, T. (2001). *Qualitative Research Interviewing*. London: Sage.

The books listed above provide excellent further coverage on the topics of data collection outlined in this chapter and are well worth a look before you decide to collect your own data.

5 Collecting data 2: questionnaires and psychometric tests

- This chapter introduces you to further methods of data collection, including questionnaire design and measurement.
- The importance of using an existing questionnaire, where possible, is emphasised.
- The process of developing a new questionnaire, where necessary, is described.
- This chapter will also introduce you to the field of psychometrics and its two key watchwords: reliability and validity.
- A selection of 'ready-made' reliable and valid tests are described, which you might consider using in your research.

INTRODUCTION

Real skill is required to collect data and without knowledge of the appropriate techniques of data collection the quality of your results may be questioned. This chapter is devoted to questionnaire design and psychometrics. Questionnaires are useful for collecting data from numbers of people in a systematic way. They are particularly valuable for development, social and applied (e.g. health) psychology research. As previously noted in Chapter 4, these chapters address only issues of data collection and not analysis, which is dealt with in Parts 2 and 3.

5.1 Questionnaires

Questionnaires are a particularly valuable method of data collection as they allow you to collect data from large numbers of people. Questionnaires are useful if you want to know something about the incidence of some behaviour or the opinions, beliefs or attitudes of large numbers or groups of people. So, questionnaires could be used to discover the beliefs of students about environmental issues or attitudes towards hunting with dogs. They are also useful if you want to measure something that is not directly observable (a theoretical **construct**). As psychologists, we can rarely measure constructs such as 'depression' directly. It may be possible to measure the consequences of depression, by using a questionnaire where participants can self-report their symptoms. However, gathering data from large numbers of people may be at the expense of the amount of information or detail you can collect. But with good questionnaire design you should be able to maximise the quality of data collected without increasing the size of the questionnaire unnecessarily. The field of psychometrics is concerned with the development of good psychological questionnaires. A good questionnaire is one that has **reliability** and **validity**. These two features are described in more detail later on in this chapter.

Questionnaires are useful for more than just collecting large amounts of data. They are often used as a convenient way of collecting background data (age, sex, ethnicity, etc.) in studies of all kinds and in the form of psychometric tests used to assess, for instance, cognitive ability or personality traits. They are also used to measure the effect of some intervention or treatment (such as a short course of psychotherapy) on the well-being (in terms of, for instance, anxiety or depression) of participants.

- Questionnaires can be used in all types of study design, including experiments.
- The term 'survey' is used to describe a study design where the questionnaire is the primary focus.
- Questions in questionnaires are often called questionnaire **items**, particularly in psychology. Personality scales and tests are said to contain 'items' rather than 'questions'. We use both terms interchangeably in this chapter.
- The term **scale** is used to describe a set of items that measure something psychological or something which is not measurable directly (a **construct**). Several scales might be published as an **inventory**.

5.2 The first rule of questionnaire design: don't reinvent the wheel

It is important not to 'reinvent the wheel' by developing a new questionnaire or scale unnecessarily. If a reliable and valid questionnaire exists for the construct you are interested in, use it or improve it (reliability and validity are described below). There are three reasons why this is the most sensible strategy:

1 Creating a new questionnaire takes a long time.
2 You will be able to make sense of your results and interpret them in light of the existing literature.
3 Other researchers will understand what you have claimed to measure. You will find it far easier to defend your study if the questionnaire or test is widely respected in the field.

As discussed in Chapter 3 a great many questionnaires simply present old wine in new bottles. Psychologists are very good at creating 'jangles' for constructs – different labels for what are essentially the same thing. For example, many different personality tests all claim to measure traits such as 'negative emotionality' or 'trait negative affect'. These are all jangles for Neuroticism. The term 'jingle' refers to giving different constructs the same name, a less common but equally wasteful exercise. This warning applies to questionnaires and tests regardless of how you use them. If you are conducting a survey or an experiment, the same principle applies. It also applies when the test is an 'outcome' measure in an experiment. For example, if you conducted an experiment (Chapter 6) to evaluate the impact of an intervention on depression scores, it would be very unwise to design a new questionnaire to measure depression. Use an existing, validated measure (in this case, the General Health Questionnaire, Hospital Anxiety and Depression Scale, or the SF-36 MCS scale would be appropriate).

5.3 General principles, types and structure of questionnaires

If you have decided to study a topic where the constructs have not been defined, or explored, it may be necessary to design a new questionnaire. Be very careful if you claim to be studying a 'new' construct. Researchers frequently claim to have discovered a 'new intelligence', a new 'cognitive domain' or another 'personality trait'. It later turns out that they have produced a jangle for cognitive ability or one of the big five personality traits. Most differences in personality traits, for example, can be understood in relation to the big five framework. Most cognitive skills are already well researched, in the hierarchical model of cognitive ability. These are explained in more detail later in the chapter.

General principles

There are a variety of general principles that inform good questionnaire design. One of the first principles is that you should keep the questionnaire as short as possible. Questions should be included only if you have good reasons for their inclusion (it is no good putting in a question 'just in case'!). People will find any excuse for not completing a questionnaire. We have all been there – approached by someone in the street or sent a questionnaire in the post. Did you take the time to complete the questionnaire? It is important that you design a questionnaire that is quick and easy to complete unless there are very strong reasons for doing otherwise. Research invariably involves a trade-off between the parsimony (simplicity) of the method of data collection and the depth of information gathered. You need to think about this balance and make the appropriate decision about ease of completion versus depth of information.

Readability

Another principle of questionnaire design is to ensure that it is written in language appropriate for your respondents (this is dealt with in more detail below). Many researchers overestimate the reading ability of the general population. You can test the readability of your questionnaire in Microsoft Word, in the spell checking facility. First make sure that this option is switched on. Click on **Tools, Options, Spelling and Grammar**. Check that both **Check grammar with spelling** and **Show readability statistics** are both ticked, then click **OK**. Next time you run the spelling and grammar check (**Tools, Spelling and Grammar**), readability statistics are displayed at the end of the process.

- Passive sentences are difficult to read, and should be avoided.
- Flesch Reading Ease is a score from 0 to 100 (higher scores indicate text that is easier to read)
- Flesch–Kincaid Grade Level converts the score into a US school grade level. This should be as low as possible; preferably 7th (age 12–13) to 8th grade (age 13–14) at an absolute maximum.

As a general rule, because some participants may have low levels of reading ability, you should improve the readability of your questionnaire. This can be achieved easily by reducing the length of sentences, and reducing the number of syllables in the words. For example, the first sentence of this paragraph requires a grade level of 14, which is degree level! This can easily be reduced by changing the sentence to 'Some people are not good readers. You should make your questionnaire easier to read.' This has a grade level of 3 (age 8–9), which is far more acceptable.

Attach a Participant Information Sheet

All questionnaires should begin with a Participant Information Sheet which tells participants about the study. It should explain clearly what it is about and why people should spend the time to complete your questionnaire. It should explain who you are and give contact details in case your respondents wish to ask questions about the study. It is also important to inform your respondents about what you intend to do with the data and whether you can assure them of anonymity and/or confidentiality. In fact, you would need very strong justification for being unable to protect the confidentiality of your participants. One final purpose of the introductory statement is to 'sell' your project. You need to maximise participation so you should tell people why your work is important and why you need their help. If you will ask sensitive questions, warn people on the Information Sheet so that they can choose whether or not to provide *informed* consent.

Attach a consent form

Depending on your institution and the nature of your study, you may need to attach a separate consent form. A consent form records the date, name and signature of each participant, indicating that they have read the Participant Information Sheet and agree to take part in the study. Some researchers combine the Participant Information Sheet with the consent form. If you have a separate consent form, make sure that this is detached from the questionnaire and stored separately in a secure location. Names that can be linked to the questionnaire (e.g. by ID number) are a threat to anonymity. Talk this through with your tutor or contact your relevant ethics review committee for advice specific to your project.

Stages of design

There are a number of stages that you need to go through to carry out a questionnaire study. Obviously the first stage is to decide on a topic to research and then develop your research question(s). This should be followed by careful planning and design of your questionnaire. This will include making decisions about the range and type of questions to include (open versus closed questions) and careful thought about question wording. Following the design of your questionnaire (discussed in more detail below) you should always **pilot** your questionnaire.

All questionnaires should be piloted – that is, tested out on a small number of people – before being widely distributed. Piloting will enable you to 'iron out' the flaws in your questionnaire and make sure that you are asking the right questions and providing the appropriate response options. It is often a good idea to sit with your pilot participants while they complete the questionnaire so that you can get feedback about it as you go. If your participants need to ask you questions then you may need to do some more work on your questionnaire. Finally, you should always ask for detailed feedback after your participants have completed the questionnaire. Was it relevant? Was it easy to complete? Could they express their responses as they wanted to?

Once you have piloted your questionnaire you should make sure that you address all the problems raised by your pilot participants. Do not just write them off. There is no point in carrying out a pilot study unless you use it as a check on the quality of your questionnaire. Remember to pay attention to the layout of your questionnaire – it should be clear (and ideally aesthetically pleasing) to your participants. In addition, the layout should enable you, the researcher, to read the responses off the questionnaire easily and enter them into the appropriate analysis software package (see Chapter 9).

Following successful piloting and revision of the questionnaire you will want to administer your questionnaire. This is where you distribute your questionnaires to your participants. It is important to distribute your questionnaire to an appropriate sample that will enable you to meet your study aims (see the section on sampling below). After your respondents have completed the questionnaire you will need to collect the questionnaires and enter and analyse your data.

Question types

Open versus closed questions

Open-ended questions (see Box 5.1) often generate more detailed information than closed questions, but at a cost. They increase the size of questionnaires and have a dramatic effect on how long it takes to complete a questionnaire. There is also a danger that many people will not complete open-ended questions at all (in order to complete the questionnaire as quickly as possible), resulting in very patchy data. It is advisable to avoid using open-ended questions without good grounds for including them (just wanting to know more about a topic is rarely a good reason). Open-ended questions need to be focused so you avoid essay responses that you can do little with. Furthermore, you need to know what form of analysis you can use to interpret the data you collect (of course this is true for any type of question but especially true of open-ended questions). However, there *are* good reasons for using open-ended questions. They enable you to collect richer data than closed questions – akin to data collected through interviews. They also avoid the problem of imposing the researcher's structure on the respondents. One of the commonest criticisms of questionnaires comprising closed questions is that they limit possible responses. Indeed, in extreme cases you could collect data that have little or no real meaning to the participants – they could follow the structure you supply and routinely answer the questions without any thought.

Closed questions require very careful wording and thought about the appropriate type of response options. You need clear, unambiguous questions and response options that enable people to complete the questions quickly and easily. You do not want people to feel frustrated and confused because they cannot work out what the question is asking or how to respond appropriately. There are some obvious benefits to using closed questions. Perhaps the most important is that they enable you to collect reliable information that is easily analysed. They also make a questionnaire easy and quick to complete for your participants. Finally, they provide a reliable way of making people respond to the issues you are interested in by avoiding the danger of open-ended questions where people tell you much more than you need to know. There are many different types of response option, ranging from 'yes/no' responses to Likert scales (where you respond from 1 (strongly agree) to 7 (strongly disagree), for instance). Some are shown in Box 5.1 and this issue is discussed again in the 'Measuring attitudes' section.

Box 5.1

Information box

Examples of open-ended and closed questions

Open-ended questions

1 What do you think about the government policy on university tuition fees?
   _____
   _____
   _____

2 Briefly state what you think are the reasons for eating organic produce.
   _____
   _____
   _____

Closed questions (with differing response options)

3 Do you think hunting foxes with dogs should be banned?   Yes ☐ No ☐

4 Adoption of children should be more accessible (circle one number below):
   Strongly agree   1   2   3   4   5   6   7   Strongly disagree

5 I think the Internet is (circle a number for each line below):

Good	1	2	3	4	5	6	7	Bad
Interesting	1	2	3	4	5	6	7	Uninteresting
Useful	1	2	4	5	5	6	7	Not useful
Strong	1	2	4	5	5	6	7	Weak
Active	1	2	4	5	5	6	7	Passive

5.4 Writing questions and measuring attitudes

Writing questions

One of the most crucial elements of questionnaire design is how you word the questions. Badly worded questions will frustrate and confuse your respondents. Furthermore, they may also result in you collecting information that is not valid. However, there are a number of well-known rules that should enable you to construct questions that are clear and effective.

Ask one question at a time

This might seem obvious but there is more to it than meets the eye. One of the commonest problems people encounter when first writing questions is keeping them simple. It is all too easy to make a question too complex. So, keep it simple and make sure you are not trying to do too much with each question (if it *can* be worded as two questions then it *should* be). Asking people if they agree that 'Fox and badger hunting should be banned' is asking two questions. Some people may have different views about each type of hunting. This might be an interesting phenomenon to study.

Avoid ambiguous questions

As before, you need to keep things simple, but this time so that you avoid ambiguous questions (questions that have more than one meaning). When we write questions we obviously know what we mean but it is surprising how often this can seem ambiguous to other people. The question 'Fox hunting should stop when the fox goes to ground' refers to the fox going underground. Some people might think that it refers to the fox stopping on the ground, or being killed on the ground. The best way to check this is to pilot your questionnaire thoroughly.

Avoid double negatives

When asking people if they agree with questionnaire items such as 'Fox hunting should not be banned', double negatives make the question more difficult to follow. If the response options ranged from 'agree' to 'disagree', people might hesitate as they try to work out if they are agreeing with the ban, or that there should *not* be a ban.

Tell respondents if your questions are going to be sensitive

Be careful how you ask questions about 'sensitive' topics – you do not want people to find your questions offensive or shocking. At best they may miss the question out (and missing data can be a real problem which should be avoided) and at worst you may receive complaints about the offensive nature of your questions. One technique for avoiding shocks and surprises is to work towards the more sensitive questions gradually, giving explanations and even warnings (if necessary) of why you need to ask these questions. Ideally, the Participant Information Sheet should warn participants what kind of questions will be asked. The 'foot in the door' technique, increasing the sensitivity of questions once people have started the study, is generally not ethically acceptable. People may feel obliged to finish something they agreed to complete. The worst possible approach is to try to slip a question about a sensitive issue in among other more innocuous questions in the hope people will not notice – believe us, they will!

Questions should be neutral rather than value-laden or leading

You should always try to keep your questions neutral rather than value-laden. We often let our own value systems slip into our work without realising it. However, when designing questionnaire items we must pay particular attention to this issue. In addition, try to avoid using emotive language (unless there is some theoretical reason to justify it, of course). An example of a question that is value-laden is, 'Do you agree that the terrible cruelty of fox hunting should be banned?' A better format is 'Fox hunting should be banned' accompanied by a Likert scale (strongly agree = 1 to strongly disagree = 5). An example of a leading question is, 'Would you generally refrain from buying battery farmed eggs?' It is clear from the word 'refrain' that the participant is being led toward a desired response. A better alternative is, 'How often do you buy battery farmed eggs?' (1 = not at all to 5 = once a week). The response options capture the full range of battery buying behaviour. The phrase 'How often' suggest to the respondent that it is acceptable to report that they do buy battery eggs.

Avoid technical terms or jargon

Whether you are carrying out an interview or writing a questionnaire, you should avoid technical terms or jargon. For example, 'Drag hunts are preferable to standard fox hunts' only makes sense to those who know what drag hunts are. In fact you should avoid any language that may alienate your respondents. What may be familiar to you may not be familiar to your respondents. So the bottom line is, keep it simple. If you need to include technical terms (e.g. what a unit of alcohol refers to), add a short explanation.

Control for response sets

Another problem that needs to be avoided when designing a questionnaire is the effect called **response bias** or **response sets**. These are consistent sources ('sets') of polluting information that can influence the questionnaire responses. There are two response sets that you should be concerned about.

Social desirability is where a respondent attempts to 'look good'. This may involve them providing answers that are honest, but positively biased (**self-deception**), or answers that portray them in the best possible way (**impression management**). This does not always involve people lying – it often happens without people being aware they are doing it. One strategy for dealing with such social desirability effects is to include a social desirability (sometimes called a 'lie') scale. A social desirability scale consists of a series of questions (included among your other questions) that if responded to consistently show someone acting in a 'saintly' way (for instance, that 'you never lose your temper' or 'you always say "thank you"') which is just not realistic. If you find participants responding in this 'saintly' way you would generally exclude them from your analysis. The Socially Desirable Response Set Five-Item Survey (SDRS-5) is a short measure that can be incorporated into your questionnaire as a measure of the strength of socially desirable responding (Hays *et al.*, 1989). Responses are presented as 'Definitely True' (1), 'Mostly True' (2), 'Don't know' (3), 'Mostly false' (4) and 'Definitely false' (5). Listed below are items from the SDRS-5:

- How much is each statement TRUE or FALSE for you?
    - I am always courteous even to people who are disagreeable (1 = 1 point).
    - There have been occasions when I took advantage of someone (5 = 1 point).
    - I sometimes try to get even rather than forgive and forget (5 = 1 point).
    - I sometimes feel resentful when I don't get my way (5 = 1 point).
    - No matter who I'm talking to, I'm always a good listener (1 = 1 point).

If you observe high scores on this scale (e.g. 5 points), consider removing the data from this participant.

Response acquiescence is the tendency to agree rather than disagree with statements (it is also worth noting that there is a similar but smaller tendency to consistently disagree with statements). The easiest way to tackle this problem is to make sure that your questions are not all positively (or negatively) worded. In the SDRS (see above), three of the questions refer to 'underside' behaviour, so people with response acquiescence would receive an approximately neutral score. By making your questions unpredictable (including a variety of response options if possible) you force your respondents to think about each question (or at the very least give the respondent who always responds positively (or negatively) a neutral score, rather than an extreme one).

Sampling

An appropriate sample is vital for carrying out good quality research (see Chapter 3). Box 5.2 should act as a reminder of some of the commonest types of sample.

Box 5.2

Information box

Sampling strategies

Random sampling

This type of sampling involves the selection of participants at random from a list of the population. This generally involves random selection by computer or through the use of random number tables. This should give each person the same chance of being included in the sample.

▶

Box 5.2 *Continued*

Stratified random sampling

This involves dividing the population into a number of groups or strata where members of the group have some characteristic in common (e.g. strata for social class or sex). There is then random sampling from those strata in proportion to the number of people in the population as a whole.

Snowball sampling

Snowball sampling involves identifying one or more individuals from the population of interest (e.g. known drug users) and then using these participants as informants to identify further members of the group. These participants are then used to identify further participants and so on until you have enough people in your sample. This approach can be seen as a form of **purposive sampling**, which is useful when there are difficulties in identifying members of the population.

Convenience sampling

This is unfortunately one of the commonest approaches to sampling and probably the worst as it does not produce representative findings. In essence, convenience sampling involves choosing the nearest and most convenient persons to act as respondents. It is, however, sometimes the only possible sampling strategy and may be acceptable as long as its limitations are acknowledged.

Response rates

Unfortunately, many questionnaire surveys suffer because of low **response rates**. The response rate is the percentage of questionnaires completed and returned from those distributed. But what is a low response rate? Well, how long is a piece of string? It depends – on your topic, sample, questionnaire, survey design etc. Some journals will not accept studies that fail to reach a defined threshold for response rates (e.g. 70 per cent). It is sensible to compare your response rate with that of other similar studies. However, there are a number of ways of maximising your response rate (over and above the techniques discussed here on good questionnaire design), which can be summarised as follows (for a full review of methods which have proven effectiveness, see Edwards *et al.*, 2002):

- Keep your questionnaire as short as possible.
- Stick to a clear, relatively conservative layout.
- Include a pre-paid envelope with postal surveys.
- Send a reminder after one or two weeks have passed.
- Give advance warning – by a letter or postcard.
- Offer a small incentive if possible (e.g. entry to a prize draw).

We are aware that some of these methods have cost implications – use only those which are cost effective for the resources and time you have available.

Measuring attitudes

Attitude measurement generally relies on more careful measurement than an average questionnaire. This is because attitudes are often elusive, with people unaware that they possess them. Consequently, researchers interested in exploring someone's attitudes need to use particular approaches that are sensitive to this issue. Attitude scales do not usually use questions but a list of statements with which the respondent has to agree or disagree. An attitude scale generally consists of a list of such statements, all different but attempting to tap some consistent underlying attitude. Two of the most widely used forms of attitude scale are detailed below.

Likert scales

A **Likert scale** (Likert, 1932) is a five- (seven-, or sometimes more) point scale where respondents are able to express how much they agree or disagree with an attitude statement (see Box 5.1, question 4 for an example). There is more to developing a Likert scale than just assembling a list of statements about the attitude object. In order to develop a reliable scale you will need to carry out the following steps:

1 Produce an equal number of positive and negative statements about the attitude object. These constitute the scale items.
2 Ask the respondents to rate each scale item on the provided five- or seven-point response options (strongly agree to strongly disagree) according to how much they agree or disagree with the statements. However, some researchers prefer to use an even number of response options, so that participants tend away from responding 'unsure' or 'neither agree nor disagree' to many items.
3 Add up the scores on each item to give the respondent's overall attitude score (remembering to reverse the scale of negatively worded items – so that high scores are positive and low scores are negative responses).
4 Carry out an item analysis (see below) on the attitude statements in order to find those that discriminate most strongly between people with high attitude scores and those with low attitude scores.
5 Reject those items that are poor at discriminating between high scores and low scores but try to keep an equal balance of positive and negative items.

If you follow the five steps above, you should have a scale comprising items that directly (and indirectly) tap a person's attitude towards some behaviour or event of interest to you. It would also be advisable to determine the Cronbach alpha coefficient (see below) for the scale you have devised as a further check on its internal reliability.

Semantic differential scales

The **semantic differential scale** (Osgood *et al.*, 1957) is an alternative to the Likert scale that takes a more indirect approach to assessing a person's attitude towards some behaviour or event (see Box 5.1, question 5 for an example). It was designed to move beyond the arguably simplistic notion of an attitude as cognitive belief (as is generally assumed with Likert scales). Semantic differential scales rely on the ability of people to think in metaphors and express their attitudes by drawing parallels with other aspects of their experience. A semantic differential scale requires the respondent to indicate their thoughts and feelings towards the attitude object on a scale consisting of bipolar opposite adjectives. Once you have produced a scale with a number of suitable pairs of adjectives (from previous studies and pilot work), you can then assess the internal reliability by calculating a Cronbach alpha coefficient on the scores produced by a set of respondents. Semantic differential scales have been shown to have good reliability values and correlate well with other attitude scales (go to Box 5.3).

5.5 Psychometrics

Psychometrics is an area of psychology concerned with the quality of scales and items designed to measure psychological constructs (e.g. personality traits, cognitive ability). Quality is assessed using two criteria: reliability and validity. The importance of reliability and validity for measurement in psychology was initially discussed in Chapter 3. They are clearly very important when collecting data with questionnaires. Reliability concerns the internal properties of a scale (does it 'hang together'?). Validity concerns the external properties of a scale (does it correlate with other variables or other scales?). There are several different kinds of reliability and validity. Correlations are used to evaluate the strength of these criteria. Please see Chapter 12 to learn about correlations.

5.6 Reliability

Internal consistency

When developing a new scale, demonstrating internal consistency is one of the most important things to do. There are four ways to test internal consistency.

Split-half reliability

When we wish to calculate the split-half reliability we need to split the test items into two groups (for instance, even numbered items in one group and odd numbered items in the other group). We give a group of participants one set of questions (even numbered) on one occasion and then the same group of participants the other set of questions (odd numbered) some time later. We can then calculate the split-half reliability coefficient (r_a) by inserting the correlation coefficient (r) between the score obtained from the two sets of questions (gathered on two separate occasions) into the following formula:[1]

---

[1] Do not worry about this formula at the moment. We will be covering statistics in Part 2. You will learn how to use SPSS in Chapter 9 and correlation coefficients are described in Chapter 12.

> **Box 5.3**
>
> **Activity box — Design and critique a questionnaire**
>
> 1. In your pair, choose one of the following areas for investigation:
>   a. Safer sex behaviour
>   b. Gender
>   c. Health
>
> 2. In your pair, establish a specific research question involving one of these three topics which can be appropriately answered by a questionnaire. For example:
>   a. How does alcohol consumption affect the use of condoms in casual sex?
>   b. How does gender interact with friendship behaviours and understandings (level of intimacy, type of activities, topics of conversation, expectations, etc.)?
>   c. What is the relationship between attitudes towards smoking or drinking and carrying out these behaviours?
>
> 3. Decide on the sections that will make up the questionnaire and the order in which they will appear.
>
> 4. In your pair, try to design sample questions (about enough for two pages of A4) for the questionnaire which address the research question you have decided on. For example, you could use open-ended questions, fixed response questions, or Likert scales. Along with each question you design you should write down its pros and cons.
>
> 5. Each pair should now swap their questionnaire with another pair to critique it. You should also tell the other pair what your research question is. The other pair should critique the choice of question type and overall design.
>
> 6. Communicate your criticisms to the other pair constructively! Try to highlight weaknesses and strengths. But do not criticise unless you can suggest a better alternative! Each pair should then improve their questionnaire in line with the criticism (if it is valid).

$$r_a = \frac{2r}{1+r}$$

However, while the split-half method solves the problem of memory effects (as the participants do not get the same items on more than one occasion), it does not provide a solution to practice effects. Participants may still be able to learn how to respond to items by completing the test on more than one occasion. Furthermore, the allocation of items into two groups may, depending on the method in which they were allocated to the two groups, give different results. Finally, many tests comprise multiple subsets of items (or subscales) which may limit the possibility of splitting the items into two groups.

Inter-item reliability

This statistic is similar to split-half reliability. It is essentially the 'average' correlation between each and every pair of items.

Item-total reliability

Here, each item is correlated with a score comprising of the total of the other items. In a ten-item scale, scores 1 to 9 are summed, and item 10 is correlated with that score. This is repeated for every item, and the average correlation is calculated.

Alpha reliability

Alpha reliability (also called **Cronbach alpha** after its creator) is similar to split-half reliability except that the process is repeated for every random pair of splits! In practice, researchers tend to report only the alpha reliability score. Therefore, there is no need to report the three alternatives above. Unless you want to have a nervous breakdown, we strongly recommend not attempting to do this by hand! SPSS can calculate alpha reliability for you. Values of 0.70 or higher are considered acceptable. However, psychological scales that require more introspection (thinking inwardly about what response to give) than tests of skills are likely to have lower internal consistency. Values of 0.60 or higher are sometimes considered acceptable (Youngman, 1979).

If you wish to calculate a Cronbach alpha reliability test this is very easy using SPSS. You will need to read Chapters 9 and 10 to learn the basics of SPSS. You can then simply select **Analyze** from the top menu bar and then **Scale** and **Reliability Analysis**. You then use the Variable Picker button to move the variables you wish to check for reliability into the **Items** box. When requesting a Cronbach alpha with SPSS it is worth checking the box for '**Scale if item deleted**' (available in the **Statistics** box) as this will give you the alpha coefficient for the scale with items removed (so you can determine (and then remove) less reliable items and maximise the alpha coefficient). If you decide to remove poorly performing items, it is good practice to administer the new set of items to a new sample. This is often not feasible for small-scale research projects – another reason why using existing questionnaires is preferable. Questionnaire development may involve several amendments to items before it becomes a reliable scale or inventory.

Item analysis

Item analysis is a method of producing a questionnaire scale with higher internal reliability by identifying items that discriminate well between high attitude and low attitude scores. First, for each item calculate the correlation between each person's score on that item and their score on the test as a whole (the summed score of each item). Second, identify the top and bottom overall scores (10 per cent or 15 per cent generally) on the test. Third, calculate the total scores of these two groups of people for each item in the test. If these two (extreme) groups scored very differently on the item then it is highly discriminative – if not then it is low in discriminating between the two groups and should be discarded.

Test–retest reliability

This form of reliability is particularly important for scales designed to measure constructs that are supposed to be stable. If a test of Conscientiousness, a trait that is claimed to be stable, produces very different scores each time it is measured, then either (1) it can hardly be a reliable measure of that construct or (2) the construct itself is not stable. Test–retest reliability is less important for constructs that we expect to change over time, such as physical or mental health status. Values of 0.7 or higher are considered good, but become stronger evidence if the time between testing is extended. At least three months is required. The LBC1921 study (see Box 5.4) is unique in that the two measures of cognitive ability were recorded 66 years apart. Test–retest reliability, when demonstrated over a long period, can be interpreted as evidence that a construct is **stable**.

While the test–retest measure of reliability is an obvious way of determining whether we are getting consistent responses to our measure, there are a number of limitations. The principal problem is that we test the same participants twice. Participants may remember the test and simply repeat their earlier responses (rather than thinking about their individual responses to the test items). Furthermore, even if participants cannot remember individual items there may be a problem due to practice (a **practice effect**). If the participants have the opportunity to respond to the same test on two occasions they may learn *how to* respond to certain types of questions. This is particularly common with tests of cognitive ability where, for instance, participants often improve their scores on problem-solving questions given the opportunity to practise responding to these types of items. Memory and practice effects can both artificially inflate the correlation coefficient between the two tests, thus distorting our evaluation of the reliability of the test.

Inter-rater reliability

Scales designed to measure constructs such as personality traits can be said to have inter-rater reliability if two observers agree in the ratings they have given. That is, the two independent sets of ratings correlate highly. For example, suppose that a researcher thinks that personality traits can be observed in horses. They create a new personality trait scale that is designed to measure conscientiousness in horses. It might contain items such as 'Keeps a clean and tidy stable' or 'Grooms regularly'. If two horsekeepers rated a horse's behaviour independently on this scale, we would hope for inter-rater reliability – a high degree of correspondence between both sets of ratings.

Parallel forms reliability

Researchers often need to create a scale that closely resembles an existing scale. This method for evaluating the reliability of a test requires us to produce two equivalent versions of the same test. When creating a test (or measure) of something (whether it be a measure of attitudes, personality traits or anything else for that matter) it is commonplace to develop multiple items designed to measure the same thing. This enables test developers to create two versions of the same test. Many standard psychometric tests have alternative forms. By creating pairs of items when developing a test and then separating them, we can create two different versions of the test (based on equivalent items) and carry out an **alternate forms reliability** test. This involves us giving the two versions of the test to the same group of participants on two separate occasions. We can then calculate a correlation coefficient for the two tests on the same people. For example, the International Personality Item Pool provides a free version of the NEO-PI-R, a popular measure of the **Big Five** personality traits (see Box 5.5). This allows researchers and students, who may not have the resources available to pay for the proper NEO-PI-R, to use an equivalent test. The high correlation between both tests provides evidence of parallel forms reliability. This means we can be confident that both tests are essentially the same.

However, as you might have already guessed, this approach, although solving the problem of memory effects, does not solve the problem of practice effects. But if there are so many problems with us giving the test to the same group of participants, why don't we use two groups (matched for criteria, such as age, sex, etc.)? Well, we are afraid that there are as many, if not more, problems in establishing reliability with this approach. Firstly, we have the problem of knowing what variables are going to be key criteria in matching the groups. There might be age effects for attitudes towards animal welfare but we do not necessarily know this. Furthermore, we may find that other attributes (such as education, social class, religion and so on) also affect responses to our test. In fact, we can never really know exactly how to match our participants – we can only try our best using the knowledge and evidence available to us. It is therefore often, though not always, a better bet to carry out a reliability test using the same group of participants and attempt, as best we can, to lessen the effect of memory and practice on our evaluation of the test.

Box 5.4 Study box

An unreliable measure of 'cognitive styles'

Peterson, E. R., Deary, I. J., and Austin, E. J. (2003). The reliability of Riding's Cognitive Style Analysis test. *Personality and Individual Differences*, **34**, 881–91.

Unlike widely researched constructs such as personality traits and cognitive ability, the cognitive styles literature is in its infancy. Cognitive styles, it is claimed, are preferred ways or 'styles' of thinking and learning. Different people might have different ways

Box 5.4 *Continued*

that they like to process information. For example, when learning something new, you might tend to use images rather than verbal information and prefer looking at the whole picture rather than analysing small details. There are few reliable and valid measures of 'cognitive style' available. The reliability of one of the few measures available, Riding's Cognitive Style Analysis (CSA) test, was called into question by researchers at the University of Edinburgh. They developed a computerised form of the test to use in their study because the original test did not provide data about the individual items, only a total score for each scale. Their new measure correlated highly with the original test (r = around 0.7) and therefore had parallel forms reliability (and concurrent validity). The wholist-analytic dimension was fairly stable one week later (r = 0.6) but the verbal-imagery dimension was not (r = 0.5). We might wonder what the point of measuring a cognitive style is if it changes after just one week. Furthermore, while the wholist-analytic dimension had reasonable split-half reliability (r = 0.7), the verbal-imagery dimension did not (r = 0.4). This demonstrated that the original measure, claiming to be a reliable measure of cognitive styles, was not in fact reliable at all. The study showed that more work was needed to improve the psychometric qualities of measures of cognitive styles.

Before moving on, we need to emphasise that reliability is necessary, but not sufficient, to demonstrate validity (Kline, 2000). That is, a scale can be reliable but not valid. However, a scale cannot be valid if it is unreliable! Reliability is the bread, and validity the butter, of scale development. You can eat bread on its own, but not butter. A good test is comprised of good items, reliable and well validated.

5.7 Validity

Face validity

Face validity refers to what a scale 'looks' like. Do the items seem to measure the construct, or do they not seem sensible? Scales with poor face validity, even if they are reliable, may leave participants confused and suspicious. If you designed a set of tests to measure cognitive ability, the tests should look like they measure cognitive skills. Adding items such as 'What is your favourite colour?' or 'What are your hobbies and interests?' would threaten face validity. However, face validity is not necessarily desirable. Items which are face valid mean that participants know what you are trying to measure, and could 'fake good' their responses (see above on response sets). This has been a concern in occupational testing, where personality tests are sometimes used in selecting job applicants. In summary, face validity can enhance participants' acceptance of a scale, but it is not necessarily connected with other aspects of validity. Face validity is sometimes a red herring. The other types of validity, now described, are more important.

Content validity

Content validity is similar to face validity, but the items are judged to be appropriate by experts in the field. For example, you might consult a researcher with experience in the area of depression, if you wanted to develop a new test to measure depression. Have all the relevant symptoms been included? If you were developing a test based on a literature review of a construct, you would want to ensure that all the content is covered in the scale (content coverage). For example, forensic psychologists developed a scale to measure **sensational hobbies and interests**. Sensational interests have rather violent, macabre or strange content (e.g. weapons, fighting, mercenaries, black magic). The psychologists drew on the forensic literature, clinical experience, and conversations with their colleagues. A list of 19 sensational interests was developed (see Egan *et al.*, 2001), which they argued has good content coverage of the 'sensational interests' construct. The process of establishing content validity is quite subjective, but is often necessary to ensure that important items are not missed.

Criterion validity

Criterion validity is concerned with whether the test gives results in agreement with other measures of the same thing. There are two main types of criterion validity used by psychologists: **concurrent** and **predictive**.

Concurrent validity

Concurrent validity is shown by a high correlation between two tests, which are taken at the same time. It is essentially the same as parallel forms reliability. The problem with both is that the 'other' test is assumed to be the gold standard scale that actually measures the construct. There may not be a suitable alternative form which you can use. If there were, you might not need to develop a new scale in the first place! Concurrent validity is normally assessed when researchers need to create a new test for a specific reason (for example, see Box 5.4).

Predictive validity

Predictive validity is shown when a scale predicts another variable. The other variable is the 'criterion' variable. The criteria should be variables different from the construct which the scale is supposed to measure. For example, it would be inappropriate to claim that a scale measuring reasoning ability had predictive validity because it predicted memory skills. Reasoning and memory are closely connected because they are part of a more general construct, cognitive ability. When assessing or reporting predictive validity, it is important to check that the criteria are truly 'external' to the scale. It might be tempting to evaluate a measure of conscientiousness by asking someone how tidy their desk is (a criterion variable). However, if the scale contains items such as 'I like to tidy up' and 'I love order and regularity' then there is too much overlap between the scale and their criterion. The tidiness of someone's desk is not external to the scale content. Objectively measuring the tidiness of someone's desk might be better (at least the criterion is not part of the questionnaire), yet there is still too close a correspondence between the scale and the criterion. It can be difficult to think of criteria that are truly external. Personality trait researchers have focused on health behaviours and health outcomes, because they are external, important 'real-life' outcomes. For example, scales designed to measure the trait Conscientiousness have been shown to predict many different kinds of health behaviours, and health outcomes (Bogg & Roberts, 2004). If a conscientiousness scale predicts objectively measured health outcomes, then we know that it has predictive validity. Predictive validity does not mean that the validity is important. We can still ask, 'so what?' Does the construct have any applied implications? It may be possible to use research about a construct, for example, to improve health (Hagger-Johnson & Pollard Whiteman, 2008).

Ultimate validity

Ultimate validity is a term coined to describe the predictive validity for the ultimate real-life outcome – mortality (O'Toole & Stankov, 1992). Conscientiousness is predictive of all-cause mortality (deaths from any causes) and cause-specific mortality (deaths from specific causes). This is a truly external criterion. It doesn't explain why personality might be associated with age of death, but it clearly demonstrates that the scale is measuring something important.

Population validity

Although **population validity** is not commonly referred to in the research literature, it is still worthy of mention. This type of validity is commonly a problem in journalistic reporting (and especially among pop psychologists on radio or television) when, for instance, they make claims about all men on the basis of research on a particular group of men. There is a danger in simply believing that our findings on a small sample of people will generalise to all members of the population from which our sample came. We need to be cautious about making claims of this kind. Effective methods of sampling (discussed below) are one important way of trying to increase the population validity of a study and therefore its **generalisability**.

Construct validity

All of the forms of validity described above are used to demonstrate construct validity, also called the **nomological network**. This is a network of research evidence surrounding and supporting the validity of a construct. Originally, this term was used to describe 'the interlocking system of laws which constitute a theory as a nomological network' (Cronbach & Meehl, 1955: 290). Psychological theories and scales rarely reach the status of laws, so the term has instead been used to refer to a network of correlations which support (not 'prove') a construct. Where specific aspects of reliability and validity are like 'flowers', construct validity is a bouquet of flowers. Taken as a whole, confidence is gained in the existence of constructs such as 'personality traits' and 'cognitive ability' because a large network of studies has built up around them, supporting the validity of the construct. Construct validity is crucial to psychologists, because the constructs which they use are precisely that – constructs. They are variables we cannot observe directly, developed from theories and research studies. Reliability and validity are evaluated in the service of construct validity, the overall aim. Construct validity takes a long time, usually many years, to develop. In the short term, there are two ways to quickly evaluate the viability of a scale in terms of construct validity. Both evaluate the pattern of correlations with existing scales. Therefore, they assume that there is already a good measure of the construct available. These are now described.

Convergent validity

If a test has convergent validity, it should correlate with tests that measure the same construct, but also 'related constructs'. In the SF-36 (page 111), the Physical Component Summary correlates with other measures of physical health, and measures of health that are related to physical aspects of health. Therefore, it has convergent validity. The measures all converge on the 'physical' health construct.

Discriminant validity

If a test has discriminant validity, it should not correlate with tests that measure different constructs, nor with unrelated constructs. In the SF-36, the Physical Component Summary does not correlate highly with measures of mental health, nor with measures related to mental health, such as anxiety or depression. Therefore, it has discriminant validity – it can discriminate between physical and mental health measures.

Summary

It takes a lot longer to demonstrate validity than it takes to demonstrate reliability. No single research study can provide all of the necessary evidence that a scale has reached the 'gold standard' of construct validity. When developing your own scale, you are not expected to achieve construct validity on your own. When evaluating existing scales, you should consider the wider nomological network. Validity is comprised of several different pieces of evidence and should be considered as a whole. This may involve looking for separate reports in research papers, or looking at the test manual if the scale is from a published inventory.

5.8 Psychometric tests

Psychometric tests are **standardised** forms of questionnaires designed to measure particular traits or personality types. By standardised we mean they have been tested on large numbers of participants, had their reliability ascertained and norms established for particular groups of people. The items will often be published as a set of scales called an **inventory**. This enables other researchers to use these scales (with confidence) without having to pilot and test the reliability of the scale. Because the tests are standardised we can compare the responses/scores we get from each of our participants (or group) with those responses/scores established as the statistical norm for a particular group of people. It should be noted that there have been some doubts raised over the validity of many psychometric scales in widespread use. While we can be assured of their reliability, the same cannot be said for their validity. This is because each test is based on an underlying theory (of personality or intelligence, for instance) that may be subject to considerable criticism (see Gould, 1996, for further discussion of these issues).

Personality inventories

Research into personality traits fell out of favour during the 1970s. This was partly because of a misunderstanding that small correlations with behaviour proved that traits did not exist (see Matthews *et al.*, 2003, for a historical review and discussion of recent developments). However, it was partly because there were simply too many different measures of personality in the literature. After years of disagreement, most personality researchers have agreed on a set of five dimensions. These are sufficient to capture most of the variability in traits. Most other personality traits or personality types you will encounter in the literature fit into the big five as blends of more than one trait. For example, 'shyness' is a combination of low Extraversion and high Neuroticism. Psychoticism is a blend of low Conscientiousness and low Agreeableness. Older tests, such as the Eysenck Personality Inventory (EPI) and Minnesota Multiphasic Personality Inventory (MMPI), are used in occupational contexts but are increasingly considered out of date by personality researchers. The big five provides a shared framework for making sense of the different kinds of traits that can be measured. A choice of different big five measures is shown in Box 5.5.

> **Box 5.5**
>
> **Information box**
>
> **Big Five personality inventories**
>
> **NEO-PI-R and NEO-FFI.** These two inventories are the most popular in the psychological literature. The shorter NEO-FFI (120 items) provides Neuroticism, Extraversion, Openness to Experience, Agreeableness and Conscientiousness (the big five). The longer NEO-PI-R (240 items) adds facets to each of the five traits, providing more detail. For example, Conscientiousness can be divided into Competence, Order, Dutifulness, Achievement-Striving, Self-Discipline and Deliberation. Most constructs that you will encounter in the literature are simply blends of different traits and facets, and are available in the NEO-PI-R.
>
> > Costa, P. T., Jr., & McCrae, R. R. (1992). *NEO PI-R Professional Manual*. Odessa, FL: Psychological Assessment Resources, Inc.
>
> **The International Personality Item Pool (IPIP).** This website provides free versions of the NEO-PI-R, NEO-FFI and many other tests. It also has a 50-item and 100-item big five measure available.
>
> > http://ipip.ori.org/ipip/
>
> **Mini-markers.** Saucier's mini-markers are 40 adjectives that provide a robust big five structure. Respondents are asked to rate themselves on adjectives that describe their traits. The mini-markers work just as well as other inventories, and may save time.
>
> > Saucier, G. (1994). Mini-markers: A brief version of Goldberg's unipolar big-five markers. *Journal of Personality Assessment*, **63** (3), 506–16.
>
> **Very brief versions.** Two very brief measures are also available, both of which contain just 10 items. These are not recommended if you need a detailed trait assessment, but perfect if you want to add the big five to a larger study:
>
> > Gosling, S. D., Rentfrow, P. J. & Swann, W. B., Jr. (2003). A very brief measure of the Big Five personality domains. *Journal of Research in Personality*, **37**, 504–28.
>
> > Rammstedt, B. & John, O. P. (2007). Measuring personality in one minute or less: A 10-item short version of the Big Five Inventory in English and German. *Journal of Research in Personality*, **41**, 203–12.

Cognitive ability tests

Cognitive ability tests are designed to measure quality of intellectual functioning. They are sometimes converted into a single summary score, called the intelligence quotient, or **IQ**. There are many different kinds of intellectual skills, such as speed of information processing, reasoning, vocabulary, logic and memory. On average, people who score highly on these tests tend to score highly on other tests. This led researchers to argue that a single, underlying aptitude drives cognitive ability (the general intelligence factor, or g). Administering tests of cognitive ability is relatively straightforward, but is time consuming. The application of these tests has attracted much criticism, particularly in the context of educational and occupational testing. The general factor can be identified in samples of people, but does not necessarily apply to the individual. It is important to avoid reductionism (in this case, reducing individual differences to one number only). Some people are good at mathematical skills, but poor at verbal reasoning, for example. The solution is to ensure that you measure both general and specific skills, and interpret scores with caution. It is also important to acknowledge other skills valued in society, such as artistic skill, musical ability or the ability to tell a good story. Many tests of cognitive ability encompass a rather narrow range of skills and may also lack cultural sensitivity and cross-cultural validity. However, be suspicious of claims that there are 'multiple intelligences'. Very often, tests designed to measure a 'new' kind of intelligence are later found to correlate with g, or to measure other aspects of the person, such as personality traits or cognitive styles. Cognitive ability research is regaining popularity because of its role in preventing cognitive decline, dementia and Alzheimer's disease (see Box 5.6).

Box 5.6 Study box

Preventing cognitive decline in the elderly

Deary, I. J., Whiteman, M. C., Starr, J. M., Whalley, L. J. & Fox, H. C. (2004). The impact of childhood intelligence on later life: Following up the Scottish Mental Surveys of 1932 and 1947. *Journal of Personality and Social Psychology,* **86** (1), 130-47.

Early cognitive decline is a precursor to debilitating illnesses such as Alzheimer's disease. But does cognitive ability during childhood predict cognitive decline in later life? This question was once unanswerable, because measures of cognitive ability in childhood are usually not recorded. Clinicians face a difficult task when faced with patients who think their memory is beginning to fail. How would they find out what it used to be like? Researchers at the University of Edinburgh realised that IQ data was available for a cohort of Scottish schoolchildren born in 1921. In 1932, every child in the country sat an IQ test. In 1997, they began locating those who were living in and around Edinburgh, then aged 76, to take part in a study. The study will be used to learn about the factors involved in cognitive ageing and the prevention of dementia and Alzheimer's disease. A **battery** of cognitive ability tests was administered, including:

Moray House. This test was the original cognitive ability measure taken in 1932. It includes 75 questions assessing different kinds of skills, including word classification, reasoning and arithmetic.

Logical memory. This is a scale from the Wechsler Memory Scale. Participants are asked to recall the contents of two stories, after a short time interval.

Raven's progressive matrices. This test is popular with psychologists because it measures non-verbal reasoning ability. The items are patterns and shapes, so there is no

> **Box 5.6** *Continued*
>
> confounding from verbal ability and language. It correlated with the Moray House test, originally administered in 1932, providing evidence of convergent validity.
>
> The researchers found that those with higher cognitive ability scores in childhood were less likely to have dementia later in life. They also had better health status today. The results highlight the need to do more research into cognitive ability, its impact on health inequalities and the role of the education system in tackling them.
>
> More information about the ongoing Lothian Birth Cohort Studies can be found at: www.psy.ed.ac.uk/research/lbc/LBC.html

Measures of mental and physical health status

It may be useful to measure mental and physical health outcomes, particularly if the aim of a study is to test a psychological intervention. If health has increased after the intervention, compared to a control group who didn't receive an intervention, this provides evidence for the effectiveness of the intervention. Mental health outcomes can be measured using the General Health Questionnaire (GHQ) or the Hospital Anxiety and Depression Scale (HADS). However, these scales concentrate on anxiety and depression. The SF-36 Health Outcome Survey (36 items) is particularly attractive because it provides a general mental component summary (MCS) score and physical component summary (PCS) score. In fact, it is becoming difficult to justify *not* using the SF-36 in quantitative health research. Eight subscales provide scores on different and important aspects of health: physical functioning, role physical, bodily pain, general health, energy vitality, social functioning, role emotional and mental health, It has been extensively validated and comes in shorter forms, such as the SF-8 (eight items long). The SF-36 questionnaire and scoring instructions are available from: www.rand.org/health/surveys_tools/mos/

Further reading

Deary, I. (2001). *Intelligence: A Very Short Introduction*. Oxford: Oxford University Press.

> This book is a short overview of cognitive ability assessment, including a historical review and recent developments in the field.

Kline, P. (2000). *A Psychometrics Primer*. London: Free Association Books.

> This book should belong on the shelf of any psychologist involved in test development.

Matthews, G., Deary, I. & Whiteman, M.C. (2003). *Personality Traits*, 2nd edn. Cambridge: Cambridge University Press.

> A comprehensive introduction to the history of personality trait research, measurement strategies and unanswered questions.

Oppenheim, A. N. (2000). *Questionnaire Design, Interviewing and Attitude Measurement.* London: Continuum.

Sapsford, R. (2006). *Survey Research.* 2nd edn. London: Sage.

Sapsford (2006) and Oppenheim (2000) provide excellent further coverage on the topics of questionnaire design and psychometric testing outlined in this chapter and are well worth a look before you decide to collect your own data.

17 Fundamentals of qualitative research

- This chapter begins by revisiting the discussion about qualitative and quantitative research methods and data analysis introduced in Chapter 1.
- Further links are made between qualitative epistemology and methodology.
- Finally, this chapter looks at the strengths, limitations and varieties of qualitative methods.

INTRODUCTION

This part of the book is concerned with demonstrating the use of qualitative methods in psychology. This particular chapter returns to some of the issues raised in Chapter 1 about philosophy, methodology and the differences between quantitative and qualitative methods. So, we need to revisit the philosophical assumptions that underpin the distinction between qualitative and quantitative research methods. However, before this, there is a brief reminder of some of the major issues already introduced.

If you remember, we discussed the question of 'what is science?' in Chapter 1. Everyday (or common-sense) understandings of science recognise it as the careful collection (through experience) of information about the world that enables us to establish facts and therefore build theories about the world. This accumulation of knowledge then enables us to control and change the world for the better. So scientific research, from this position, is the acquisition of knowledge based on experience that is objective. Chapter 1 also introduced the distinction between inductive and hypothetico-deductive approaches to research. Most quantitative research subscribes to the hypothetico-deductive approach that was advocated by the philosopher Karl Popper. In contrast, most qualitative research will embrace a more inductivist approach. That is, qualitative research will seek to avoid imposing a particular theoretical perspective on the questions being asked, data being collected and process of analysis.

Finally, Chapter 1 covered the basic distinction between qualitative and quantitative research. Quantitative research is that concerned with the quantification (counting) of phenomena while qualitative research is that concerned with the qualities of phenomena. Later in this chapter we revisit this distinction to draw out further distinctions and also discuss whether it continues to be an important way of categorising psychological research in the twenty-first century. However, we first wish to highlight some more philosophical concepts (and some more technical terms) that are important for understanding quantitative and qualitative research methods and the distinctions that may be drawn between them.

17.1 Philosophical underpinnings: the old paradigm

Epistemology

Epistemology is a philosophical term that is very commonly used, and although it sounds ferocious it has a very simple meaning. In short, epistemology concerns those questions we ask about our knowledge of some phenomenon. Or, in other words, epistemology is the branch of philosophy concerned with the varieties and validity of our knowledge of aspects of the world. Why do we need to know about this? Well, we need to know about epistemology because people (psychologists and philosophers) disagree (very profoundly) about what we can say *we know* about people. And these disagreements are key in understanding why some psychologists use quantitative methods modelled on the natural sciences to make truth claims about people and the world and others reject these completely. So, if you ever hear or read something where people are discussing the epistemological foundations of a theory or approach, they are talking about the philosophical assumptions concerning the question of what we can say we know about something. So, for instance, do we believe that our approach enables us to discover the truth of a real knowable world (the more traditional scientific approach – positivism, see below)? Or do we believe that our approach enables us *only* to identify some personally subjective, socially and historically contingent knowledge about a person's particular way of understanding the world (as we might expect in a phenomenological study, see Chapter 19)? But remember, these questions do not have certain answers. Psychologists disagree strongly about the knowledge claims we can make about our research and this is why the traditional scientific approach has come under fierce attack over the past 20 years or so.

Positivism

Positivism is a broad concept (often used together with empiricism to define a very traditional view of what science is – empiricism was covered in Chapter 1) that very simply means there is a simple, unproblematic relationship between our perception of the world and the world itself. If we are positivists we will believe that through systematic study of the world we can describe and explain what is really out there. Furthermore, the nature of the external world determines what we can say about it. There is ultimately some truth waiting to be discovered about the object of study. The goal of research for positivists is to provide objective knowledge about the world (or people living in the world if you are a psychologist); that is, knowledge that is impartial and unbiased. Once again, similar to developments in empiricism, understandings of positivism have moved on from this fundamental position. Very few psychologists today would class themselves in a very simple way as positivists, believing that our perception of people and events in the world is unproblematic (and unaffected by our preconceptions and presuppositions). However, psychologists may subscribe to some modified form of positivism (and similarly empiricism) and believe that there is a real, knowable world out there to investigate (albeit one understood through our perception of it). A great deal of research in biological and cognitive psychology (and in some developmental and social psychology) would be of this kind; its epistemological position is one based on a particular view of science that is positivist and empirical, principally using a hypothetico-deductive approach to knowledge acquisition. This type of research is invariably, though not necessarily, quantitative research. However, there is a growing body of research in social and developmental psychology which does not subscribe to positivism, or the hypothetico-deductive approach, but is more sceptical of what we can say we know about the world. This work tends to use inductive methods to generate descriptions of and theories about people and the world in which we live. This body of research is invariably, though not necessarily, qualitative research.

Criticism of the scientific approach

But what is wrong with the view outlined above? Surely psychology is *the* scientific study of people and should therefore use a scientific epistemology that emphasises the objective (empirical) collection of data through a hypothetico-deductive approach. Well, as we mentioned above, for many psychologists the discipline is just like this. But there is a growing group of people who think this approach is, at best, only one, and certainly not the only, way to understand human nature and, at worst, a fundamentally misguided way of carrying out research within psychology. And the principal factor underpinning these disagreements is the different beliefs about the epistemological assumptions underpinning the various methodologies.

What is wrong with the scientific approach to psychology? Well, there is not really the time or space to enter into this debate fully here. If you wish to read more about this, read some of the books listed in the Further reading section of this chapter. However, we will briefly run through a few of the criticisms levelled at positivist research (and also quantitative research more generally) to give you a feel for the arguments being made against the, still dominant, quantitative approach to social research. Perhaps the most important criticism concerns the notion that reality can be defined objectively and that there are psychological phenomena 'out there' that can be described and measured. This view is very difficult to justify. Most qualitative psychologists believe that psychological phenomena exist within (or between) the minds of people and are therefore always subject to interpretation. Furthermore, quantitative techniques of measurement invariably obscure this interpreted level of understanding through the imposition of highly structured tools onto the phenomena in question. At a more general level this problem arises because the social sciences and psychology in particular have attempted to use the natural sciences as a model of practice. Although natural sciences techniques have undoubtedly demonstrated their utility within that field, it is almost certainly the case that they are inappropriate for studying human nature. People are not passive phenomena waiting to be measured but active agents who change over time and who change their own worlds. Sodium from 50 years ago will still demonstrate the same qualities as sodium today, but people from 50 years ago are very unlikely to demonstrate the same qualities. In fact, the same person studied over only a very short time is likely to differ and change. Finally, the attempt of researchers within psychology to remain objective, one of the most important aims of positivist quantitative research, is flawed, for it is inevitable that the views of the researcher will influence the research process in any number of ways. The influence of the researcher and their views is apparent from the first question asked through to the interpretation of the findings found. Furthermore, many qualitative researchers would argue that not only is the attempt to remain objective flawed but it is also unnecessary. For it is only with recognition of the active involvement of the researcher in the research process that understanding can truly emerge.

Changing awareness of qualitative methods within psychology

While it is clearly the case that quantitative approaches to psychological research are still dominant within UK and US psychology, the criticisms from qualitative perspectives have had an impact. The desired change is more minor than many qualitative psychologists would wish but there is change, particularly in the United Kingdom and Continental Europe, nonetheless. Not only is there growth in qualitative research in Europe but there is also greater awareness and recognition of these perspectives among quantitative psychologists. Recent guidelines setting benchmarks for the discipline from the British Psychological Society and the Higher Education Council for England recognise the need for qualitative research methods to be taught alongside quantitative methods within an undergraduate psychology curriculum. Furthermore, although there are still differences of opinion, the arguments are no longer so vociferous and many more psychologists are using both quantitative and qualitative methods in their research programmes (see Chapter 24 on mixed methods). Whether the criticisms from qualitative researchers will ever impact fully is unknown, and for now at least the quantitative approach remains dominant, but at least it is a little more tolerant of qualitative approaches than before.

17.2 Philosophical underpinnings: the new paradigm

There are a number of philosophically and politically informed positions within the social sciences that have provided strong criticism of the positivist approach to research within psychology. We consider three of these below and present some of the implications of these positions for psychological research.

Social constructionism

Research from a socially constructed perspective is concerned with understanding the various ways in which people might construct their social reality. This approach has become more and more important in UK psychology since the 1980s. Unlike the traditional positivist approach, research from a social constructionist perspective recognises the fact that all experience is historically and socially contingent. That is, social phenomena are not simple unchanging events that we can measure but events that need to be understood in a specific way within particular social and historical conditions. Let us give you an example. Only a short time ago homosexuality was categorised within the psychological professions as a mental disorder. The diagnostic manuals (DSM and ICD) listed homosexuality alongside rape and paedophilia as a psychological problem in need of treatment and cure. Although not everyone accepts homosexuality within our society, things have changed. Homosexuality is no longer considered to be a disorder but just another aspect of sexual life in these late modern times. And people who are lesbian, gay and bisexual are, thankfully, no longer subjected to terrible treatments in an attempt to 'cure' them of their 'illness'. Changes such as these are important, for if one simply subscribed to a positivist view of psychology then how could this be explained? This is not simply a case of psychologists identifying a psychological phenomenon (homosexuality) and then measuring it, but something much more complex than that. This change has come about because times have changed (historical change) and with it attitudes within society (social change) such that homosexuality is no longer considered psychopathology. Social constructionists believe that all knowledge is like this, mediated by historical and social conditions, and that psychologists must recognise this within their research programmes and not simply believe that they are measuring things in a way that is neutral (or objective).

Feminism

The feminist critique is an important one that has had a tremendous impact on the discipline. Many of the problems with traditional positivist methodologies were highlighted and subjected to severe and sustained criticism by feminist scholars. First-wave feminists in the 1970s argued that women were either invisible or pathologised within the discipline. Psychological research either studied men exclusively or set out to draw comparisons between men and women where women would invariably be found to be inferior to men. Research of this kind served to maintain the status quo at that time when women were treated differently from men and given fewer opportunities. Feminist writers challenged both the epistemological and methodological foundations of this research in a way that was impossible to ignore. Psychological research was invariably conducted by men on men, or if women were involved they were found to be wanting in comparison to men. Feminist writers argued that this was not due to some inherent feminine weakness but to the bias of the researchers and their procedures.

A particularly useful and significant element to evolve from the feminist critique of positivist research has been the recognition of the role of the researcher within the research process. As we have already mentioned, quantitative positivist research attempts to limit the influence of the researcher through the use of particular methods. Feminist scholars argued that not only was this approach flawed but it was also unwise, for good research comes with a recognition of **reflexivity**, that is, the role of the researcher within the research process. Feminist research particularly, but also much qualitative research more generally, requires account to be taken of reflexivity within the analytic process. Here the researcher cannot remain hidden behind the mask of methodology but must instead 'come out' and be recognised for their role in producing the findings. This issue will be discussed again in some of the chapters that follow.

Queer theory

The criticism from queer theory is a new one for psychology and has yet to impact, but we believe it will, for it is a radical critique that problematises much within the discipline. Queer theory entails a conceptualisation of sexuality that sees sexual power embodied in different levels of social life (enforced through boundaries and binary divides such as masculine and feminine or men and women). What queer theorists are engaged in is the problematisation of sexual and gender categories (and all identities more generally). That is, no longer can we assume that sexual and gender categories such as 'masculine' and 'feminine' represent some underlying reality about the world. Instead they represent ways in which society may be categorised for various political aims. At its most extreme we see a willingness to interrogate areas not usually seen as the terrain of sexuality and the transgression of all conventional categorisations and the breaking of boundaries. So, what does this have to do with psychology? Well, very obviously it is tremendously important for how we understand the psychology of sex and gender. In combination with the feminist critique these categories become increasingly problematic and open to interpretation. But more broadly, queer theory provides a challenge to many of the, often very subtle, heterosexual assumptions that underpin knowledge within the discipline in much the same way as feminist theory offers a challenge to the many sexist assumptions that underpin knowledge. This critique is yet to impact on psychology but it will, and you are forewarned, so be prepared.

17.3 Revisiting the qualitative versus quantitative debate

How important is this divide – philosophically?

We have covered this issue a fair amount previously (in this chapter and Chapter 1). To summarise, there are distinct epistemological positions that can be taken by researchers within the social sciences. Philosophers have provided the foundation for these positions and continue to argue which is right and which is wrong (even when they do not believe we can ever know when something is right or wrong). Some psychologists believe (and argue) very strongly that their philosophical position is correct and that all others are wrong. One of the most vociferous debates of this kind in recent times in the United Kingdom came about with the arguments advanced by the discourse analysts (e.g. Potter & Wetherell, 1987). They argued very strongly that much previous research, and most especially positivist research, was fundamentally flawed. Instead of studying internal mental processes they argued that psychological research should be concerned with language use. This debate has not been resolved and so continues in UK psychology today, but it is no longer so vociferous. This is the strongest position taken and many others believe and advocate their own philosophical standpoint without expending too much energy arguing with others who may disagree. This has resulted in the proliferation of different methodologies within psychology and, some would argue, fragmentation of the discipline (Langdridge & Butt, 2004).

How important is this divide – practically?

The distinction between qualitative and quantitative research is clearly important on a practical level. By and large, the claims made about the world differ in quite dramatic ways and clearly the methods employed by quantitative and qualitative researchers are different. However, things are not totally clear cut, for some methods are used in quantitative and qualitative research. And furthermore, an increasing number of researchers are using both quantitative and qualitative methods together within the same research project (see Chapter 24). So while many qualitative methods developed within the context of a critique of quantitative methods, researchers are beginning to see the utility of a practical strategy to research where illumination of the topic under investigation becomes clearer with a multi-method approach. But how do we do this? Surely these approaches are so different, with different epistemologies, aims and methods, that they can never be combined? Well, firstly, people advocating a **pragmatic** approach to research would argue that the epistemological questions must be put to one side, for (i) the main concern is with what works, and (ii) these questions are never likely to be settled. So, we bracket off the philosophical questions – well, the philosophical debate at least – for we cannot forget the philosophical issues when it comes to the question of what our methods allow us to say about the world. What about the differing aims of quantitative and qualitative methods? Well, this divide is potentially one of the strengths of a multi-method approach, for with such a strategy we get the possibility of investigating a phenomenon where we ask different questions and get different answers. This gives us the possibility of **triangulation,** where multiple perspectives enable us to truly understand the phenomena of interest. Triangulation generally concerns the desire to gain multiple perspectives within a qualitative approach but it can also involve the use of multiple perspectives from different traditions (Flick, 2002). Quantitative research may tell us, for instance, how many people experience depression, while phenomenological qualitative research may help us understand what it is like to experience depression. By taking different perspectives and using different methods we get the possibility of greater understanding of the topic (see Chapter 24). This strategy seems to be growing within psychology, and most particularly within applied areas, but it remains controversial, for there are those who argue that the epistemological differences cannot and should not be ignored since they concern fundamental questions about the nature of the discipline.

How important is this divide – politically?

As you have probably guessed by now, the divide is clearly an important one politically. The very fact that some people call themselves quantitative and others qualitative means that the label matters. And in this case the label really does matter, for although things are changing, and there is growing acceptance of qualitative approaches, there are still arguments and issues on both sides. Very simply, the quantitative approach to psychology remains dominant and with this dominance come certain advantages. Firstly, quantitative research is more likely to get funded than qualitative research. Secondly, quantitative research is more likely to get published than qualitative research. This is important for academics, for career advancement is invariably dependent on securing funding and getting published. It is obviously also important for the discipline more generally, as qualitative research will remain sidelined if funding and publication rates do not increase.

17.4 Limitations of the new paradigm for the social sciences

Up until now we have been advocating qualitative methods and highlighting their advantages over quantitative methods, but it is important to recognise their limitations too. Imagine you wished to increase the number of people wearing condoms when having sex. This is important, for if we increase the number of condoms worn we will decrease sexually transmitted diseases such as HIV. Now imagine we carried out a discourse analysis of talk about condom use. Will this help us implement a new health education intervention (like a pamphlet promoting condom use) to increase condom use? Well, it might provide some insight, but as the concern with discourse analysis is language use we doubt whether it will provide us with simple answers that can quickly and easily be incorporated into a pamphlet we can distribute. Similarly, a phenomenological study may give us insights into the experience of negotiating condom use among a small number of people and these may be key insights that help with the pamphlet, but we cannot know whether they apply to more than the 12 people in our sample. So, while qualitative research may be helpful to some extent, a quantitative approach, where we sample a representative number of people and ask them about their attitudes towards using condoms, may well enable us to identify quickly and easily relevant variables that can be incorporated into our health education leaflet.

Now, we have given just one example, which arguably demonstrates the (practical) superiority of a quantitative approach in one specific situation, and therefore why, we believe, qualitative research cannot and should not be the only approach used by psychologists. However, there are as many other examples which, we believe, demonstrate the superiority of qualitative research and clearly demonstrate why quantitative research should not be the only approach. There are countless examples on both sides that demonstrate the utility of quantitative and qualitative methods in achieving some outcome. Whether a particular approach is useful will depend on the questions being asked and, as you might expect, there are many questions left to be asked by psychologists. It is for this reason that we believe qualitative and quantitative perspectives both have a part to play in improving our knowledge of human nature. There is clearly good and bad research from both perspectives but let us not let that cloud our judgement and obscure the possibility of a constructive future where both have an equally valued place.

17.5 Varieties of qualitative methods and analysis

Epistemology and methodology

We have talked about the debates concerning different epistemological positions and it is important to think about their impact on **methodology** and **methods** used. As Willig (2001) makes clear, it is important to clarify the differences between methodology and methods, for the link between epistemology is necessarily close with one (methodology) and not the other (methods). Methodology concerns the 'general approach to studying research topics' (Silverman, 1993: 1), while methods are the specific techniques used to carry out research within a general position. The methodological approach taken by a researcher will clearly be strongly influenced by their epistemological standpoint. If, for instance, you are sceptical about psychology as an objective scientific study of human nature then you are unlikely to locate yourself within the traditional quantitative paradigm. Instead you might embrace a more critical methodological position such as social constructionism. Here the link between your epistemological position and methodology is clear and necessary. However, there is not such a necessary relationship between your epistemological position and method. But your methodological position *will limit* the range of methods that are appropriate. It is unlikely, though not impossible, that a social constructionist would employ experimental methods. Similarly, a quantitative researcher using the hypothetico-deductive approach is unlikely to employ semi-structured interviews. So, although there are links between epistemology, methodology and method, these are *often important but not always necessary*.

Qualitative methodologies

There are many different epistemological and methodological positions and therefore, as you might expect, many different qualitative methods. This is one of the biggest problems for people new to qualitative research. Quantitative research is, by comparison, simple and clear cut. Everyone knows where they stand and what to do. Good quantitative research has certain common foundations, with only variations in, for instance, methods of data collection and techniques of statistical analysis. There are not fundamental differences in methods that determine the very nature of your research questions, design, methods of data collection and analysis. Well, qualitative research is not that simple and at first glance it will appear complicated and probably confused. However, once you move beyond this first impression, things are not as complicated as they look.

The first thing to recognise is the different approaches to qualitative research that you might encounter. Chapters 19 to 22 outline what we consider to be the most important theoretical approaches to qualitative research within psychology. However, there are (many) other approaches that you may encounter and we are sure some people will feel we have made some terrible omissions. The chapters include the following qualitative approaches: phenomenological research, grounded theory, discourse and narrative research. These can be divided at a very simple level into two groups:

1 those that emphasise meaning for the participants (phenomenology and grounded theory), and
2 those that concentrate on language use (discourse analysis).

Participants' understanding of their own experience is emphasised and prioritised with the first group of methods. The key factor underpinning the second is, however, recognition of the dynamic nature of language. Language does not simply describe the world but plays an active part in constructing the world. Discourse analysts are not concerned with understanding the experiences of participants, like the phenomenologists, but they might be concerned with how people construct meaning through language use. Things are complicated somewhat by narrative approaches to research (Chapter 22) as they effectively combine elements of both of the above, though with some narrative methods concentrating more on meaning and others on language use.

However, things are even more complex than this, for even within the particular approaches listed above there are further distinctions and sometimes sharp divisions. For instance, there is not one way of doing grounded theory but several and the two founders (Glaser and Strauss) each now occupy opposing positions about which is correct. Similarly, there is not one approach to narrative research, discourse analysis or phenomenology but many. Sometimes these differences are minor and have only a marginal impact on, for instance, an element of the analysis of data. However, some of these distinctions are major and profoundly alter the whole research process. In the chapters that follow we outline some of the divisions though not all. If you wish to know more about any particular perspective then it will be crucial that you read further about it. The chapters in this book provide only a brief introduction. If you wish to carry out research from any qualitative perspective it is important that you read more, much more.

Commonalities in qualitative research

Although there are many differences between the different theoretical perspectives, there are a number of similarities and common features that provide a distinction between qualitative research and quantitative research. Following Hammersley (1992) we outline some of the commonalities here. It is important to note, however, that none of these distinctions is cast in stone. Like much in the social sciences, there will always be exceptions that disprove the rule. So, it is important that you think through these distinctions rather than simply remember them. Firstly, as you already know, qualitative research is concerned with the qualities of phenomena and not their quantification. This does not mean that qualitative research is less precise than quantitative research, just that it has a different focus. Instead of looking for causal relationships, qualitative researchers will tend to prefer to describe or uncover the quality of the phenomenon being investigated. Secondly, and perhaps most importantly, qualitative research has a focus on meanings rather than on behaviour. Variables are unlikely to have a place in qualitative research. This is because the research will prioritise the experience of the participants (or the construction of meaning through language) and any attempt to define variables in advance of this inevitably entails imposing a particular way of seeing the world on a participant. Thirdly, as discussed above, qualitative research rejects the natural science model of scientific endeavour. Research will rarely employ a hypothetico-deductive approach wherein we seek, through the use of controlled settings, to test an explicitly formulated hypothesis and make predictions about the world. Qualitative research is concerned with identifying processes rather than with predicting outcomes. Fourthly and finally, qualitative research is almost always naturalistic. Qualitative researchers study people in their natural environments and seek to capture the richness of such settings. No attempt is made to control 'extraneous variables', for there can never be extraneous variables in qualitative research. The 'noise' is part and parcel of the phenomenon and to (attempt to) exclude it from an investigation is to lose the essential richness of a person's experience.

Further reading

Burr, V. (2003). *An Introduction to Social Constructionism*. 2nd edn. London: Routledge.

> An excellent and very clear introduction to this topic. If you wish to grasp the emergence of this new approach to psychology then this book will be invaluable.

Denzin, N. K. & Lincoln, Y. S. (2005). *The Sage Handbook of Qualitative Research*. 3rd edn. London: Sage.

> A mammoth and expensive book, so one to borrow from the library. It is extremely comprehensive and includes excellent material on reflexivity, feminism and a whole lot more.

Smith, J. A., Harré, R. & Langenhove, L. (1995). *Rethinking Psychology*. London: Sage.

> Excellent coverage of many of the debates within psychology from a wide variety of qualitative positions. It is now a little dated but includes coverage of phenomenology, discursive and feminist approaches. The companion volume *Rethinking Methods in Psychology* is also excellent and worth reading.

CHAPTER B5
Sampling

Contents
Approaches to sampling   154
Choosing a sampling approach   171
References and further reading   173

In context

In this section we look at the ways of deciding which data to gather to include in your research. We are rarely in a position to collect data from all the cases, contexts and situations that are relevant to our research questions. If we are going to select only some of the potential data sources – people, documents, cases – then we have to make some decisions about how we are going to do that. Only in the ten-yearly census is data collected about every member of the UK population, and even then there are some groups – for example, homeless people – who are often excluded. If you are using secondary data or documentary data you will still need to think about how you decide what to include, and to be aware that somebody else – a researcher or an official perhaps – has already made some decisions about who or what is included in the data or document. Broadly speaking, there are two ways of approaching the task: a probability sample or a purposive sample, and which way you choose depends on the nature of your research question, the data you want to gather and whether you are gathering quantitative or qualitative data (or both). However, while the two approaches are quite different, they can be regarded as being at two ends of a spectrum, and you may find that you are using a combination of approaches – particularly if you are using a mixture of data collection methods.

PART B: Preparing for research

    B1: Planning a research project
    B2: Reviewing the literature
    B3: Research design
    B4: Choosing methods
▶   B5: **Sampling**
    B6: Research proposals

The selection of some cases from a larger group of potential cases is called sampling. Our approach to sampling is closely related to our choice of research design and methods, and reference will be made to research designs and choice of methods considered in B3 and B4. Throughout this section we will use researching volunteering as the basis of our examples.

> ### Example B5.1
>
> **Is volunteering good for you?**
>
> *[Volunteering is] an activity that involves spending time, unpaid, doing something that aims to benefit the environment or individuals or groups other than (or in addition to) close relatives.* (Commission on the Future of Volunteering, 2008)
>
> A report prepared for the Office of the Third Sector in the Cabinet Office by the National Centre for Social Research and the Institute for Volunteering Research found that in 2007 just under three-fifths of their population sample had been involved in formal volunteering with an organisation, with two-fifths doing so at least once a month. Volunteers said that the benefits of volunteering were enjoyment, personal achievement and satisfaction in seeing the results of their volunteering; 51 per cent said that it made them feel less stressed and 44 per cent said it improved their physical health (Low et al., 2007).

We will also bear in mind throughout this chapter that time and other resources are important factors in the choice of data collection methods and approaches to sampling. Research can be undertaken at many different levels, with researchers bringing a wide range of skill resources, time and financial support. Here we aim to provide guidance on the choice of sampling approach for a university student undertaking research as part of a programme of study, but we will also refer to larger-scale and more heavily resourced research examples. This will enable you to have a better understanding of other research which you may read and use as part of your study.

> ### Your research
>
> **Research quality check – generalisability and transferability**
>
> One of the first questions we need to address when thinking about how we are going to choose our data sources is how we will want to use the data when we have gathered it.
>
> 1. Do we want to be able to use the data from our sample to tell us about the population from which it was drawn? If, for example, we are collecting data about school pupils, do we want to be able to show how the data from our sample can be *generalised* – that is, said to be likely to be similar to that of *all* school pupils in the UK, in our local town or to school pupils in state-run schools?
>
> 2. Do we want to be able to collect data that will enable us to explore in depth the experiences, opinions or behaviour of particular people, cases or situations? Are we, for example, asking questions about the way particular educational settings impact on the behaviour of particular groups of school pupils? We may then want to consider how far our findings could be *transferred* to other similar situations or settings.
>
> We will consider these questions in relation to each different approach to sampling.

An important note: although throughout this chapter we will often refer to and use examples that are based on selecting individual *people* to take part in research, much of what is included here is appropriate for the selection of *cases*, *documents* and time and context *periods* for observation. Selection is always part of research design, and you must be aware of the criteria and approach you are using when you decide to collect data from any sources. The relevant sections in C3 and D3 will provide material to consider in addition to this chapter.

Approaches to sampling

In Figure B5.1 we have arranged the different approaches to sampling in a spectrum. At one end of the spectrum are the sampling approaches that are based on statistical theory, and which aim to produce a sample that can be shown to be highly representative of the whole population – or all the potential cases – in terms of relevant criteria: **probability samples**. At the other end of the spectrum are approaches to sampling that are concerned with selecting (usually fewer) cases that will best enable the researcher to explore the research questions in depth, and to work with the data collected to identify and explore theoretical ideas: **purposive** and **theoretical samples**.

probability sample
A sample that can be shown to be highly representative of the whole population – or all the potential cases – in terms of relevant criteria.

purposive sample
A sample of selected cases that will best enable the researcher to explore the research questions in depth.

theoretical sample
A sample of selected cases that will best enable the researcher to explore theoretical ideas.

population
In statistical terms, population refers to the total number of cases that can be included as research subjects.

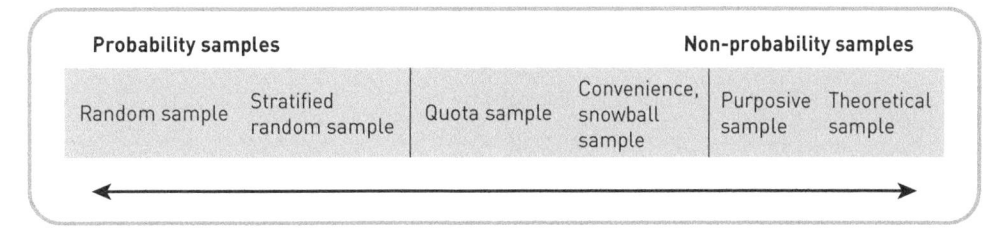

Probability samples				Non-probability samples	
Random sample	Stratified random sample	Quota sample	Convenience, snowball sample	Purposive sample	Theoretical sample

Figure B5.1 A spectrum of different approaches to sampling

Statistical sampling – or selecting a probability sample

One approach to sampling is to use probability or statistical theory to help you to select a sample that is representative of the **population** from which it is taken. This approach is most commonly used when designing experimental and survey research (B3) and where the data being gathered is quantitative in nature. Selecting a sample in this way enables the researcher to undertake a statistical analysis of the data (D3).

What is . . .

Population
In statistical terms, population refers to the total number of cases that can be included as research subjects. For example, a population may be:
- all the people who live in a country;
- all the students studying at a particular university;
- all the undergraduate students studying sociology at any UK university at a particular time;
- all the newspaper articles published in the UK referring to student volunteering during a particular month.

The key characteristics of a probability sample are as follows:

- Each member of the population has a known (and usually equal) chance of being selected for the sample. This assumes that the members of the population are known – that is, that they can be individually identified. If this is not the case, then other sampling strategies may need to be adopted.

- Each sample member is chosen at random and it cannot be predicted which members will be chosen.
- The sample is usually selected to be representative of the population on the basis of certain known characteristics, for example, age, gender, socio-economic group and so on, which are relevant to the research study.

Random samples and stratified samples

In a random sample every case has an equal chance of being selected.

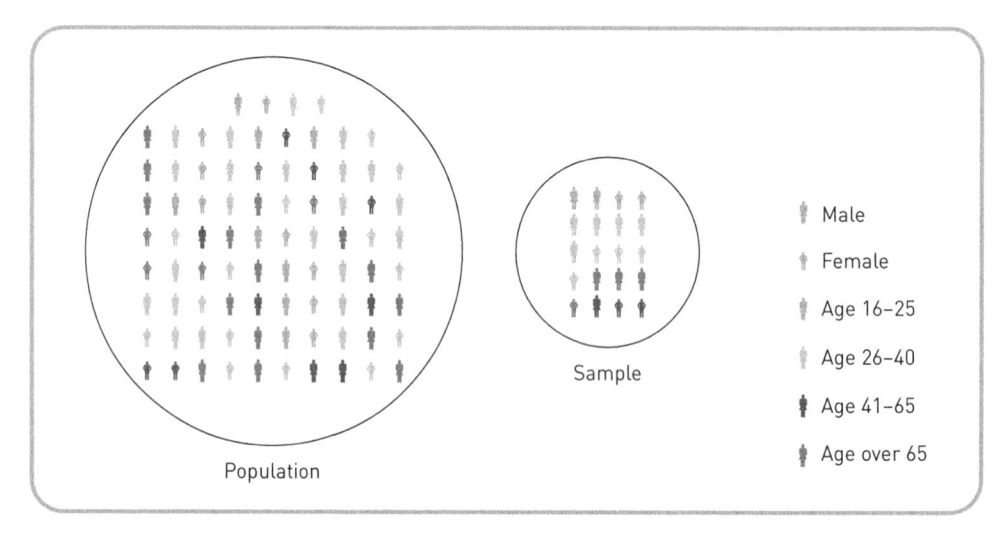

Figure B5.2 Selecting a random sample from a population of men and women aged over 16 years (A)

A random sample may or may not include cases with particular characteristics in the same proportions as they are found in the population. So in Figure B5.2 the sample does include the age groups represented by colours and male and female symbols in similar (but not exact) proportions.

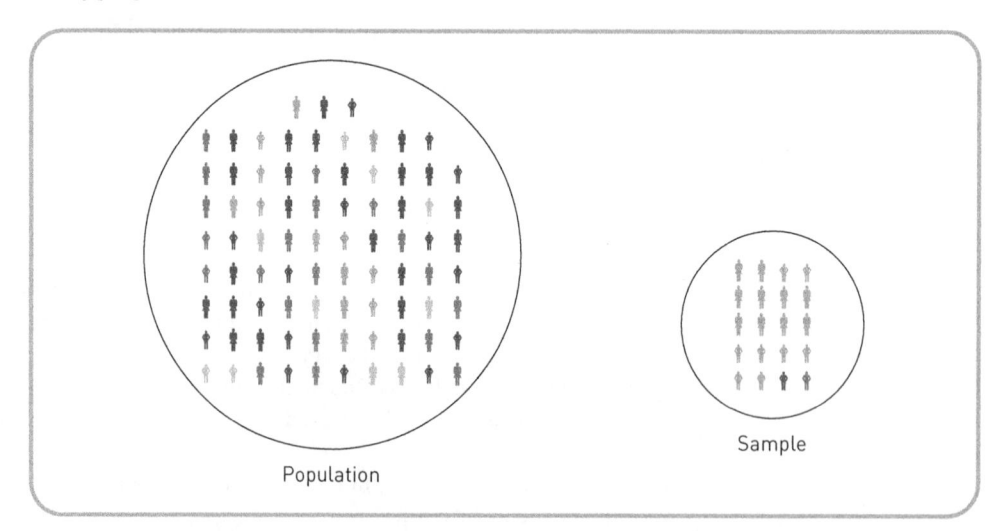

Figure B5.3 Selecting a random sample from a population of men and women aged over 16 years (B)

In Figure B5.3, you will see that the random sample includes all the green symbols and only two others. Taking a random sample can *potentially* produce this type of result, and would clearly have implications for research that was designed to look at the different experiences of, for example, people aged 16 to 25 years and those aged 41–65 years, as only one of the second group has been included.

stratification
A method of organising a population in order to improve the representativeness of a sample.

The probability of selecting a sample that is so unrepresentative of the population is low, but it is one that must be considered (see below). To improve the representativeness of the sample we can introduce some **stratification**, while still ensuring that all the population cases have an equal chance of being included in the sample.

> ### Think about it . . .
> #### Statistical probability of selecting a sample from a population
> There are many possible samples of 20 people that could be selected from 100 people. The possibilities increase if the population is much larger – for example, there are even more ways of selecting 1,000 people from 50,000,000. Statistical probability theory can be used to show that most of these samples will closely resemble the characteristics of the population. If, for example, we found from our sample that, on average, people who visited their doctor infrequently undertook volunteering activities five times a year, how likely is it that people in the whole population (in this case, the doctor's patient list) who visit their doctor infrequently also have an average of volunteering five times a year?
>
> Using statistical theory, we can say that if we took lots of different samples from the same population, we would find that the distribution of the average (mean) number of volunteering activities would be a normal distribution. This is a bell-shaped curve graph, as shown in Figure B5.4 below. If we assume that the population mean is at the high point of the bell curve (that is, coinciding with the highest numbers of sample means), then we can say that our particular sample mean will lie within two **standard deviations** of the central point in 95 per cent of cases. The standard deviation is a statistical measure of how the cases – in this case the averages (means) of each of our samples – are distributed around the mean (in this case the assumed population mean).
>
> [Bell curve showing percentages: 2.5%, 13.5%, 34%, 34%, 13.5%, 2.5% across standard deviations from -3 to 3]
>
> Figure B5.4 A normal distribution

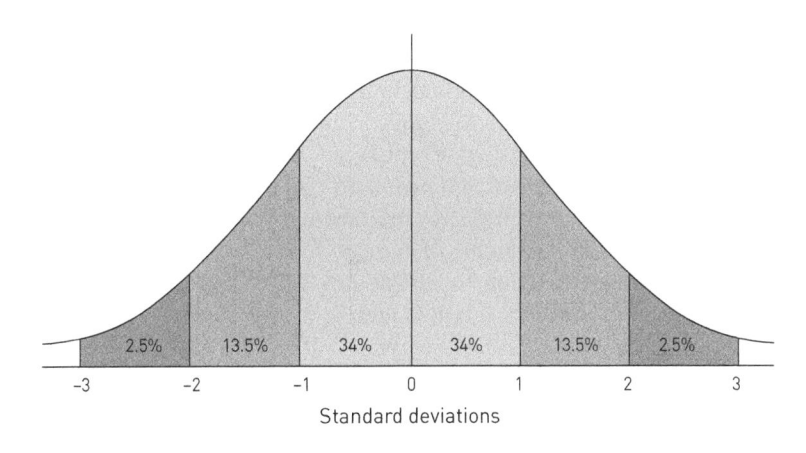

What is . . .

Standard deviation
The standard deviation is a statistical measure of how the cases – in this example the averages (means) of each of our samples – are distributed around the mean (in this case the assumed population mean).

> **Your research**
>
> Further reading for students who want to understand more about statistical sampling: D. B. Wright and K. London (2009) *First (and Second) Steps in Statistics*, 2nd edn, London: Sage.

> **Example B5.2**
>
> **Sampling: volunteering and health**
>
> A doctor wants to explore the links between volunteering and physical and mental health among her adult patients who are aged 65 or under. She has heard of some research that shows that people who volunteer tend to be healthier. She would like to find out which of her patients do volunteer, but does not have the resources to survey all of them.
>
> She has two ideas about how she might sample her 5,000 patients.
>
> (a) She might ask her administrator for an alphabetical list of all her patients aged between 16 and 65 years and then select 500 (1 in 10) patients at random using random number tables to decide which patients to include (random number tables are lists of numbers generated at random, usually by a computer).
>
> (b) She might devise a questionnaire and ask her receptionist to give this out to the first 500 patients aged between 16 and 65 years to come to the surgery during a particular month.
>
> Which of these, (a) or (b), would be a random sample?

In Example B5.2, approach (a) is a good method for selecting a random sample – although it still may not be the best way of getting a useful sample, as we shall see. First, though, let us consider what the problem is with approach (b). Although we cannot predict who would be the first 500 people to visit the surgery, people who have chronic diseases or who need to see their doctor on a regular basis would have a much higher chance of being included in the sample than those who rarely have cause to visit their doctor's surgery. As the research is trying to distinguish between people on the basis of their physical/mental health and ill health, this sample would not be an appropriate way to select people for this research.

Let's now consider sample approach (a) in a little more depth by thinking about the research question. The researcher is interested in people who do and do not volunteer, and in their health. From what she knows about the subject, she suspects that there will be differences that relate to people's ages, genders and perhaps ethnic group. She also knows that most younger people are in good health, and that as people get older they are less likely to be so. If she wants to be able to explore these questions, she needs to ensure that her sample is going to include all of these different combinations of people. To do this, she will need to know more about her population, so that she can select a sample that is representative of the population in relation to these characteristics.

To do this, the doctor will first need to find out the proportions of her patients who are in each of the categories. She might start by drawing this diagrammatically, as in Example B5.3. Note that she has decided to use a **proxy definition** of health by separating her patients into two groups – those who visit the doctor's surgery infrequently, and those who are frequent

proxy definition
A 'rule of thumb' definition which stands in for a more detailed and sophisticated way of defining something.

attenders. This proxy definition is standing in for a more detailed and sophisticated way of defining health, as a means of ensuring that the sample includes the range of people she needs in order to be able to address her research questions.

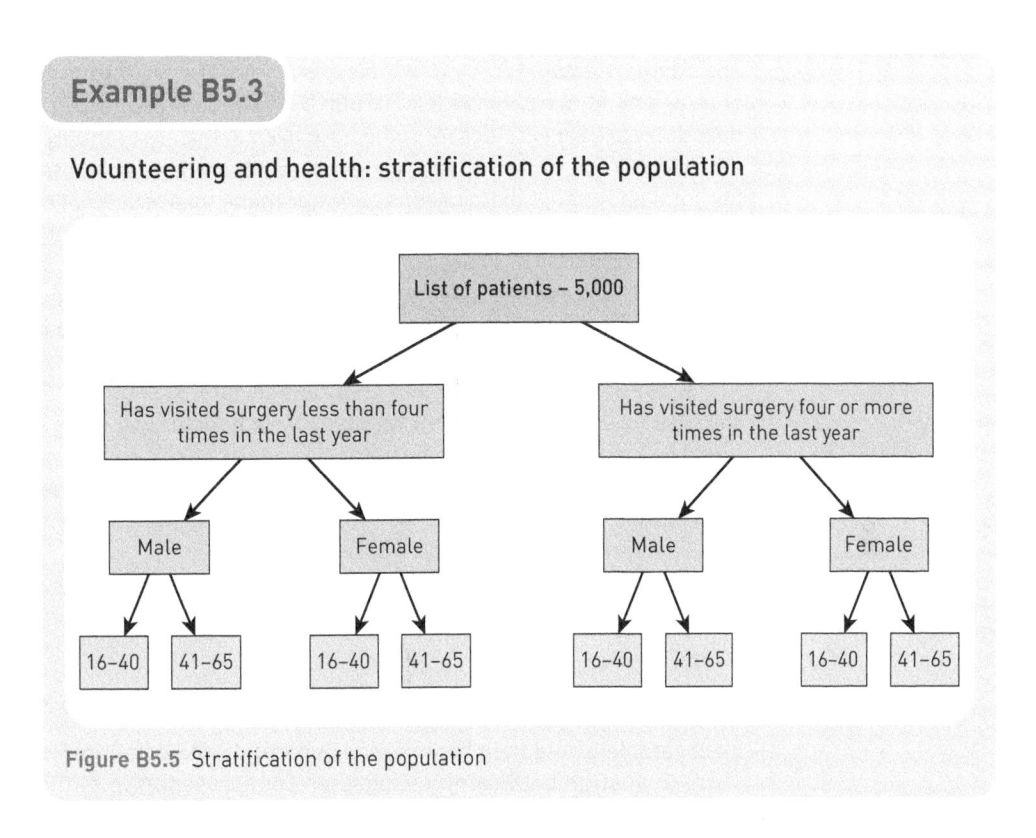

Example B5.3

Volunteering and health: stratification of the population

Figure B5.5 Stratification of the population

Her sample, then, should include the sample proportions of people in each group. For example, if there are 500 women aged between 41 and 65 years who have visited the surgery less than four times during the last year, then:

$$500/5{,}000 \times 500 = 50$$

So 50 women in this category should be included in the sample. These women can be selected at random from the list of 500 women in this category.

Think about it . . .

If there are 300 men aged 16–40 who are frequent attendees, how many should be included in a sample of 500?
What if there were just 30 men in this age group who were frequent attendees? Do you think this would be a sufficient sample of this group?

In this example, the population has been stratified, or organised into categories at three levels, to enable the doctor to select a sample that will help her to address her research questions. The levels of stratification are:

1. Frequency of visiting the surgery
2. Gender
3. Age.

> ### Example B5.4
>
> #### Volunteering and health
>
> The doctor is also interested in the experiences of people from two minority ethnic groups among her patients. One group have lived in the area for many years, while the others are recent migrants who have lived in the area for only a year or so. Their ethnicity is recorded on their case notes. Each group is only a small percentage of her total patient list (both groups together make up about 5%, or 250), so her initial sample is likely to include just a few of each group. The doctor therefore decides to take an additional sample, made up of people from these two minority ethnic groups. In this case she selects a higher proportion of the total population, 1 in 2, to ensure that her sample is large enough to enable her to analyse her findings on the same variables of age and gender as her larger sample.
>
> However, when she comes to analyse her data, she cannot simply add the two samples together, because the samples have been drawn using different **sampling fractions**, and patients of the two ethnic groups had the chance of being selected in both samples. The doctor can analyse the two samples and present the findings for each sample separately, and the findings from the two samples can be compared using percentages rather than raw numbers.
>
> An alternative, or additional, approach would be to select two samples:
>
> A: from the total population excluding the two ethnic groups – using a sampling fraction of 1 in 10;
>
> B: from the two ethnic groups using a sampling fraction of 1 in 2.
>
> Each sample would then be analysed separately and compared using percentages. Then, to analyse both samples together as representative of the total patient list, the doctor would need to reduce the weight of sample B. To do this she would need to divide any results from sample B by 10/2 = 5 as the patients from the two ethnic groups were five times more likely to be selected than the other patients.
>
> Table B5.1 Volunteering and health sample data
>
> | Gender | (1) Data from sample A | (2) Data from sample B | (3) Weighted data from sample B Column 2/5 | (4) Total of sample A and weighted sample B Column 1 + Column 3 |
> |---|---|---|---|---|
> | Male | 225 | 75 | 15 | 240 |
> | Female | 250 | 50 | 10 | 260 |
> | Total sample | 475 | 125 | 25 | 500 |
>
> Note that the data gathered from *all* those included in sample B is used and the weighting is applied to it. Do not be tempted to simply select, for example, 25 out of the 125 patients from the small ethnic groups to include and exclude the remainder.

Stratified samples are also used to enable researchers to minimise the time and resources required, particularly in large-scale interview surveys which draw samples from across a large geographical area. Most large-scale surveys undertaken by government departments take this approach, as the 'Real research' box on p. 160 shows. In this example, the researcher

cluster sample
A sample consisting of cases selected because of their proximity to one another.

first selected wards (geographical, local government areas). By selecting geographical areas first, the researchers ensured that their sample would not be spread across *every* area of England and Wales. This is called a **cluster sample**, because the sample is clustered (in this case geographically) and thereby reduces the time and resources needed to access the selected cases. As you will see from the 'Real research' example, a stratified sample can be very complex. Few researchers have the time and resources to design and then gain access to such a large, complex sample. However, the example demonstrates the different elements and stages of a stratified sample which can be useful to a student researcher seeking to create a representative sample from a defined population.

Real research

The Citizenship Survey 2005

The Citizenship Survey 2005 was commissioned by the Home Office to find out the views of the population in England and Wales on a range of issues. The survey included questions about views on the locality, racial and religious discrimination, volunteering, and rights and responsibilities. Face-to-face interviews were carried out by interviewers from the National Centre for Social Research. The technical report on this research can be found at www.communities.gov.uk/publications/communities/2005citizenshipsurveytechnical (accessed 21 July 2009). Findings from the research can be found at www.communities.gov.uk/publications/communities/2005citizenshipsurveycross (accessed 21 July 2009).

The sample

A nationally representative sample of 10,000 adults in England and Wales, and an additional sample of 4,500 people from minority ethnic groups.

How was the sample selected?

A sample of addresses was drawn from the Royal Mail Postcode Address File using a two-stage sampling approach:

1. A random sample of 663 wards was selected using Census Area Statistics.
   (a) Before selection the wards were sorted into three groups according to the percentage of minority ethnic group population within the ward (less than 1%, 1–18%, over 18%).
   (b) Within these groups wards were sorted by Government Office Region.
   (c) Within each Government Office Region, wards were sorted into three groups based on the percentage of head of households in non-manual occupations.
   (d) Finally, within each group, wards were sorted by the proportion of males in the ward who were unemployed.
   (e) The sample of 663 wards was selected at random from the stratified list with the probability of inclusion being proportionate to the number of addresses within the ward.
2. Within each selected ward, 25 addresses were selected at random.
   (a) If an address included more than one household, the interviewer selected three households to interview at random using a systematic procedure.
   (b) One person aged 16 or over was randomly selected from each household by the interviewer, again using a systematic procedure.

> The additional minority ethnic groups sample was drawn as follows:
>
> 1. The wards that had a relatively high proportion (over 18%) and medium proportion (1–18%) of people from minority ethnic groups were used for this sample.
>   (a) In each of the medium density wards, the two addresses before and after the addresses already chosen were selected for screening. Respondents at the chosen addresses were asked if there were people from minority ethnic groups living at these addresses. If so, then the interviewer called at these addresses.
>   (b) In the high density wards, an additional 110 addresses were chosen and screened by the interviewer for respondents from people from minority ethnic groups.
> 2. An additional sample of wards was drawn from a further 150 wards (not included in the core sample) with a high density population of people from minority ethnic groups. The same stratification process was used, and 110 addresses were selected for each ward. These were then screened for people from minority ethnic groups.
>
> **What was the response rate achieved?**
>
> **Core sample**
>
> Of the 16,575 addresses selected:
>
> > 1,543 addresses: were not suitable – e.g. empty, non-residential, demolished
> > 338 addresses: no contact – unable to establish eligibility
> > 3,923 addresses: refused to take part
> > 595 addresses: unable to take part through e.g. illness, language
>
> A total of 9,691 interviews were carried out.
>
> *Minority ethnic groups sample*
> 7,171 households selected including eligible adults (i.e. from a minority ethnic group)
> 4,390 interviews were carried out

Probability sampling – the practicalities

If you are thinking of using probability sampling, there are a number of questions to think about at this stage.

What are the relevant characteristics of the population that should be represented in the sample?

At this stage, you should already be thinking about how you will analyse the data you gather, and be able to identify the characteristics or variables that you will be using to distinguish between different cases. For example, if it is clear from your research question or hypothesis that you will be looking for similarities and differences between people of different age groups, or between articles from different types of newspaper, then you will need to ensure that cases are selected to include these. By stratifying your population using these characteristics, you can ensure that you include similar proportions of each group in your sample to those in the population (as the doctor did in the example). If you keep in mind both your research questions and your plans for analysis, your sample will be designed to ensure that you are collecting data from cases that will provide data that can be used to address those questions.

Is there an accessible list – or sampling frame – of all the members of the population from which a sample can be drawn, and which gives the information required to be able to draw a stratified, representative sample?

sampling frame
A list of all the members of a population from which a sample may be drawn.

In many cases it will not be (easily) possible to draw up or have access to a list of all the members of the population from which the sample can be drawn (a **sampling frame**). This could be because, quite simply, no such list exists. When drawing a sample for the Citizenship Survey, the researchers were unable to use a list of all the addresses in the UK where people from minority ethnic groups lived, because no such list existed. Instead, the researchers used census data to identify the wards where people from minority ethnic groups were most likely to be found.

Even if a list of your population exists, you may not have access to the details about the people or cases on the list that you need in order to draw the sample. This may be because the information is confidential, or because the person who holds the list, sometimes called the 'gatekeeper', is unwilling to give you access to it. While the doctor in the earlier example did have access to her own patient list, she may be unwilling to give a student researcher access to the information required for the student to undertake the research on volunteering. There are a number of reasons that a gatekeeper may not give you access to the information you need to draw a sample. The data may be confidential and covered by the data protection legislation or the gatekeeper may have a professional or other responsibility for the people you wish to involve in your research and may be concerned for their well-being (A5). These are ethical issues and you may need to consider whether you will be able to access the people or settings in the way that you wished. Other reasons for denying access may relate to the gatekeeper's lack of time to help you or lack of interest in the research you are proposing, particularly if the research is not seen to be of value to the gatekeeper or her organisation.

quota sampling
A sampling technique that selects a certain number, or quota, of cases, on the basis of their matching a number of criteria.

If you do not have access to a population list, you may need to consider other approaches to gathering a sample, including **quota sampling** and **snowball sampling**, which are discussed later in this chapter – see pp. 164 and 166.

How large a sample should be drawn?

snowball sampling
A sampling technique where members of an initial sample are asked to identify others with the same characteristics as them, who the researcher then contacts.

This is not an easy question, as a number of different aspects need to be taken into account. First of all, thinking statistically, it is generally the case that if you are selecting a representative random sample from a known population, increasing the sample size means that the generalisability of the sample data to the population increases, and the **sampling error**, or likely variation of the sample mean from the population mean, decreases. However, it is not the case that the bigger the population, the bigger the sample required. Market research and opinion poll organisations often depend on a sample size of 1,000 from the adult population of the UK as the basis of their research. It can be shown that the additional benefits derived from increasing the sample size become smaller as the sample size increases and the time and resource implications of increasing the sample size begin to take precedence over the marginal reduction of the sampling error.

sampling error
The likely variation of the sample mean from the population mean.

However, for a student undertaking research with limited time and resources, the sample size is more likely to be influenced by the resources available and the ease of access to the sampled cases. Seek advice from your tutor or supervisor on this, as she will be able to advise you of any guidelines and look with you at the particular issues relating to your research. It is important, though, to be aware of the limitations of a smaller sample and to discuss these in your research report or dissertation.

A further matter to consider with regard to sample size: remember that, like the doctor in Example B5.2, you are likely to want to analyse data for groups within the sample – for example, look for differences between men and women of different age groups. If your overall sample is small, you will find that the data relating to (for example) men aged 16–24 years is based on very few cases. This will limit the usefulness of the data and may mean that you are not able to undertake the analyses you have planned.

A final point to remember is that there will be some non-responders – people who do not agree to take part in your research – and some whom you may not be able to contact.

It is advisable to select your sample with this in mind and to select at least 10% more than you hope to gain responses from.

Is there any bias within the sampling frame or the method of sampling which may affect the sample?

When considering your sampling frame – that is, the list of people or cases that may be included in your sample – you need to check that the list has not been compiled in such a way as to exclude particular cases or groups. It was noted earlier that even the official UK census cannot claim to include every member of the population. You need to be aware of cases and groups of people who may be missing from the list. In the volunteering example, we saw that collecting a sample by giving questionnaires to the first 500 patients to come to the surgery could **bias** the sample towards people who made more frequent visits to the doctor. In this example we might also consider the gender of the doctor and question whether male and female patients were equally likely to choose a female doctor. By selecting the sample from only her own patient list, the doctor may be selecting a sample that is biased towards people who made a particular choice.

bias
Prejudice in favour, or against, a group individual, perspective, etc.

Is the sample accessible? And likely to participate or respond?

Before drawing the sample, you also need to think about how accessible the sample you have chosen will be. Will the selected people or cases be available to you at the time you are required to carry out your data collection? Will you need to travel? If you are planning an email survey, will all of your sample have access to and be regular users of email? Are there likely to be any language or comprehension difficulties?

Here we are highlighting another source of potential bias, because you may not have the same access to all of your sample, and they may not all have the same opportunity to participate in your research. You should expect that there will be some people who will not participate in your research, and record evidence of the **non-response**. Non-response can occur for a variety of reasons:

non-response
This occurs wherever an invited participant declines to be involved in a research project, perhaps because they refuse, are ill or are inappropriate.

- non-contact – the researcher is unable to contact the selected person;
- refusal – the selected person does not wish to take part in the research;
- the selected person is unable to take part through, for example, ill health, language or holidays;
- the selected person is not appropriate – usually because the information about the person was inaccurate.

As a researcher, you need to do what you can to minimise non-response. This is best done through good preparation and forethought.

Your research

Research quality check: probability samples and generalisability

- Are there significant omissions from the population list which may lead to bias?
- Is the sample selected randomly?
- Are your analysis groupings sufficiently large (at least five cases in each group)?
- Have you considered bias that may be introduced through lack of access and non-response?
- Is the probability sample of sufficient size to support statistical analysis and claims of generalisability to the population?
- Have you included a discussion of the limitations of your sample in your research report or dissertation?

Non-probability sampling

We have already noted that when you are embarking on a small piece of research with limited time and resources, you are unlikely to be able to create a sample that is (a) large or (b) meets all the requirements of a random probability sample. In this section we introduce some approaches to sampling that are perhaps more suited to the scale of research work most students undertake. These approaches may be suitable for small-scale experimental and cross-sectional survey research designs.

Convenience sampling

With limited time and resources, student researchers may have little choice but to select a sample on the basis of its convenience or ease of access. In fact, if we look at a selection of research studies, we will often find that the context in which the research is set has been selected from a much wider range of possibilities because the researcher has easy access to it. Typically a student researcher may select an appropriate setting from which to obtain as many responses as possible, for example, her own university department, a community centre or meeting place, a shopping centre or a sports club.

Example B5.5

Volunteering and health

The doctor in our example begins by defining the population for her study as all her own patients; in other words, the patients to whom she has easy access. She is not attempting to draw a sample from the total adult population of the UK. However, she does go on to select a probability sample from her 'convenient' population.

Example B5.6

Student volunteering

A student interested in researching the prevalence and nature of volunteering among the student population decides to select participants from his own programme group and his hall of residence and email a questionnaire survey out to all those listed. He hopes for a good response, particularly from those he knows well!

In his dissertation, he shows that he understands the limitations of this approach by pointing out that, by using this sampling approach, those who live at home or in private lettings are likely to be under-represented and those who are on his programme, Social Policy, are over-represented. He discusses the possibility that Social Policy students are more likely to volunteer than others and that those students living at home may have different opportunities to volunteer from those who live in a hall of residence.

Quota sampling

This approach to sampling includes some of the features of a **stratified sample** (a sample that is selected to ensure that certain categories and groups of people and cases are included proportionate to their presence in the population) without the use of a complete list of all the people or cases in the population and can be a more convenient way of developing a sample. In fact, it is an approach taken by many market research organisations. If you have ever been approached in the street by an interviewer with a clipboard, asking you to be involved in some research about a new brand of crisps or detergent, it is likely that the interviewer has been given a quota of interviews to complete. You may have been approached because, for example, you are male, look as if you are aged between 18 and 25 years, and have a middle-class background. The interviewer will have been given a set of criteria which she has to meet, which may include:

Five male

Five female

Three aged 18–25

Four aged 26–45

Three aged 46–65

Six middle-class

Four working-class.

Interviewers will then look for individuals who fulfil at least one, but probably more than one of these criteria. In this example, the interviewer could achieve her quota by conducting just ten interviews, provided that all of her criteria are met according to the quota she has been given. The criteria are usually derived from population data, for example, local census data, and the quotas are worked out so that the sample of individuals selected will be in proportion to the prevalence of a particular characteristic (gender, age, ethnicity, etc.) in the population. The interviewer continues approaching potential interviewees until all the quota have been filled. The interviewer will, of course, sometimes get it wrong and approach people who look as if they fulfil the quota but, on questioning them, find that they fall into the wrong age or social class grouping for her quota. The interview will then usually be ended.

Example B5.7

Volunteering and health

The doctor could use a quota sample to gather a sample of patients by giving the receptionist a quota of patients, using age and gender as the criteria, to approach and ask to take part in the survey of volunteering. This would ensure that a range of patients were included on the basis of age and gender. However, it would not include information about the frequency of visiting the doctor, and the sample would be biased towards those who attend more frequently.

Can you think of a way that this frequency of visiting could also be included in the quota criteria?

The example has given us some clues to the limitations of quota sampling.

(a) *Choice of criteria.* It may be difficult to choose criteria that are both useable in practice and relate to the research questions. For example, how would you decide whether a person in the street was middle-class or working-class?

(b) *Bias towards particular groups of people.* The choice of place and time to select the sample of participants is likely to exclude certain groups and give other groups a much higher chance of being included. Market research is often carried out in town centre shopping areas during working hours, i.e. between 9 a.m. and 5 p.m. People who are busy or are in a hurry to catch a train or go to a meeting are more likely to refuse to take part in an interview, while those who are not busy, or are perhaps unemployed, may have more time and be more willing to participate. In addition, interviewers (and researchers!) may be more likely to approach people who look to them as if they are likely to take part, or who look friendly and less likely to refuse.

(c) *Non-random selection.* Data from a quota sample of people cannot be regarded as statistically generalisable to the population, because the way the sample is collected does not give every member of the population a calculable chance of being included.

Snowball sampling

As we noted above, some populations are quite hard to find because there are no lists of such people or cases, nor are there obvious places where the cases may be found. These 'hidden' populations are sometimes associated with behaviour that is seen as less socially acceptable or criminal. However, all sorts of other behaviour and characteristics can be hidden from the researcher, for example, their 'informal volunteering' as in Example B5.8. A snowball sample starts with a few people who are known to be the type of people the researcher wants to involve in the research. The researcher may make contact with them through a shared meeting place, an internet site or through personal contacts of her own. Then each member of the initial group is asked to suggest others with the same characteristics, and the researcher will then contact them, and so on. Given that people who have certain characteristics or behaviour are often part of a network of similar people, this approach to sampling can be quite fruitful, particularly if it is combined with a quota sampling approach which seeks out people with specific characteristics, for example different ages and ethnicities.

> **Example B5.8**
>
> ### Informal volunteering
>
> A researcher wants to include 'informal' volunteers in her research. She has defined an 'informal' volunteer as someone who carries out tasks and activities for others who are not family members, without payment. She is particularly interested in people who help out their neighbours on a fairly regular basis by, for example, doing their shopping or gardening.
>
> She selects a neighbourhood and begins by identifying a few 'informal' volunteers through visiting the local church, mosque and community centre. She then asks them if they know other people in their street or nearby who are also 'informal' volunteers, and so on, until she has built up a sample that covers most of the streets in the neighbourhood.

Comparing a non-probability sample with the population

The characteristics of a non-probability sample can in some cases be compared with those of the total population. If comparable data about the whole population is available – for example, the proportions of male and female and the proportions in each age or socio-economic group for the area in which the research is carried out – this can be used to see how closely the sample resembles the population. Although a non-probability sample cannot be used to generalise to the population *statistically* as a probability sample can, in research where the non-probability sample does resemble that of the population closely, this should be discussed in the research report.

> **Your research**
>
> **Research quality check: non-probability samples**
> - Have you clearly set out how the sample was drawn up?
> - Have you identified possible sources of bias and, where possible, tried to address these?
> - Have you set out the limitations of your sample in terms of what claims you are able to make from your findings?
> - Have you identified the strengths of your sample in terms of good use of resources, identification of suitable cases, response rates and suitability to address the research questions?

Purposive sampling

The final approach to sampling may be regarded as being at the other end of the spectrum we introduced at the beginning of this chapter. **Purposive sampling** and theoretical sampling are both approaches that are non-probability based samples and are quite deliberately so. These approaches are generally associated with small, in-depth studies with research designs that are based on the gathering of qualitative data and focused on the exploration and interpretation of experiences and perceptions. This includes case studies, some cross-sectional studies, ethnographical and Grounded Theory designs (B3).

In these approaches to sampling, there is no attempt to create a sample that is statistically representative of a population. Rather, people or cases are chosen 'with purpose' to enable the researcher to explore the research questions or develop a theory. The cases are selected on the basis of characteristics or experiences that are directly related to the researcher's area of interest and her research questions, and will allow the researcher to study the research topic in-depth. The cases chosen are those that can reveal and illuminate the most about the research area.

What is . . .

Purposive sampling
Ritchie and Lewis (2003: 79) usefully set out different approaches that may be taken to creating a sample:
- **Homogeneous sample** – where all the cases belong to the same group or have the same characteristic. This enables an in-depth and detailed investigation of a particular social phenomenon.
- **Heterogeneous or maximum variation sample** – here, ensuring that there is variation between cases means that cross-cutting common themes can be identified.
- **Stratified purposive sampling** – perhaps the most common way of selecting a purposive sample is to select from within groups of cases where there is some variation between the groups to enable the groups to be compared. The groups may be derived on the basis of information already held from a survey or population data.
- **Extreme case sampling** – here cases are chosen because they are extreme or deviant, and can therefore shed light on a social phenomenon from a different perspective from that which is normally taken.
- **Intensity sampling** – cases are selected that 'strongly represent the phenomena of interest'.

- **Typical case sampling** – here cases are selected that can be regarded as typical or 'normal'.
- **Critical case sampling** – cases are selected on the basis of the way they are 'critical' to a process or phenomena.

Theoretical sampling

theoretical sampling
A sampling technique in which the initial cases are usually selected on a relatively unstructured basis; as 'theory' begins to emerge from the initial data, further cases are selected to explore and test the emerging theory; this continues until there is no new theory emerging and theoretical 'saturation' is reached.

Theoretical sampling is a variation of purposive sampling which is based on the ideas and processes of Grounded Theory (B3). It assumes that data collection, analysis and the sampling of cases are going on concurrently, and that sampling of new cases for data collection continues until there is no further data emerging from each additional case. The process is described by Glaser and Strauss (1967: 45) as

> data collection for generating theory whereby the analyst jointly collects, codes, and analyses his data and decides what data to collect next and where to find them, in order to develop his theory as it emerges.

Thus the initial cases are usually selected on a relatively unstructured basis. As 'theory' begins to emerge from the initial data, further cases are selected to explore and test the emerging theory. The researcher is also interested in identifying 'negative cases' – cases that do not conform to the emerging theory, as it is from these cases that the theory can be amended and developed. This continues until there is no new theory emerging and theoretical 'saturation' is reached.

Purposive sampling – the practicalities

The approach to designing and gathering a purposive sample draws on other non-probability techniques which we discussed earlier in this chapter. Convenience, quota and snowballing samples are all commonly used approaches to gathering participants or cases for a purposive sample. As we have seen in the sample and volunteering example, it may be possible to use data gathered using a probability sample, as data is then available to help the researcher to purposefully select participants for the more in-depth study.

What is the population from which the sample will be selected?

When designing a purposive sample, we are using population in a similar way to when drawing a probability sample, in that it needs to be defined in terms of its characteristics, and particularly in terms that are relevant to the research study. However, we are not seeking to identify all possible members of the population in order to be able to draw a sample from them. Rather, we are looking at the relevant characteristics and thinking about the context in which a population with those characteristics may be found.

> **Example B5.9**
>
> **Volunteering in hospitals**
>
> A researcher is developing a study of people who volunteer in hospitals. He starts by considering the context – the hospital – and finds out about how hospitals are organised through reading and searching the internet. By visiting a local hospital, he is able to find out more about the opportunities for volunteering in the hospital. This helps him to identify people and organisational structures that may help him to identify potential participants for his study.
>
> Thinking a bit more about his research questions and the hospital, he then wonders whether volunteering in a large city-centre hospital is different from volunteering in a small local hospital, so he finds a smaller hospital and finds out more about the context before deciding to include volunteers from both hospitals in his study.

What are the characteristics or criteria for selection?

The criteria for selection within a purposive sample usually derive from the research questions themselves and the type of purposive sample. For a small-scale piece of research undertaken by a student, a sample that is stratified – or a quota sample – based on the key areas and issues you are identifying in your research questions is the most common approach to take.

As with probability sampling, it is important at this stage to also be planning the initial stages of your analysis. In particular, you should be aware of groups of cases, based on such variables as age, gender and ethnicity, that you may wish to compare for similarities or differences. You should also think about the differences and similarities you might expect to find based on your reading of other research and theory in the topic area, and ensure that you are including cases within your example that will enable you to explore these initial ideas. From this, a sample matrix (see Ritchie and Lewis, 2003: 101) can be developed, as shown in Example B5.10, which will enable you to identify potential participants.

How many cases should be included?

Purposive sampling is usually used as part of research designs that include in-depth study, gathering and working with qualitative, in-depth and detailed data. The number of cases is typically small by comparison with a probability sample, for the following reasons:

(a) Research that uses qualitative data is not usually concerned with being able to generalise to a population, or the prevalence of a particular characteristic in the population.

(b) There are diminishing returns to be gained from the data gathered from each additional case. Because we are not attempting to demonstrate the prevalence of a particular characteristic in the population, there is no requirement to go on looking for further examples.

(c) Gathering qualitative data is very time- and resource-consuming, and the data gathered is itself rich in detail. Few researchers have the resources, or the need, to include large numbers of cases.

That said, the question of how many cases to include remains. For most student projects, it is likely that a maximum of around 20 individual interviews will be feasible (though in some circumstances it may be less – check your regulations), and for many it will be unnecessary to include even as many as this. Much will depend on time and resources. Perhaps even more, it will depend on the access to participants and their willingness to participate in the research. Setting out the criteria for selection as shown in the matrix in Example B5.10 can be very helpful in terms of identifying the minimum and maximum number of cases you want to include.

Of course, if you are using purposive sampling to sample for a focus group, then you may be seeking to include rather more individuals (C5). And if you are using a case study design, you will want to first consider your selection of cases (B3) before perhaps gathering a sample of individuals or groups from within each case.

> **Example B5.10**
>
> #### Volunteering and health – a mixed-methods approach
>
> The doctor who is interested in her patients' volunteering experience primarily wants to study the way volunteering and mental well-being are linked. She is interested in the effect the volunteering experience has on the way her patients feel. To undertake research on this, she wants to explore patients' experiences and perceptions in depth and so decides to select a small sample of patients from those who completed her questionnaire who do volunteer.

NOTE: At this stage she does not want to spend time and resources interviewing people with no volunteering experience and who are unable to shed any light on the research questions.

She is interested to see whether men and women of different ages have different experiences and perceptions of volunteering, and she still feels it would be interesting to include some people who visit the surgery frequently and some who visit infrequently. However, she also wants to ensure that she includes people who are in paid employment as well as those who are not. She is able to use her initial questionnaire to identify potential participants on the basis of a matrix. She has the resources to interview about 16 people.

Table B5.2 Volunteering and health – a purposive sampling matrix

Age	Frequent visits to surgery		Infrequent visits to surgery	
	Male	Female	Male	Female
16–40	2 or 3	2 or 3	1 or 2	1 or 2
41–65	2 or 3	2 or 3	1 or 2	1 or 2
Total	10		6	
Not in paid employment	4–6		3	
Paid employment	4–6		3	

Is the sample accessible?

The initial research regarding the sample context will usually include the opportunity to find out how accessible the potential participants in the research are likely to be. When using purposive sampling we are not so concerned with non-response as we are seeking to fulfil the selection criteria rather than ensuring that our sample is based on probability of inclusion. However, you do still need to minimise the possibilities of non-response by ensuring that you consider how best to encourage informed participants. The research report or dissertation will usually include a discussion of the ways that access to participants was achieved, any difficulties in terms of refusals to participate and how any difficulties were overcome.

Your research

Research quality check: purposive sampling

- Have you a good understanding of the research context and the potential participants?
- What type of purposive sample are you using?
- How do the criteria for selection relate to your research questions?
- Have you justified your sample size and composition in terms of the analytical approach you plan to take?
- Have you identified the strengths of your sample in terms of your research questions and the claims you hope to be able to make for your analysis, the development of theory or the transferability of your findings to other contexts?

Choosing a sampling approach

At the beginning of the chapter we said that the approach you take to sampling will depend on your research questions, the nature of the data you want to collect, whether the data is quantitative or qualitative and the methods of data collection you decide to use. We also suggested that the different approaches to sampling can be thought of as a spectrum. In Figure B5.6 we have mapped each of the research designs and data collection methods across the sampling spectrum. This shows that for each research design you have a range of approaches you can take to sampling and selecting your research cases, people, documents or observations. In practice any researcher faces limitations to the possibilities available to them and these will significantly determine the eventual sample used in the research. The research quality checks for each approach can be used to help you to assess the strengths and limitations of the approaches available to you.

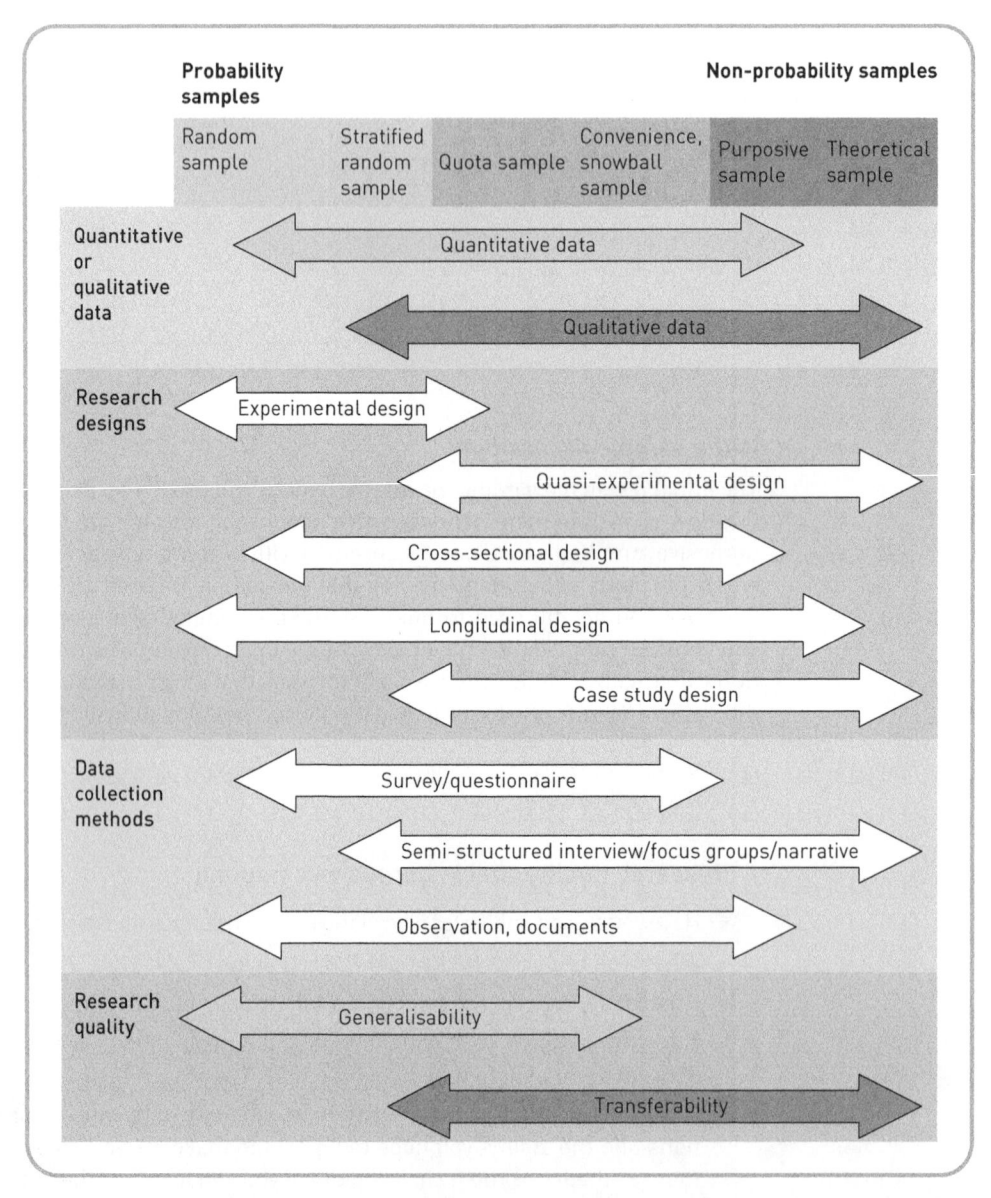

Figure B5.6 The sampling spectrum and research design, data collection methods and quality

The sampling approach chosen determines the claims you can make for your findings in relation to the wider social context from which they were drawn. In general terms we can say that the findings from probability samples may be generalisable to the population from which the sample is taken whereas the findings from a purposive sample can be considered in terms of their transferability to other settings or cases. However, in most small-scale research, including student research projects, great care must be taken in terms of the claims you can make for your findings on the basis of the sample you have selected.

> **Your research**
>
> **Thinking about your research topic and research questions: which sampling approach (or approaches) will you choose?**
>
> A probability sample may:
>
> - enable you to generalise to your population;
> - enable you to use statistical techniques to analyse your data.
>
> BUT
>
> - Do you have access to population lists – all the selected cases?
> - Do you have the time, resources and skills to carry out the research in this way?
>
> A non-probability sample may:
>
> - enable you to make good use of your time, resources and skills;
> - enable you to achieve a 'good enough' sample for the size and scale of your research;
> - enable you to target the cases that are most likely to be of relevance to your research.
>
> BUT
>
> - Have you considered possible sources of bias in your sample?
> - Can you justify the use of this sampling approach in your research report or dissertation and identify the limitations?
>
> A purposive sample may:
>
> - enable you to select cases on the basis of your research questions;
> - enable you to gather in-depth data from a small number of cases;
> - enable you to make good use of your time and resources.
>
> BUT
>
> - Do you have a good understanding of the criteria you will use to select cases?
> - Do you have access to cases that meet those criteria?
> - Can you justify your sampling approach and the criteria used in your research report or dissertation?

References and further reading

Commission on the Future of Volunteering (2008) *Report on the Future of Volunteering and Manifesto for Change,* London: Volunteering England.

Glaser, B. G. and Strauss, A. L. (1967) *The Discovery of Grounded Theory: Strategies for Qualitative Research,* New York: Aldine de Gruyter.

Low, N., Butt, S., Ellis Paine, A. and Davis Smith, J. (2007) *Helping Out: A National Survey of Volunteering and Charitable Giving,* London: Office of the Third Sector.

Moser, C. (1958) *Survey Methods in Social Investigation,* London: Heinemann.

Ritchie, J. and Lewis, J. (eds) (2003) *Qualitative Research Practice: A Guide for Social Science Students and Researchers,* London: Sage.

Wright, D. B. and London, K. (2009) *First (and Second) Steps in Statistics,* 2nd edn, London: Sage.

18 Transcribing, coding and organising textual data

- This chapter begins by stressing the importance of transcription not only in terms of accuracy but also as part of the analytic process.
- Approaches to transcription are introduced.
- The chapter then moves on to consider first order, second order and third order coding as first stages in a thematic analysis of textual data.
- Finally, this chapter looks at ways of organising and presenting textual data.

INTRODUCTION

Once you have collected data through audio recordings of semi- or unstructured interviews, the next step in most qualitative research is to transcribe the material. Transcription is the process of turning the spoken word into written form. You may think this is a simple process but, like so much in the social sciences, it is a lot more involved than you may think. For a start, there are many different ways of transcribing and these vary from one methodological position to another. Secondly, transcription is hard work. Ask anyone who has had to transcribe just one or two interviews and they will confirm this! Qualitative research is not an easy option. You may not have several hundred questionnaires to code and enter into SPSS but transcription and analysis of qualitative data, in almost all cases, will take much longer. Finally, transcription is not simply a mechanical task, for properly understood it constitutes the first stage of analysis. There is more about this below.

It is worth noting that before the widespread use of audio recorders the only way to collect data from interviews or through participant observation was through field notes. As you might imagine, making written notes during an interview or during breaks in an observation is very difficult and will not produce a word-for-word record of what went on. Field notes should be as accurate as possible and record what was said by whom. They also offer the possibility of the researcher recording their impressions during an interview or observation. Field notes should be made at the time, or as soon after an interview or observation as possible, to maximise their reliability. However, you cannot expect field notes to be as accurate as a transcribed audio recording. But the inability to capture everything that was said word for word may not be as much of a problem within some research projects as you might think. Research seeking to understand what it is like to live a certain way that involves, for instance, longitudinal participant observation invariably involves an attempt by the researcher to enter the person's 'lifeworld' (see Ashworth, 2001) or way of perceiving the world. This means that it is less crucial to record every single spoken word for this is not crucial to understanding. Instead, understanding may come from immersion in the world and the development of empathy with the people you are studying. However, field notes are very rarely used in interviewing and really only remain as a method of data collection in participant observation (and even there researchers now often use Dictaphones to record their thoughts and observations).

Once you have some data in spoken, written or even visual form (we may analyse visual material as well as written material – more on this in Chapter 21 on discourse analysis), you will want to carry out some form of analysis. In most qualitative research the first stage would involve coding the data. Coding is the process of describing and understanding your data through the systematic categorisation of the data. Almost any thematic or discursive analysis begins with coding in an attempt to organise and manage the data. However, there will be differences in the process of coding depending on the methodology being employed. Many qualitative analyses are forms of thematic analysis where the aim of the analysis is to draw out themes of meaning. Sociologists (and some psychologists publishing in multidisciplinary journals) may report thematic analyses without too much regard for whether the methodological position of their work is grounded theory or phenomenology. Psychologists (and most certainly the editorial boards of psychology journals) tend to be much more concerned with methodological issues, especially in qualitative research, and therefore often need to justify their methods through reference to some methodological system such as grounded theory. In this chapter we explain different ways of coding textual data and then move on to discuss thematic analysis. In later chapters in this section of the book we cover other qualitative positions which have a number of similarities (analytically speaking) to thematic analysis, such as interpretative phenomenological analysis (IPA) and grounded theory.

18.1 Purposes and principles of transcription

As we stated above, there is a lot more to transcription than first appears. It is the first stage in a considerable amount of qualitative research and is a vital stage. Without good quality transcription your research will suffer. A transcript produced must be fit for purpose and the purpose will vary from one methodological position to another. A discourse analyst will want a much more detailed transcript than a phenomenologist. This is because the focus of a discourse analysis is with the micro-level organisation of language. A phenomenologist, on the other hand, will be much more concerned with more macro-level content. However, even a phenomenologist will want a clear and (very important!) accurate transcript. At the simplest level a transcript will record what was said by whom in a simple chronological order (see Box 18.1).

> **Box 18.1**
>
> **Information box**
>
> **Simple transcription – an example**
>
> Int: So, tell me what led you to feel this way.
>
> Res: Well I don't know really. I guess it all began when I was younger and started to feel pressure from my parents to lose weight. I was big uh big boned you might say eh? But the pressure to lose weight and more uhm weight just got worse even so I felt ur no I mean it got worse no matter what I did. And then the names started you know piggy my little fat boy and stuff like that.
>
> Int: And how did that make you feel?
>
> Res: Err well uh it was awful. I cried myself to sleep and just wished I could be smaller.
>
> Int: Smaller?
>
> Res: Yea I jus jus wanted to disappear you know urm lose er become smaller and smaller so no one could see me and call me those names.
>
> As you have probably guessed, 'Int' stands for interviewer and 'Res' for respondent. Very often a transcript will use names instead to identify the interviewer and respondent. They may be false names but using a name reminds us that there is a person here taking part in our research and not an unknown subject.

As you can see from Box 18.1, transcription at this level is simply the transformation of the spoken word that has been recorded into the written word verbatim (word for word). This needs to be done as accurately as possible and in most research this involves no attempt to 'correct' what was said: that is, grammar is not corrected, nor are any colloquialisms, mispronunciations and so on. The attempt is to reproduce in written form as accurately as possible exactly what was said. It is also usual practice to transcribe what both the interviewer and interviewee said, so prepare yourself for listening to yourself on the recording. The reason for this is that what the interviewer says is as important as what the interviewee says. Context is crucial in most qualitative research and the context for what an interviewee says includes the interviewer and their questions, comments and statements.

18.2 Systems of transcription

There is no universal system for transcription. The simple approach detailed above is adequate for much qualitative research but not all. Those approaches to research that focus on language and language use, such as discourse analysis, some forms of narrative analysis and conversation analysis (which is mentioned in Chapter 21), require a much more detailed level of transcription. But there are many different approaches to the analysis of language and different approaches tend to use different systems of transcription. Even within the same approach there are disagreements over which system of transcription to use.

What do we mean by 'system'? Well, when we said the approach detailed above was simple, that was not an understatement. While a verbatim record that focuses on the content of what was said may be adequate for a phenomenological analysis or grounded theory, it is most certainly not adequate for discourse or conversation analysis. This is because it does not record the conversation in sufficient detail. The important thing to remember is that spoken language not only involves verbal information but also the **prosodic** (phonological elements of spoken language such as intonation and stress), the **paralinguistic** (non-phonemic aspects of language, such as whether a word was said in a joking manner or seriously) and the **extralinguistic** (non-linguistic elements of speaking, such as gestures).

The very fine level of analysis in which a discourse or conversation analyst engages includes analysis of all these aspects of language, for they believe (and argue very strongly) that this information is *necessary* for understanding what is meant in an utterance (O'Connell & Kowal, 1995). This means that we need to include more information than simply verbal information in a transcript if we wish to conduct a linguistic analysis of this kind. Therefore we need a comprehensive system to record and code all this extra information into a written form. No system is perfect, however, and there are therefore arguments over which system is best and/or most appropriate for a particular form of analysis. One of the most widely used transcription systems is the Jefferson system. Gail Jefferson developed this system and a complete description can be found in Atkinson & Heritage (1984). See Box 18.2 for an example and very brief introduction to some features of this system.

Box 18.2
Information box

The Jefferson system of transcription

P: well if you wanna the::n   [wot you mean
I: yes
P: is that I (0.5) can see ((sighs)) him

Box 18.2 *Continued*

I: (1.5) if <u>you</u> want to I guess =

P: = great I knew you would understand

What the symbols mean:

:   A colon indicates that a speaker has stretched the preceding vowel sound (the more colons the greater the stretch)

[ ]   Square brackets between lines of speech indicate overlapping talk

(2.0)   Numbers in brackets indicate a pause timed in tenths of a second

__   Underlining indicates speaker emphasis in a word

=   An equals sign means there is no gap between two utterances

... and there are many more symbols than this.

As you can see, this is a much more complex form of transcription that takes even longer to carry out than the simple transcription described previously. A great deal more detail is included that conversation and (many, if not all) discourse analysts believe is necessary to understand what is going on within a piece of talk. While the Jefferson system is widely used, there are many other systems that transcribe more information and are therefore even more complex (and at times almost unreadable). In addition, some authors have raised concerns over Jefferson's system (e.g. O'Connell & Kowal, 1995).

The most important thing to remember about transcription is that the system employed must be fit for the purpose. If you wish to conduct a phenomenological analysis you will probably be satisfied with the simple system of transcription where only the verbal content of speech is recorded. The Jefferson system may well record more detail of what occurred in the speech being transcribed but it offers no benefit if that extra information is not going to be used in an analysis. On the other hand, if you wish to conduct most forms of discourse or conversation analysis it is vital that you use a comprehensive and very detailed system such as the Jefferson system or it will be impossible to carry out your analysis.

18.3 Transcription as analysis

We mentioned earlier that transcription could also be understood as the first stage of analysis and not just as a tedious and mechanical process necessary when gathering qualitative data. But why is this? One of the first elements of any qualitative analysis is becoming familiar with your data. It is vital that you get a feel for your data and one of the best ways of doing this is to transcribe the audio material yourself. When transcribing speech you are forced to listen to every detail in an attempt to get an accurate written record. No matter how hard you try, you are unlikely to listen this closely if you already have transcripts of your audio recording that someone else has produced.

Transcribing your own data also enables you to maintain a link between the raw data (your tapes or digital recording) and your transcript. It is important to maintain this link so that you do not rely on the transcripts too much and forget the audio recording. Information is missed with any transcript (no matter what system is used) and this information can only be recovered by listening to the recording. Sometimes we need to listen to a person to really understand what is going on and we will therefore need to return to the recording. Listening to the recording is also useful for reminding the researcher that the transcript belongs to a person (there is always the danger of forgetting this).

As you transcribe you can also begin the process of analysis more formally. When you are transcribing you should have a notepad handy so that you can make notes that occur to you. Notes of these kinds are called **memos** and are part of the data analysis strategy that stems from grounded theory (more about this in Chapter 20). In brief, a memo is a note to yourself from your reflection about the data. They are a useful way of beginning the process of theory development from the 'bottom up'. Later, when you are coding and categorising your data, your memos will provide information that may inform your analysis and theory development. Grounded theorists make memos as they code their data and it is a sensible thing to do during the process of transcription as well.

While we have stressed the value of transcription as a first stage in the analytic process, there are many researchers (ourselves included, we must confess) who get others (secretarial staff and research assistants) to transcribe their data for them. We have all done it ourselves once, for sure. The arguments above should be considered in context. The context in question, for us at least, is academic life. Academics these days rarely have the time available for this part of the research process. Pressure to carry out research and publish is immense and academics have found it necessary to employ strategies to maximise their output, and getting others to transcribe their data has increasingly become a necessary strategy. This is much more difficult for discourse and conversation analysts, for the complex system of transcription they use requires considerable expertise which is not widely available.

18.4 Coding qualitative data

Once you have a transcript you need to start the process of analysis proper and for thematic analysis this involves **coding**. Coding is very simply the process of assigning labels (or codes) to your textual data. Codes are usually applied to chunks of data. These chunks may be words, phrases, sentences or even paragraphs. The important thing to remember about coding is that it requires a human hand. The reason for human involvement is that coding entails the ascription of descriptors according to meaning in the text rather than simply because a word or phrase appears. So, you may have different words, phrases and sentences coded together and similar words, phrases and sentences coded differently (because of, for instance, the different contexts in which they appear). Coding is creative but it should also always be consistent and rigorous. There is no room for sloppiness here any more than in the statistical analysis of quantitative data.

In a thematic analysis three levels of codes are usually recognised (other forms of analysis such as discourse analysis will code data differently). These are **first**, **second** and **third level** (or **order**) **codes**, with the differences reflecting the differing levels of interpretation being applied to the text. Most people begin with a very basic descriptive level of coding and work upwards in a systematic manner towards a more interpretative level. However, not everyone goes through three levels and some people code once and then move on to the thematic analysis stage without multiple layers of codes.

First order coding

First order or descriptive-level coding is the most basic level of coding and the start of the analytic process where textual data are organised and categorised. Box 18.3 gives an example of this level of coding.

Box 18.3

Information box

First order descriptive coding

Whenever I feel down about my weight (WEIGHT) I make myself some comfort food (FUFC) or nip to the shops and buy crisps, biscuits or cake. I indulge myself (IMY) in this pleasure but then regret it afterwards (LREG).

Codes:

WEIGHT – Concern over weight

FUFC – Food used to provide comfort

IMY – Indulge myself with food when feeling down

LREG – Feel regret later after indulging in food

As you can see, this level of coding is very descriptive. There is minimal interpretation but it still requires care and thought. Guided practice is the best strategy for improving your ability to code effectively. If you look at the example, chunks of meaning are being coded ('feeling down about my weight' is coded as WEIGHT or concern over weight). Throughout the rest of the transcript you will look for further discussion of concern over the person's weight (if it occurs) and also code these chunks as WEIGHT. Similarly, any further mention of feeling regretful after indulging in food would be labelled LREG.

This is not a static process, however, for you may need to revise initial codes as you proceed through a transcript and/or as you move on to another transcript. In fact it is rare that your initial codes will be adequate for the task. You may find that a code such as WEIGHT is too crude to capture the meaning in the text adequately and it should therefore be understood in two ways (e.g. concern over weight because of others – WEIGHTO – versus concern over weight because of self – WEIGHTS). So, the initial code becomes subdivided. It is equally possible that you may need to combine codes if you realise that there is too much overlapping meaning. Nothing is cast in concrete. Your analysis must always be driven by your data and not by your desire to stick with your list of codes. Now have a go yourself (see Box 18.4).

Box 18.4

Activity box — **First order coding**

Make sure you have a partner for this exercise.

1. Individually read through an interview that you have transcribed or another piece of text that you have available (anything will do – you could use text from a newspaper, for instance), making short notes where appropriate ('memos') of ideas that occur to you about the meaning of the text.

2. Discuss your initial ideas with your partner and then write a short paragraph summary of these ideas.

3. Individually construct a small number of (first order) descriptive codes (four or five) which could be applied to the interview. At this level codes should simply describe what is going on in the text. Resist the temptation to explain – just describe what is there. This stage is all about categorising (or grouping) the text into units of meaning. Give a clear explanation of how each of the codes should be applied. Remember, try to create codes that apply to quite large chunks of text, i.e. represent some unit of meaning, value, action or activity. Chunks will probably be one or two sentences, though they may be shorter or longer than this.

4. Compare your descriptive codes with those of your partner. Compare them in terms of:

   - agreement/disagreement;
   - overlap of meaning (are they really about the same thing?);
   - more general or less general (does one code incorporate several other codes as sub-codes?);
   - separate concepts (no overlap at all);
   - how clearly and unambiguously they are defined.

Box 18.4 *Continued*

5 Make notes on the following:

- how easy or hard it was to make the codes unambiguous;
- problems you encountered in applying the codes to the transcripts;
- how well you think the codes capture the meaning of the interviews.

Second order coding

This level of coding entails somewhat more interpretation than first order coding. At this level these may be super-ordinate constructs that capture the overall meaning of some of the descriptive codes or they may be additional codes that reflect issues such as power, knowledge or conflict within the text (Box 18.5). You are now moving from the initial descriptive level of coding to a more interpretative level. However, you should resist the temptation to draw on grand psychological theories such as psychoanalysis. You still need to keep close to your data.

Box 18.5

Information box

Second order interpretative coding

Whenever I feel down about my weight I make myself some comfort food or nip to the shops and buy crisps, biscuits or cake (BODIMG). I indulge myself in this pleasure but then regret it afterwards (COPAREG).

Codes:

BODIMG – Participant often feels depressed about their body image and consequently indulges in comfort eating to alleviate distress. Feels they cannot control this situation.

COPAREG – Experiences cycle of pleasure and regret with food. Participant cannot break this cycle of pleasure and regret despite insight.

Third order coding

Here we are at a higher level of coding which may blur into the next stage, the thematic analysis. Codes at this level will be superordinate constructs that capture the overall meaning of some of your descriptive and interpretative codes. **Third order** (or **pattern**) coding involves moving from the initial descriptive level of coding to a more interpretative level of coding (Box 18.6). This is now the time to draw on psychological theories to aid your interpretation of the data. So think through relevant theoretical ideas that may inform the generation of themes of meaning within your text. Be careful, though, for your analysis must still be grounded in your data.

> **Box 18.6**
> **Information box**
> **Third order pattern coding**
>
> Whenever I feel down about my weight I make myself some comfort food or nip to the shops and buy crisps, biscuits or cake. I indulge myself in this pleasure but then regret it afterwards. (COABUSE)
>
> **Code for whole segment**:
>
> COABUSE – Cycle of abuse. The participant's relationship with food and their body is indicative of much of the way they relate to their own body. They feel alienated from their body, ashamed of it and abuse it in an attempt to exact some sense of control over their body and their emotions.

18.5 Thematic analysis

It is in fact only a short step from pattern coding to the next stage in a thematic analysis, which is to draw out the overarching themes in your data. Pattern coding sometimes results in this situation anyway, which is why some people do not recognise three distinct levels of coding. Once you have gone through the systematic process of coding your data, you will then want to draw out the higher-level concepts or themes. There will usually be only a few (often three or four) themes in a transcript on a particular topic and these will represent more general concepts within your analysis and subsume your lower-level codes. In a sense you were always building to this level of analysis. Look at the study described in Box 18.7 to get a feel for the level we are talking about.

> **Box 18.7** **Study box**
>
> Grogan, S. & Richards, H. (2002) Body image: Focus groups with boys and men. *Men and Masculinities*, **4** (3), 219-32.
>
> This study used focus groups with boys and young men to explore the way in which they understood issues such as body shape ideals, body esteem and so on. The study included focus groups of boys and men aged 8, 13, 16 and 19–25. The group facilitator encouraged

Box 18.7 *Continued*

discussion about issues concerned with body image. The focus groups were tape-recorded and then transcribed. The data were then subjected to a thematic analysis. The themes represented the important overarching issues raised by the boys and men in the focus groups about body image. Themes included: *the importance of being muscular, fear of fat, being bothered or not with exercise, social pressure* and *power and self-confidence*. The theme *fear of fat*, for instance, concerned the beliefs that boys and men were responsible for being fat or not and demonstrated weakness if they were fat. In addition, it was accepted, even by those who felt themselves to be overweight, that blame and ridicule should be associated with being fat. Overall, the authors looked at these themes in relation to recent discussion about changes in attitudes to the male body and the increase in men being concerned with body image.

18.6 Organising and presenting the analysis of textual data

It is important to understand how to present a thematic analysis when reporting such work. Chapter 26 outlines the structure of quantitative and qualitative reports and journal articles but we would like to show how findings from a thematic analysis should be presented here. A thematic analysis will produce anything from a couple of themes to quite a number depending on the topic and size of project. How many themes are appropriate will depend on the data but it is unlikely that you will get into double figures. In published research, which we believe offers the best model for any report, you will see a fairly standard way of presenting findings from a thematic analysis. In the findings, analysis or results/discussion sections of a report, authors will generally structure the findings in terms of their themes. So, the authors of the study mentioned above in Box 18.7 started their results and discussion section (results and discussion sections are nearly always combined in qualitative research – more on this in Chapter 26) with a brief introduction and then went on to present their findings about *The Importance of Being Muscular*. This theme was used as a subheading and then followed with discussion of its meaning and quotes in support of the arguments. The authors then went on to discuss the other themes. See Box 18.8 for an example of what this section of a research paper (and any report of this kind) should look like.

> **Box 18.8**
>
> **Information box**
>
> **Presenting findings from a thematic analysis**
>
> Example (fictional and deliberately kept short).
>
> **Results/discussion**
>
> This study identified a number of themes arising in the context of young people's concern with their bodies. These included the following: Cycle of abuse, Re-visiting the past and The yo-yo experience.
>
> **Cycle of abuse**
>
> Several participants talked in ways that showed the relationship with food and their body is indicative of much of the way they relate to their own body. They often felt alienated from their own bodies, ashamed of them and sometimes abused them in an attempt to exact some sense of control.
>
> Jayne: Whenever I feel down about my weight I make myself some comfort food or nip to the shops and buy crisps, biscuits or cake. I indulge myself in this pleasure but then regret it afterwards.
>
> As you can see, Jayne demonstrates the classic cycle of excessive eating and consequent regret (Jones & Evans, 1999). Even though she demonstrates insight it is clear that this is something she sees as beyond her control.
>
> Int: Tell me how you feel when you do this.
>
> Fred: I know it is wrong but I cannot help myself I I really can't stop so I jus kinda take out all my frustration any way I can and I end up in a mess.
>
> Fred is typical of many we interviewed when he talks about the frustration felt with these feelings of lack of control and regret [and so on ...]
>
> **Re-visiting the past**
>
> As discussed in previous research (Matthew & Milton, 2000), all participants talked of a time in the past when things were different [and so on ...]

As you can see from the example in Box 18.8, themes are presented and discussed in relation to previous literature on the topic. The example is fictional and somewhat short. In journal articles you will generally see more extensive discussion of each theme and greater use of quotes. Themes emerge from the data and are presented in a report in a systematic way, theme by theme. Each theme presents some discussion of its meaning along with data, in the form of quotes, in support of the arguments being made. Themes will generally consist of a number of arguments and also several quotes. The key issue with the presentation of findings is clarity. You need to express your findings clearly and succinctly so that readers can understand your statements and arguments. In addition, you need to convince readers of what you found and it is here that you need to present data (quotes) in support of your findings.

Further reading

Miles, M. B. & Huberman, A. M. (1994). *Qualitative Data Analysis: An Expanded Sourcebook*, 2nd edn. London: Sage.

> This is a truly excellent book for understanding the practicalities of qualitative research. Very few books actually tell you how to conduct a qualitative analysis of data in as much detail as this book. There is detail on coding and analysis and a wealth of further information. Our only warning is to remember that while this book provides information about thematic analysis more generally, the authors also concentrate on their own particular methods for qualitative analysis (such as the use of matrices) grounded in the sociological tradition and which are only some amongst many methods used for the analysis of such data.

25 The ethics and politics of psychological research

- This chapter begins by explaining why ethics are so important in psychological research.
- It then covers the fundamentals of ethics in psychological research, drawing on the guidelines produced by the British Psychological Society (BPS).
- Finally, this chapter discusses wider political issues in research.

INTRODUCTION

Now this is a chapter you may think you can skip. No! Ethics are an absolutely vital element for conducting psychological research in such a way that it does not harm other people. You might think 'I wouldn't deliberately harm anyone' and we are sure that is quite true, but research can impact negatively on people that you might not have thought about. And this is the reason for working through this chapter *before* conducting any research of your own! If you need persuading about the need for ethics, read about the history of psychology and you will quickly become aware of some of the atrocities that psychologists have committed, all in the name of scientific advancement. In the past, there were very different attitudes towards psychological research and much less consideration of ethics. This situation led to some astonishing studies being conducted that we now consider highly unethical. Research was often conducted with little or no consideration of the impact on the 'subjects' taking part (they were not 'participants'). Research was often at any cost and many people were harmed as a consequence.

Probably the most fundamental ethical principle is that researchers should treat their participants with respect. It is the responsibility of the researcher to ensure that no harm comes to their participants and this is a responsibility that must be taken seriously. After all, none of us (we hope) want harm to come to people who, by volunteering to take part in our research, are doing us a real favour! One way of emphasising this changed attitude to ethics is the change in term used for people taking part in research. People who were interviewed or experimented on were previously 'subjects', and this was a good description of their role – they were 'subjected' to the procedure (whether it was an interview or an experiment). The British Psychological Society (BPS), the governing body for psychology in the United Kingdom, now insists that researchers use the term 'participants' instead. This is because we should no longer be 'subjecting' people to our research. They should be 'participating' in the research. While this may seem a trivial change, it is an important first step. Changing the term we use for people helping us in our research encourages us to think about them as fellow human beings and therefore treat them with the respect they deserve.

A particularly contentious aspect of psychological research is that concerned with experimenting on animals. We have personal views about this form of research which we will put aside in this chapter. There are clear ethical guidelines about animal research which must *legally* be adhered to. This will no doubt satisfy a number of people that everything is being done to minimise harm to animals within the context of the need for such work. Others will feel differently, believing that there is a fundamental problem with this kind of research which no ethical guidelines can solve. This is a complex debate and there is not space to do it justice here. We will present the ethical guidelines for animal experimentation for your information later in the chapter and then leave this issue for you to debate among yourselves.

25.1 Ethical fundamentals

The ethical principles that researchers subscribe to today did not emerge out of thin air. They are the result of a very long tradition of philosophical work on ethics and morality. This work has been concerned with many different issues but particularly with understanding how and why we distinguish between actions that are right and those that are wrong. It is therefore important to learn (very briefly) about some of this philosophical work to improve our understanding of ethics and why we adhere to the principles that we do today. If you are interested in ethics and philosophical thinking about ethics then there are some suggestions for further reading at the end of this chapter.

Key issues in philosophical ethics

By and large, moral/ethical philosophers treat morality and ethics interchangeably (Singer, 1993). Ethics are generally understood as a system of moral principles and not as a distinct enterprise. Therefore, ethical principles stem from moral positions we take about issues and not from some 'independent' ethical way of thinking about our actions and effects. It is important to recognise that acting in a moral (ethical) way does not mean acting in a *necessarily* conservative fashion. When people speak of 'falling moral standards' they are invoking a particular view of morality (often a conservative one) and not a generally agreed view of morality. It is entirely possible to conceive of something like casual sex as moral *or* immoral and therefore increasing casual sex in our society as either a 'fall in moral standards' *or* a 'rise in moral standards'. These debates are grist to the mill for practical ethical philosophers and should remind us all that ethical guidelines are *guidelines* that should not be blindly followed but important principles that require careful thought and consideration.

There are two distinct schools of thought in philosophical ethics: **consequentialism** and **deontology**.[1] According to **consequentialism**, the rightness or wrongness of any act depends upon its consequences. It therefore follows that one should act in such a way as to bring about the best state of affairs (of goodness, happiness, well-being, etc.). The exact nature of the best state of affairs is, of course, open to debate. **Utilitarianism**, a particular subtype of consequentialist ethics, emphasises the role of pleasure or happiness as a consequence of our actions (Raphael, 1981). However, there is no reason why we should not seek to maximise many other factors (such as liberty, equality of opportunity, etc.) instead. According to **deontology**, however, there are certain acts that are right or wrong in themselves and not *necessarily* in terms of their consequences (Gillon, 1986). This is essentially a moral theory whereby certain acts must or must not be done regardless (to some extent) of the consequences of their performance or non-performance. There are, however, two well-established problems for deontological ethics. The first concerns the difficulty of how we know which acts are right or wrong *in themselves*, and the second concerns the difficulty of distinguishing between acts and omissions. If you want to know more about the debates between these two positions you should consult some of the further reading suggested at the end of this chapter.

These two philosophical positions clearly have implications for what we consider to be ethical research. One obvious example concerns the arguments about animal experimentation. A consequentialist may argue that the ends justify the means. That is, the immediate consequence of animal experimentation may be some suffering to the animals concerned, but the later consequence is the possibility of saving human lives, which justifies the earlier consequences. This consequentialist argument in favour of animal experimentation (you could equally make a consequentialist argument against animal experimentation) is itself predicated on a contentious deontological argument that human life is more important than animal life (and the animal suffering is therefore warranted by possible increases in human well-being). If, however, one does not accept this deontological presupposition, the consequentialist argument advanced above becomes more problematic. Peter Singer (1993) directly engages with these practical philosophical arguments and should be read if you want to understand more about these important ethical debates.

---

[1] Actually there are more than just two schools of thought. We know of four significant schools of thought (*consequentialism*, *deontology*, *intuitionism* and *Kantianism*) and there are probably many others. However, consequentialism and deontology are two of the most widely discussed in philosophical ethics and the most important for psychological ethics.

25.2 Confidentiality and anonymity

Confidentiality and **anonymity** are two of the most important ethical considerations in social science research. The BPS guidelines (details of these are given in the Further reading section at the end of this chapter) clearly state that information obtained about a participant during an investigation is confidential unless otherwise agreed in advance (subject to the requirements of legislation). That is, the fall-back position is one of confidentiality. No information given to a researcher by a participant should be revealed to another person (other than members of the research team, supervisors, etc.) unless prior agreement has been given by the participant. It is still important that researchers inform participants of the confidential nature of the relationship, for they are unlikely to be well versed in the BPS guidelines! Some research (often using questionnaires) may enable participants to remain anonymous. If this is the case then this should also be communicated clearly before people agree to take part. If, however, any identifying information is collected then the participants are not anonymous and this should be made clear. If confidentiality and/or anonymity cannot be guaranteed then the participants must be warned of this in advance of agreeing to participate. Many people may choose not to take part in a study where their personal information is not treated in a confidential manner. Participants have the right to expect that information they provide will be treated confidentially and, very importantly, if published, will not be identifiable as theirs.

25.3 Deception

Deception used to be commonplace in psychological research. This has changed in recent years. The BPS guidelines state that the withholding of information is unacceptable if participants are typically likely to object or show discomfort once debriefed. Furthermore, they state that participants should never be deliberately misled without extremely strong scientific (and this includes qualitative research) or medical justification. The fact that the guidelines use the word 'discomfort' demonstrates how much things have changed. 'Discomfort' is a very mild response which most of us feel at one time or another in our lives. However, it is our duty as researchers to minimise such unease and therefore to refrain from deceiving our participants about the true nature of the study without considerable justification. A distinction is made between providing deliberately false information and withholding some of the details of the study. The latter is considered more acceptable and is often necessary in experimental research. The former, however, requires considerable justification and the possible effects on a participant need to be considered carefully.

If a study does involve deception then the investigator has a special responsibility to: (i) ensure that participants are provided with sufficient information at the earliest stage (**debriefing**) and (ii) consult appropriately upon the way that the deception will be received. Debriefing is a vital part of any study involving deception. Investigators should normally provide participants with any necessary information to complete their understanding of the nature of the research as soon as possible after the deception occurred. This should be before the participants leave the research setting. So, if, for instance, you are carrying out an experiment where the true nature of the study needs to be hidden, you must make sure that all participants are informed about the real purpose of the study before they leave the laboratory. This debriefing should also be an *active intervention*. It is not enough to hand out a leaflet and let people wander off. You must make sure they have read the leaflet and are able to ask any questions they might wish about the true nature of the study. However, debriefing does not provide a justification for unethical aspects of an investigation – any deception must be justified on strong scientific or medical grounds.

Finally, if during an investigation you become aware of psychological or physical problems then the BPS guidelines state that you have a responsibility to inform the participant if you believe that by not doing so the participant's future may be endangered. We urge caution, however. If you discover some psychological or medical problem then it is very important that you consult with experienced colleagues/supervisors. How information of this kind is communicated is important and such matters must be handled with care and sensitivity. Care must also be taken if participants seek professional advice during an investigation. If the question falls outside your realm of *professional expertise* then you should *not offer an opinion* and the appropriate source of professional advice should be recommended instead.

25.4 Discomfort and harm

Researchers have a *primary* responsibility to protect participants from **physical** and **mental harm** during the investigation. It is not the responsibility of your participants to look after themselves. It is you who are exposing them to risk (however small) and it is therefore your responsibility to protect them from both physical and mental harm. The BPS guidelines state that, normally, the risk of harm must be no greater than in ordinary life. But what does this mean? Well, there is no easy answer, for some people may lead very risky lives while others do not. In general, all attempts are made to keep risk to an absolute minimum unless there are very strong scientific and/or medical grounds for doing otherwise. If there is risk associated with your study, participants should be informed of all risks and informed consent given (see below). In addition, it is important to make sure that you ask your participants about any factors that might create a risk, such as pre-existing medical or psychological conditions.

25.5 Consent

Consent is another particularly important ethical issue. The BPS guidelines are very clear that all participants should be informed sufficiently about a study that their consent to participate is properly informed. If a person consents without knowing the full nature of the research to which they are consenting then their consent is not informed and therefore not valid. This is why deception is so problematic. If participants are under 16 years old their consent should be given *plus* that of their guardian(s). This is important, for research involving children should not ride roughshod over their views even if, in law, they may not be able to give their consent (which is why we need the consent of their guardian(s)). Similarly, if you have adult participants who are unable to give informed consent then consent should be obtained from a family member or other party able to appreciate the impact of the research on the individual. It is important that researchers are aware of the fact that they are often in a position of authority (or perceived as such) which grants them influence over participants. This relationship must be treated with caution so that consent is not given under duress, however mild.

Participant observation

There may be particular ethical issues when conducting studies involving participant observation. Some sociologists have suggested that private locales ought to remain protected from the prying eyes of the social scientist and that it is unethical for a social scientist to deliberately misrepresent their identity for the purpose of entering a private domain to which they are not otherwise eligible. Furthermore, it has been argued that it is unethical for a social scientist to deliberately misrepresent the character of the research in which they are engaged. If we subscribed to this ethical position it would effectively mean the end of undisclosed participant observation for sociologists and psychologists. Needless to say, there are a number of researchers who recognise the particular ethical difficulties inherent in ethnographic research but still believe the ends (in terms of unique insight into others' lives) outweigh the means (uninvited intrusion often involving deception). These two positions involve complex arguments on both sides. If you are contemplating participant observation, it is crucial that you discuss the ethical issues early on with experienced colleagues/supervisors.

25.6 Non-participation and withdrawal

At the start of any investigation the investigators should make it clear to the participants that they have the **right to withdraw** from the study at any time. This is irrespective of whether any payment or other inducement has been given. Furthermore, participants do not have to give any explanation for their withdrawal from the study. This ethical principle is often particularly difficult for researchers. One of the hardest parts of many studies is recruitment. Until you have experienced the frustrations involved in recruiting participants you will not be able to appreciate the desperate desire to hang on to every one of them. Psychological researchers are human beings like anyone else and need to be careful that their desire to keep participants does not result in their minimising the opportunities for participants to withdraw from the study. In addition, there are genuine scientific concerns about participants withdrawing from research studies. If 'drop-out' is high a researcher might be concerned that there is some common element of the research or participants that leads them to drop out. This might have important implications for the study findings. So, while participants do not need to give an explanation for withdrawing from a study, the researcher is perfectly entitled to ask why they do not wish to continue. It is important that questions of this kind are not used to coerce participants into staying. Finally, participants have the right to withdraw *retrospectively* any consent given, and to require that their own data, including recordings, be destroyed. This can be particularly galling but recognises the fact that the data are the property of the participant and that we only have access to this material with their permission.

Observational studies

Naturalistic observation studies present particular problems for consent. If people are being observed in a natural setting, gaining consent may be problematic. It is always possible to ask people if they mind being observed, but researchers may worry about contaminating the naturalness of their observation (see also Chapter 7 for information about e-research and ethics). The general principle is that, unless those observed give their consent to being observed, observational research is only acceptable in situations where those being observed would expect to be observed by strangers. This is still not entirely clear cut, however. We will give you a real-life example. Many years ago, some students were given the task of observing a setting, making field notes and then writing up the study. They were told that this must be a public setting and that care must be taken not to intrude upon anyone's privacy. One particular group of students took this advice seriously but still ran into ethical difficulties. When they returned from their observation the tutors were rather surprised to find they had observed people in a porn cinema! Now, although you could argue that the cinema is a public place, we do not think it is a place where people expect to be observed (quite the opposite, in fact) and is therefore not an appropriate place for naturalistic observation. It is also important for researchers to pay particular attention to local cultural values and the privacy of individuals even if observing in a public place. In some cultures 'people watching' may be looked upon quite differently from how it is generally perceived in the United Kingdom.

25.7 Research with (non-human) animals

As we stated above, research using (non-human) animals is controversial. More precisely, experimenting on animals is controversial. Fieldwork with animals is generally thought to be acceptable as long as disturbance is kept to an absolute minimum. There are arguments for and against psychological research which involves animal experimentation, and it is something that you need to think about for yourself. Animal experimentation is not commonly part of an undergraduate education in psychology any more, so you will not have to engage directly with the ethical guidelines on this matter unless you decide to go on to further study or research that uses animals. However, it is important that you understand the ethical issues involved in research with non-human animals so we have presented a summary of the major ethical principles in Box 25.1.

Box 25.1
Information box

Ethical guidelines for research with animals

Adapted from the BPS 'Guidelines for psychologists working with animals' (2007).

Legal issues

All researchers working with (non-human) animals must abide by British law designed to protect their welfare. Detailed guidance on animal experimentation is given in the Animals (Scientific Procedures) Act (1986) published by HMSO. In addition, researchers engaged in fieldwork with animals must abide by legislation concerning endangered species.

Replacing the use of animals

There is an expectation that – where possible – alternative methods of research (and especially teaching) that use previous research or computer simulations instead of animals should be used. It is now commonplace to use computer simulations for students studying rat behaviour rather than running rats through mazes yourself.

Choice of species

Appropriate species of animals should be chosen in such a way that suffering be minimised. Thought should be given to the level of sentience and the natural history of the species. Knowledge of whether the animal has been bred in captivity is also important.

▶

Box 25.1 *Continued*

Number of animals

Researchers are legally required to use the smallest number of animals necessary to accomplish the goals of the research. Advice is also given about ways of reducing the number of animals used in such research.

Experimental procedures

- Deprivation and aversion techniques must be undertaken with care and with regard to the particular needs of different species. Alternatives should be used wherever possible.
- Animals should be housed in such a way that they are not subject to undue stress due to isolation or overcrowding.
- Staged encounters between predators and prey should be avoided wherever possible and natural encounters used instead.
- Proper care should be taken with surgical procedures such that stress and residual effects are minimised.
- Animals found to be suffering severe pain or distress should be humanely killed using an approved technique.

Fieldwork

Researchers studying free-living animals should minimise interference with individual animals and also the environment in which they live. Care should be taken with any procedure that requires removal (however short) of an animal from its environment.

Animal procurement

Animals used in experiments must only be purchased from Home Office approved establishments.

Housing and care

Researchers also have a responsibility of care for the conditions under which animals are kept. Animals must be kept in accordance with the regulations of the Animals (Scientific Procedures) Act (1986). Minimum requirements include: a degree of freedom of movement, food, water, and care appropriate to its health and well-being. Natural living conditions should be reproduced if at all possible.

Animals in psychology teaching

Students must not be required to carry out any experimental procedure that they consider ethically unacceptable and should be encouraged to form their own judgements about such matters. The use of live animals in teaching is prohibited unless the topic cannot be taught by any other means.

> **Box 25.1** *Continued*
>
> **The use of animals for therapeutic purposes**
>
> Animals may occasionally be used by psychologists as adjuncts to therapy. This may include the use of dogs or horses, for instance, to facilitate psychological development. In addition, animals (such as spiders or snakes) may be used for behavioural exposure in the treatment of phobias. In all cases, similar standards of care to those expected for experimental animals is required. Stress on the animal should also be minimised with it given the opportunity to retreat where appropriate.
>
> **Clinical assessment and treatment of animal behaviour**
>
> Some psychologists work with animals with disordered behaviours. Specific guidelines and a scheme for accreditation for this work have been drawn up through a collaboration of the BPS and Association for the Study of Animal Behaviour (ASAB).
>
> Source: From The British Psychological Society (2007) *Guidelines for Psychologists Working with Animals*, Leicester, UK: BPS. Copyright © 2007 The British Psychological Society. Reproduced with permission.

25.8 Equal opportunities

Equality of opportunity is generally considered an essential factor in our educational and work lives. It is also important to consider equal opportunity issues in the context of psychological research. Feminist researchers have argued that there is considerable sexism in psychological research. Robson (2002), drawing on work by Eichler (1988), identifies seven sources of sexism in research: *androcentricity, overgeneralisation, gender insensitivity, double standards, sex appropriateness, familism* and *sexual dichotomism*. We will address these issues here but the interested reader should use Robson (2002) as a starting point for further reading on this issue.

Androcentricity simply means viewing the world from a male perspective. This is a particular problem with psychological research. There has been a long tradition of developing and testing instruments on men and then assuming they will be appropriate for use with women. In addition, when comparisons are made, the male response is generally assumed to be the normal position and the female response abnormal. **Overgeneralisation** is similar and is where one studies only one sex and then generalises to the other. Care needs to be taken to avoid such sexism in research. **Gender insensitivity** is where one ignores sex as a possible variable. **Double standards** is a description for the process of treating identical behaviour by men and women differently. **Sex appropriateness** is a particular form of double standard where some behaviour (or belief, etc.) is assumed to be a female (or male) activity. So, for instance, a researcher might assume that only men are interested in casual sex. **Familism** is the tendency to treat the family as the smallest unit of analysis. This can be a particular problem for women where an individual woman's behaviour, beliefs or views are obscured with the family as the unit of analysis. Finally, **sexual dichotomism** is where men and women are treated as two entirely separate groups with no overlap at all. Some of these sources of bias are *possible* but not *necessary* sources of sexism. For instance, it may be appropriate in some cases to treat the family as the smallest unit of analysis.

In addition, researchers need to be aware of equal opportunity issues regarding age, social class, ethnicity and culture, religion, sexuality, dis/ability and so on. There are many assumptions made that serve to exclude people who are older, working class, black, gay and so on that are very subtle. It is only if we all pay attention to these issues that psychology will be able to move beyond its somewhat controversial history and transform itself into a discipline for and about *all people* and not just the privileged few.

25.9 Politics and psychological research

There has been a tradition of positivist research (which is invariably quantitative) conducted by psychologists who have assumed it is objective and therefore 'value free' or immune from politics. Thankfully, this is changing, at least in part due to the influence of qualitative research which often engages a great deal with political questions in one way or another. The very idea of 'value free' science is now largely discredited. This view has been critiqued to such an extent by philosophers of science that it is no longer tenable. The choice of a research topic, formulation of research questions, choice of methods and so on all involve value judgements of some kind. If we decide to research drug use or anorexia or attitudes to nuclear weaponry or more apparently mundane topics then we are making decisions based on a value system (our own). Similarly, the way we formulate research questions and choose some methods over others depends on the particular value system we wish to buy into. Therefore, if all research involves value judgements to some degree then it must necessarily be political. Hammersley (1995) argues that there are four ways in which values are involved in social research:

1 The very fundamental commitment to advancing knowledge is political. The fact that we prefer knowledge to ignorance immediately invokes a particular value system.
2 The need for resources in research is dependent on political decisions. Decisions about the allocation of resources are political (see Langdridge, 2006). Health psychology is an increasingly popular area of research partly because resources are increasingly being allocated to this topic. Resources are allocated to this area (and not others) for various political reasons.
3 All research relies on presuppositions reflecting the values of the researcher. The choice of topic, questions asked, etc. will be founded on these presuppositions. The presuppositions themselves will depend on the biography of the researcher and may include demographic variables such as their sex, age,

social class, ethnicity, etc., as well as their experience of education, family life and so on.

4 Social research will always have effects on people's lives. Participants will be directly affected by research through their involvement, while others may be affected through the consequences of the research findings. How findings are presented will depend on the researcher's value system.

It is therefore important that we are *critically aware* of our own value systems and the influence that they have on our work. Ignorance is no defence!

25.10 Evaluation research

Evaluation research is concerned with the evaluation of the worth or merit of an intervention of some kind. It is becoming an increasingly important form of social research as education, health and social care organisations are recognising the merit of evaluating their programmes or interventions. Evaluation research uses the standard techniques of social science research but in applied settings. So, for instance, evaluation research may involve the evaluation of an after-school homework programme to see whether it improves educational achievement, or the evaluation of the use of counselling in doctors' surgeries to reduce attendance of 'heart sink' patients, and so on. This type of research invariably raises significant ethical and political issues, which require particularly sensitive handling from the investigator. One of the unique aspects of evaluation research is the need to engage group skills, management ability, political dexterity and sensitivity to multiple stakeholders (any persons with an interest in the research). A considerable amount has been written about this form of research and the particular demands that it places on researchers (see Further reading).

25.11 The need for balance

While this chapter has been concerned with emphasising the need for ethics in psychological research, this last section offers a few words of caution about the proliferation of what we can only call an 'ethics industry'. In recent years, we have witnessed increasing concern about ethical issues and the growth of ethics committees. Ethics committees (university, health trust and so on) now routinely assess research proposals before allowing research to be conducted. This is clearly a sensible precaution that is designed to serve the needs of the public and protect them from harm. However, many researchers are worried about a growth in conservatism (in research) as a result of the growth of the 'ethics industry'. More and more researchers are having to deal with often spurious 'ethical concerns' that do nothing more than prevent good quality and important research. The *fear of harm* is often out of proportion to any *real risk*. Researchers are having to fight overly conservative ethics committees where almost any piece of research involving people raises 'ethical concerns'. This is clearly nonsense and represents a real risk to academic freedom and the future generation of knowledge. Human beings must be treated with respect but do not need to be treated with 'kid gloves', and as long as 'sensitive' topics are treated with care there should be *no* 'no go areas'. Ethical issues are important and must be accounted for but they must not be used to stifle research.

Further reading

Robson, C. (2002). *Real World Research*, 2nd edn. Oxford: Blackwell.

This book contains a chapter on evaluation research which will provide an excellent starting point if you are interested in finding out more about evaluation research. In addition, there is further discussion of ethical issues and feminist criticism of social science research. It also provides guidance on further reading.

Singer, P. (1993). *Practical Ethics*, 2nd edn. Cambridge: Cambridge University Press.

This is a fascinating book containing some extraordinary and controversial ethical arguments. Peter Singer is a leading, but very controversial, ethical philosopher who writes with great clarity and depth of argument. This book engages with a considerable range of practical ethical issues, including arguments about animal rights, abortion, euthanasia, the environment and much more besides. The arguments are always strong and demand attention but do not always make comfortable reading. Give it a go – you will not be able to forget it.

The British Psychological Society Ethical Principles for Conducting Research with Human Participants. [currently being revised]

The British Psychological Society Code of Ethics and Conduct (2006).

The British Psychological Society Guidelines for Psychologists Working with Animals (2007).

The British Psychological Society Report of the Working Party on Conducting Research on the Internet (2007).

These guidelines are all available from the BPS website (**www.bps.org.uk**). The first document is currently being revised but is the main source of information for students and academics on research ethics. The second document includes details of a code of conduct for professional psychologists, and the third document the latest details of ethical principles for working with humans and animals. The final document includes the most recent guidelines produced for conducting research using the Internet. All of the above guidelines are clear and concise and an essential source of information on this important topic.

CHAPTER 25

Evaluating and writing up qualitative research

Overview

- The evaluation of qualitative research emphasises the value of the analysis – that is the coding and theory-building process typically rather than the data collection instruments.

- Evaluating qualitative research requires a clear understanding of the intellectual roots and origins of qualitative research in psychology. Hence you need to study Chapters 17 to 24 for this chapter to be most helpful.

- Many criteria are similar in some ways to those applied to quantitative analysis. However, great emphasis is placed on ensuring that the analysis corresponds closely to qualitative ideals.

- Suggestions are made as to how a newcomer to qualitative research should tackle self-evaluation of their work.

25.1 Introduction

Surely qualitative research is evaluated in much the same ways as quantitative research? This is not so. Qualitative research may be evaluated in a number of ways, none of which can be regarded as a final seal of approval. Some of the criteria are quite close to the positivistic position (reliability and validity) but, as we saw in Chapter 17, this is eschewed by at least some qualitative researchers. Some of these prefer to emphasise the radically different philosophies which straddle the quantitative–qualitative divide if not continuum. For example, quantitative researchers take it for granted that observations should be reliable in the sense that different researchers' observations of the same events are expected to be similar. That is, different observers should observe the same thing if the data are of value. In contrast, some qualitative researchers argue that this is an inappropriate criterion for evaluating qualitative data. They point out that different readers of any text will have a different interpretation (reading) of the text. The diversity of interpretations, they argue, is the nature of textual material and should be welcomed by qualitative analysts. As a consequence, different 'readings' of the data should not be regarded as methodological flaws. The underlying difference between quantitative and qualitative researchers is not a matter of numbers and statistics. It is much more fundamental. At its most extreme, quantitative and qualitative research are alternative ways of seeing the world, not just different ways of carrying out research. It is, after all, the difference between the modern (scientific) approach with its emphasis on cause and the postmodern approach with its emphasis on interpretation.

It may be useful to consider that, according to Denscombe (2002), there are a number of features that distinguish good research *of all types* from not so good research (see Figure 25.1). Among the features that he lists are the following:

- The contribution of new knowledge.
- The use of precise and valid data.
- The data are collected and used in a justifiable way.
- The production of findings from which generalisations can be made.

These are tantalisingly simple criteria which are hard to question. Perhaps the difficulty is that they are so readily accepted. Some might suggest that we are all so imbued with positivist ideas that we no longer recognise them in our thinking. Phrases such as 'new knowledge', 'precise/valid data', 'justifiable' and 'generalisation' may be more problematic than at first appears. What is new knowledge for example? By what criteria do we decide that research has contributed new knowledge? What is precise and valid data? How precise need data be to make them acceptable in research? For what purposes do the data need to be valid to make them worthwhile? Why should worthwhile knowledge be generalisable? Should knowledge that works for New York City be generalisable to a village in Mali?

This boils down to the problematic nature of evaluation criteria. If it is difficult to suggest workable criteria for quantitative research, just what criteria should be applied to qualitative research? One approach is to recognise that much qualitative research has its intellectual roots in postmodernist ideas which, in themselves, are a reaction against the modernist ideas of traditional science and positivism. That is, it would seem that the criteria should be different for qualitative and quantitative research given this. Nevertheless, in some ways, it would seem better to seek criteria which are equally applicable to both qualitative and quantitative research. One such set of criteria is that which determines high standards of scholarship in any field. What are these criteria? Careful analysis, detachment, accuracy, questioning and insight are among the suggestions.

Validity criteria in qualitative research

Denscombe (2002)
- Contribution to new knowledge
- Precise and valid data
- Data collection and use justifiable
- Findings can be generalised

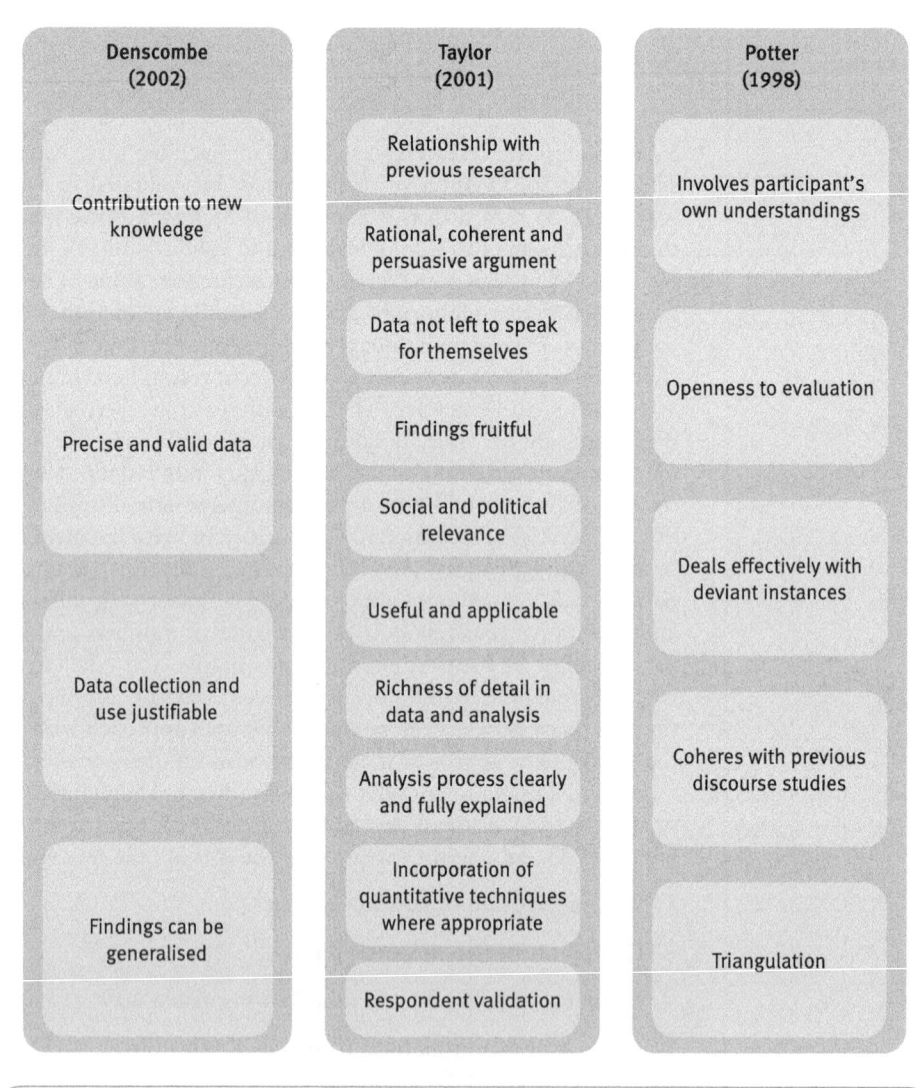

Taylor (2001)
- Relationship with previous research
- Rational, coherent and persuasive argument
- Data not left to speak for themselves
- Findings fruitful
- Social and political relevance
- Useful and applicable
- Richness of detail in data and analysis
- Analysis process clearly and fully explained
- Incorporation of quantitative techniques where appropriate
- Respondent validation

Potter (1998)
- Involves participant's own understandings
- Openness to evaluation
- Deals effectively with deviant instances
- Coheres with previous discourse studies
- Triangulation

FIGURE 25.1 Validity criteria in qualitative research

But there is nothing in such criteria which clarifies what is good psychology and what is bad. As we saw in Chapter 17, the intellectual roots of qualitative analysis are outside psychology, where different priorities exist. And why is detachment a useful criterion, for example? It hints that the researcher ideally is an almost alienated figure. Indeed, criteria such as detachment have been criticised for encouraging research to be anodyne (for example, Howitt, 1992a).

Universal criteria for evaluating what is good psychology may be a futile quest and possibly an undesirable one. Such an endeavour would seem to miss the point since epistemological bases of qualitative and quantitative research are in many ways incompatible. Many of the precepts of quantitative research are systematically reversed by coteries of qualitative researchers. For example, when qualitative researchers reject psychological states as explanatory principles, they reject much psychology. The alternative to finding universal evaluation criteria is to evaluate qualitative and quantitative methods by their own criteria, that is, in many respects differently.

25.2 Evaluating qualitative research

The distinction between qualitative data collection and qualitative data analysis is paramount (Chapter 18). If the researcher seeks to quantify 'rich' data collected through in-depth methods such as open-ended interviewing then criteria appropriate to qualitative analyses may not always apply. It is fair to say that qualitative researchers do not speak with one voice about what the evaluative criteria should be. Qualitative research is an umbrella term covering a multitude of viewpoints, just as quantitative research is.

Taylor (2001) discusses a number of evaluative criteria for qualitative research. Some of them apply to research in general but often they take on a special significance in qualitative research. Others are criteria which best make sense only when considering qualitative research. The following are some of Taylor's more general criteria for evaluating qualitative research. We will discuss her more specific criteria and those of others later:

- *How the research is located in the light of previously published research*   Traditionally in psychological research, knowledge grows cumulatively through a process which begins with a literature search, through development of an idea based on this search and data collection, to finally reporting one's findings and conclusions. This is not the case in all forms of qualitative research. Some qualitative researchers begin with textual material that they wish to analyse, and delay referring back to previous research until after their analysis is completed. The idea is that the previous literature is an additional resource, more text if one likes, with which to explore the adequacy of the current analysis and its fit with other circumstances. The delay also means that the researcher is not so tempted to take categories off the peg and apply them to their data. In some forms of qualitative analysis – especially conversation analysis – reference to the published research can be notably sparse. So the research literature in qualitative research is used very differently from its role in quantitative research. In quantitative research, knowledge is regarded as building out of previous knowledge, so one reviews the state of one's chosen research and uses it as a base from which to build further research. Traditionally, quantitative research demands the support of previous research in order to demonstrate the robustness and replicability of findings across samples and circumstances. Often, in the quantitative tradition, researchers resort to methodological considerations as an explanation of the variability in past and current findings. In the qualitative tradition, any disparity between studies is regarded much more positively and as less of a problem. Disparity is seen as a stimulus to refining the analytic categories used, which is the central activity of qualitative research anyway.

- *How coherent and persuasive the argument is rather than emotional*   Argumentation and conclusion-drawing in psychology are typically regarded as dependent on precise logical sequences. It is generally not considered appropriate to express oneself emotionally or to engage in rhetorical devices in psychological report writing. This is quite a different matter from being dispassionate or uninvolved in one's subject matter. A great deal of fine psychological writing has been built on the commitment of the researcher to the outcomes of the research. Nevertheless, the expectation is that the researcher is restrained by the data and logic. In this way, the researcher is less likely to be dismissed as merely expressing personal opinions. This is the case no matter what research tradition is being considered.

- *Data should not be 'left to speak for themselves' and the analysis should involve systematic investigation*   The meaning of data does not reside entirely in the data themselves. Data needs to be interpreted in the light of a variety of considerations of both a methodological and a theoretical nature. Few if any data have intrinsic, indisputable and unambiguous meanings. Hence the role of the researcher as interpreter of the data has to be part of the process. This interpretation has to be done with subtlety. There is a temptation among newcomers to qualitative analysis to feel that the set of data should speak 'for itself'. So large amounts of text are reproduced and little by way of analysis or interpretation offered. To do so, however, is to ignore a central requirement of research which is to draw together the data to tell a story in detail. In qualitative research this is through the development of closely fitting coding categories in which the data fit precisely but in a way which synthesises aspects of the data. Qualitative research may cause problems for novice researchers because they substitute the data for analysis of the data. Of course, ethnographically meaningful data should carry its meaning for all members of that community. Unfortunately, to push this version of the ethnographic viewpoint too far leaves no scope for the input of the psychologist. If total fidelity to the data is more important than the analysis of the data, then researchers may just as well publish recordings or videos of their interviews, for example. Indeed, there would be no role for the researcher as anyone could generate a psychological analysis. But, of course, this is not true. It takes training to be capable of quality analyses.

- *Fruitfulness of findings* Assessing the fruitfulness of any research is not easy. There are so many ways in which research may be fruitful and little research is fruitful in every respect. Most research, however, can be judged only in the short term, and longer-term matters such as impact on the public or other researchers may simply be inappropriate. Fruitfulness is probably best judged in terms of the immediate pay-off from the research in terms of the number of new ideas and insights it generates. Now it is very difficult to catalogue just what are new ideas and insights but rather easier to recognise work which lacks these qualities.

- *Relevance to social issues/political events* Qualitative research in psychology often claims an interest in social issues and politics. There are a number of well-known studies which deal with social and political issues. The question needs to be asked, however, just how social and political issues need to be addressed in psychology, and from what perspective? Mainstream psychology has a long tradition of interest in much the same issue. Institutionally, the Society for the Study of Social Issues in the USA has actively related psychology to social problems (Howitt, 1992a), for example, for most of psychology's modern history. There is a distinct tradition of socially relevant quantitative research. Given the insistence of many qualitative researchers that their data are grounded in the mundane texts of the social world, one might expect that qualitative research is firmly socially grounded. One criticism of qualitative research though is that it has a tendency to regard the political and social as simply being more text that can be subjected to qualitative analysis. As such the social and political text has no special status other than as an interesting topic for textual analysis. Some qualitative researchers have been very critical of the failure of much qualitative research to deal effectively with the social and political – concepts such as power, for instance (Parker, 1989). Since power is exercised through social institutions then one can question the extent to which analysis of text in isolation is sufficient analysis.

- *Usefulness and applicability* The relevance of psychological research of any sort is a vexed question. Part of the difficulty is that many researchers regard their work as one aspect of an attempt to understand its subject matter for its own sake without the constraints of application. Indeed, applied research in psychology has often been seen as a separate entity from academic research and often somewhat derided as ordinary or pedestrian. Nevertheless, this point of view seems to have reduced in recent years and it is increasingly acceptable to consider the application of research findings as an indication of the value of, at least, some research. It is fairly easy to point to examples from mainstream psychology of the direct application of psychological research – clinical, forensic and educational psychology all demonstrate this in abundance. Part of the success of psychology in these areas is in finding ways of dealing with the practical problems of institutions such as prisons, schools and the mental health system. Success in the application of psychology stems partly from the power of research findings to support practical activities. Qualitative researchers have begun to overlap some of these traditional fields of the application of psychology. Unfortunately the claim that qualitative research is subjective tends to undermine its impact from the point of view of mainstream psychology. Nevertheless, topics such as counselling/psychotherapy sessions and medical interview are to be found in the qualitative psychology literature. As yet, it is difficult to give examples of the direct application of the findings of such psychological research.

The above criteria are in some ways similar to those which we might apply to quantitative research. They are important in the present context since it clarifies their importance in qualitative research too. They sometimes take a slightly different form in the two types of research.

25.3 Validity

The concept of validity is difficult to apply to qualitative research. Traditionally validity in psychology refers to an assessment of whether a measure actually measures what it is intended to measure. This implies there is something fixed which can be measured. The emphasis is really on the validity of the measures employed as indicators of corresponding variables in the actual world. So the validity of a measure of schizophrenia is the extent to which it corresponds with schizophrenia in the actual world beyond that measure. This is not usually an assumption of qualitative research. In qualitative research, the emphasis of validity assessment is in terms of the question of how well the analysis fits the data. A good analysis fits the data very well. In quantitative research, often a very modest fit of the hypothesis to the data is acceptable – so long as the minimum criterion of statistical significance is met.

As we saw in Chapter 15, there are a number of ways of assessing validity in quantitative research. They all imply that there is something in actuality that can be measured by our techniques. This is unlikely to be the case with qualitative research for a number of reasons. One is the insistence by some qualitative researchers that text has a multiplicity of readings and that extends to the readings by researchers. In other words, given the postmodernist emphasis on the impossibility of observing 'reality' other than through a looking glass of subjectivity, validity cannot truly be assessed as a general aspect of measurement.

Discussions of validity by qualitative researchers take two forms:

- It is very common to question the validity of quantitative research. That is, to encourage the view that qualitative research is the better means to obtaining understanding of the social and psychological world.

- The tendency among qualitative researchers to treat any text (written or spoken) as worthwhile data means that the validity of the data is not questioned. The validity of the transcription is sometimes considered, but emphasis is placed on ways in which the fidelity of the transcription, say to the original audio-recording, may be maximised. The greatest emphasis is placed on ways in which the validity of the qualitative analysis as a qualitative analysis may be maximised. This really is the primary meaning of validity in qualitative research. So many of the criteria listed by qualitative researchers are ones which are only meaningful if we understand the epistemological origins of qualitative research. That is, there are some considerations about the worth of qualitative data which do not normally apply to quantitative research.

Potter (1998) uses the phrase 'justification of analytic claims' alongside using the word validity. The phrase 'justification of analytic claims' emphasises the value of the analysis rather than the nature of the data. He suggests four considerations which form the 'repertoire' with which to judge qualitative research. Different researchers may emphasise different combinations of these:

- *Participant's own understandings* When the qualitative material is conversation or similar text, we need to remember that speakers actually interpret the previous contributions by previous speakers. So the new speaker's understanding of what went before is often built into what they say in their turn. For example, a long pause and a change of subject may indicate that the speaker disagrees with what went before but does not wish to express that disagreement directly. Potter argues that by very carefully paying attention to such details in the analysis, the analyst can more precisely analyse the conversation in ways which are relevant to the participant's understandings. It is a way of checking the researcher's analysis.

- *Openness to evaluation* Sometimes it is argued that the readers of a qualitative analysis are more in contact with the data than typically is the case in quantitative research in which tables and descriptive statistics are presented but none of the original data directly. Qualitative analyses often incorporate substantial amounts of textual material in support of the analytic interpretation. Because of this, the qualitative analysis may be more open to challenge and questioning by the reader than other forms of research. Relatively little qualitative research is open in this way, however. Potter suggests that for much reported grounded theory and ethnographic research, very little is presented in a challengeable form and a great deal has to be taken on trust, just as with quantitative research. Even where detailed transcripts are provided, however, Potter's ideal may not be met. For example, what checking can be done if the researcher does not report the full transcript but rather selected highlights? Furthermore, what avenues are open to the reader who disagrees with an analysis to challenge the analysis?

- *Deviant instances* In quantitative research, deviant cases are largely treated as irrelevant. The participant who bucks the trend of the data is largely ignored – as 'noise' or randomness. Sometimes this is known as 'experimental error', but it is really an indicator of how much of the data is actually being ignored in terms of explanation. Often no attempt is made to explain why some participants are not representative of the trend. In qualitative research, partly because of the insistence on detailed analysis of sequences, the deviant case may be much more evident. Consequently the analysis needs to be modified to include what is truly deviant about it. It may be discovered that the seemingly deviant case is not really deviant – or it may become apparent why it 'breaks the rules'. It may also prove a decisive reason for abandoning a cherished analytic interpretation.

- *Coherence with previous discourse studies* Basically the idea here is that qualitative studies which cohere with previous studies are more convincing than ones which are in some way at odds with previous research. There is a sense in which this is a replicability issue since not only does coherence add conviction to the new study but it also adds conviction to the older studies. This is also the case with quantitative studies. But there are difficulties with this form of validity indicator. Qualitative research varies in terms of its fidelity to previous research when a replication is carried out. Some research will be close to the original and some may be substantially different. In this context, if a qualitative study is merely designed to apply the theoretical concepts derived from an earlier study then the findings are more likely to cohere with the earlier studies. Studies not conceived in this way will be a more effective challenge to what has gone before – and provide greater support if they confirm what went before.

Additional criteria for the evaluation of qualitative research are available (Taylor, 2001). These are not matters of validity, but do offer means of evaluating the relative worth of different qualitative studies:

- *Richness of detail in the data and analysis* The whole point of qualitative analysis is to develop descriptive categories which fit the data well. So one criterion of the quality of a study is the amount of detail in the treatment of the data and its analysis. Qualitative research requires endless processing of the material to meet its aims. Consequently, if the researcher just presents a few broad categories and a few broad indications of what sorts of material fit that category, then one will be less convinced of the quality of the analysis. Of course, richness of detail is not a concept which is readily tallied so it begs the question of how much detail is richness. Should it be assessed in terms of numbers of words, the range of different sources of text, the verbal complexity of the data, or how? Similar questions may be applied to the issue of the richness of detail in the analysis. Just what does this mean? Is this a matter of the complexity of the analysis and why should a complex analysis be regarded as a virtue in its own right? In quantitative research, in contrast, the simplicity of the analysis is regarded as a virtue if it accounts for the detail of the data well. It is the easiest thing in the world to produce coding categories which fit the data well – if one has a lot of coding categories then all data are easily fitted. The fact that each of these categories fits only a very small part of the data means that the categories may not be very useful.

- *Explication of the process of analysis* If judged by the claims of qualitative analysts alone, the process of producing an adequate qualitative analysis is time-consuming, meticulous and demanding. As a consequence of all of this effort, the product is both subtle and true to the data. The only way that the reader can fully appreciate the quality of the effort is if the researcher gives details of the stages of the analysis process. This does not amount to evidence of validity in the traditional sense, but is a quality assurance indicator of the processes that went into developing the analysis.

- *Using selected quantitative techniques* Some qualitative researchers are not against using some of the techniques of quantitative analysis. There is no reason in their view why qualitative research should not use systematic sampling to ensure that the data are representative. Others would stress the role of the deviant or inconsistent case in that it presents the greatest challenge to the categorisation process. The failure of more traditional quantitative methods to deal with deviant cases other than as 'noise', error or simply irrelevant should be stressed again in this context.

- *Respondent validation* Given the origins of much qualitative research in ethnomethodology, the congruence of the interpretations of the researcher with those of the members of the group being studied may be seen as a form of validity check. This is almost a matter of definition – the meanings arrived at through research are intended to be close to those of the people being studied in ethnomethodology. Sometimes it is suggested that there is a premium in the researcher having 'insider status'. That is, a researcher who is actually a member of the group being studied is at an advantage. This is another reflection of the tenets of ethnomethodology. There is always the counter-argument to this that such closeness actually stands in the way of insightful research. However, there is no way of deciding which is correct. Owusu-Bempah and

Howitt (2000) give examples from cross-cultural research of such insider perspectives. Of course, the importance of these criteria is largely the consequence of allegiance to a particular theoretical stance. It is difficult to argue for universality of this criterion.

- *Triangulation*   This concerns the validity of findings. When researchers use very different methods of collecting data yet reach the same findings on a group of participants, this is evidence of the validity of the findings. Or, in other words, their robustness across different methods of data collection or analysis. The replication of the findings occurs within settings and not across settings. This is then very different from triangulation when it is applied to quantitative data. In that case, the replication is carried out in widely different studies from those of the original study. The underlying assumption is that of positivist universality, an anathema to qualitative researchers.

Box 25.1   Practical Advice

Writing up a qualitative report

In some ways, writing up a report of qualitative research is potentially beset with problems. There are many reasons for this especially because no set format has yet emerged which deals effectively with the structure of qualitative practical reports. The conventional structure explained in Chapter 5 is clearly aimed at quantitative research and, at first sight, there may be questions about its relevance to qualitative research. However, they both have as their overriding consideration the need for the utmost academic rigour and, in part, that is what the standard report structure in psychology helps to achieve. However, we have already explained in Chapter 5 that the conventional report structure often needs some modification when quantitative research departs from the basic laboratory experiment model. By modifying the basic structure, many of its advantages are retained in terms of clarity of structure and reader-friendliness resulting from its basic familiarity. Our recommendation is that you write up qualitative research studies using the traditional laboratory report structure which you modify by adding additional headings or leaving out some as necessary. Of course, you would probably wish to consult journal articles which employ similar methods to your own for ideas about how to structure your report. These can, if chosen wisely and used intelligently, provide an excellent model for your report and are an easy way of accessing ideas about how to modify the conventional laboratory report structure for your purposes. Occasionally, you will come across a qualitative journal article which is somewhat 'off the wall' in terms of what you are used to but we would not recommend that you adopt such extreme styles.

You are writing a qualitative report in the context of the psychological tradition of academic work and you will do best by respecting the academic pedigree of this.

By adopting but adapting the conventional laboratory report structure you are doing yourself a favour. Quantitative report writing is likely to be familiar to you and you will have had some opportunity to develop your skills in this regard in all probability. Everyone has difficulties writing quantitative reports but this partly reflects the academic rigour that writing such reports demands. The reader of your report will benefit from the fact that they are reading something which has a more-or-less familiar structure where most of the material is where it is expected to be in the report. There will be differences, of course. In particular, it is unlikely (but possible) that you would include hypotheses in a qualitative report just as it is fairly unlikely that you would include any statistical analysis (but again possibly especially with techniques such as thematic analysis). Many forms of qualitative research are methodologically demanding and the analysis equally so. It would not be helpful to you to produce sloppy reports given this. Bear the following in mind when writing your qualitative report:

- The *introduction* is likely to discuss in some length conceptual issues concerning the type of analysis that you are performing. This is most likely to be the case when conducting a discourse analysis which is highly interdependent with certain theories of language. You probably will spend little time discussing conceptual issues like these when conducting a thematic analysis which is not based particularly on any theory.

- The *literature review* is generally as important in qualitative write-ups as quantitative ones. Indeed, especially when using qualitative methods in relation to applied topics, you may find that you need to refer to research and theory based on quantitative methods as well as qualitative research. While it is not common for quantitative methods to be looking at exactly the same issues as qualitative studies, there are circumstances in which each can inform the other. Although professional publications using conversation analysis often have very few references (as conversation analysis sees itself as data-driven and not theory-driven in terms of analysis), we would not recommend that students emulate this. As in any other writing you do as a student, we would recommend that you demonstrate the depth and extent of your reading of the relevant literature in your writings. You cannot expect credit for something that you have not done.

- Although preliminary *hypotheses* are inappropriate for most qualitative analyses (since hypotheses come from a different tradition in psychological research), you should be very clear about the aims of your research in your report. This helps to focus the reader in terms of your data collection and analysis as well as demonstrating the purposive nature of your research. In other words, clearly stated *aims* are a helpful part of telling the 'story' of your research.

- The *method* section for a qualitative report should be comparable to one for a quantitative report in scope and level of detail. There are numerous methods of data collection in qualitative research so it is impossible to give detailed suggestions which apply to each of these. Nevertheless, there is a temptation to give too little detail when reporting qualitative methods since often the methods are quite simple compared with the procedures adopted in some laboratory studies, for example. So it is best to be precise about the procedures used even though these may at times appear to be relatively simple and straightforward compared with other forms of research.

- Too frequently qualitative analysts fail to give sufficient detail about how they carried out their analysis. Writing things like 'a grounded theory analysis was performed' or 'thematic analysis was employed' is to say too little. There is more to qualitative analysis than this and great variation in how analyses are carried out. To the reader, such brief statements may read more like an attempt to mystify the analysis process than to elucidate important detail. It is especially important for students to explain in some detail about how they went about their analysis since, by doing so, not only does the reader get a clearer idea about the analytic procedures employed but the student demonstrates their understanding and mastery of the method. As ever in report writing, it is very difficult to stipulate just how much detail should be given – judgement is involved in this rather than rules – but we would suggest that it is best to err on the side of too much detail.

- There is a difficulty in deciding just how much data should be presented in a report. A few in-depth interviews can add up to quite a bulky number of pages of transcripts. However, in terms of self-presentation, these transcripts (especially if they involved Jefferson transcription methods) are a testament to how carefully and thoroughly the researcher carried out the analysis. Not to include them in your report as an appendix means that the reader has no idea of the amount of effort that went into your analysis but, also, the reader is denied the opportunity to check the analysis or to get a full picture of what happened in the interviews. Normally transcriptions do not count towards word limits though you might wish to check this locally with your lecturers.

- You should make sure that you include analysis in your report – sometimes researchers simply reproduce numerous quotations from their data which are weakly linked together by a simple narrative. This may not constitute an analysis at all in a meaningful sense of the term. A commentary on a few quotations is not what is meant by qualitative analysis.

- Your analytic claims should actually be supported by the data. So you need to check that your interpretation of your data actually is reflected in the excerpts that you use.

- It is possible to be systematic in the presentation of your analysis of qualitative data. A good example of this is the way in which IPA analysts (see Chapter 24) produce tables to illustrate the themes which they identify. In this way, themes can be linked hierarchically and illustrative excerpts from the data included for each theme in a systematic manner.

- Furthermore, with thematic analysis especially, it can be very helpful to give some basic statistical information about the number of interviews, for example, in which the theme was to be found or some other indication of their rates of occurrence.

- When it comes to discussing the findings from your qualitative research, you will find numerous criteria by which the adequacy of a qualitative study can be assessed in this chapter. Why not incorporate some of these criteria when evaluating your research findings?

25.4 Criteria for novices

There is probably no qualitative study that effectively embraces all of the criteria of quality that we have discussed. The criteria are not normally discussed within a qualitative report and are more often referred to in theoretical discussions of qualitative methodology. Hence, it is difficult to provide researchers new to qualitative research with a well-established set of procedures which serve as routine quality assurance checks. In this way, quantitative research is very different. Significance testing, reliability estimates, validity coefficients and so forth are minimum quality indicators. Similarly, the literature review is part of the process of assessing the worth of the new findings. Of course, many other indicators of quality are neglected in quantitative reports, just as they often are in qualitative ones.

While these criteria of the worth of a qualitative study can be seen to be intrinsically of value (once the intellectual roots of qualitative research are understood), it is likely that the complexity of the criteria will defeat some novice researchers in the field. They certainly do not gel as a set of principles to help launch good-quality qualitative research by newcomers. So in this section we will suggest some of the criteria which beginners might wish to adopt as a more pragmatic pathway to successful qualitative research (see also Figure 25.2):

- Have you immersed yourself in the qualitative research literature or undergone training in qualitative research? Analytic success is a long journey and you need to understand where you are heading.

- Why are you not doing a quantitative analysis? Have you really done a quantitative analysis badly and called it qualitative research?

- Can you identify the specific qualitative method that you are using and why? Qualitative research is not an amorphous mass but a set of sometimes interlinking approaches.

Quality criteria for novice researcher

- Have you studied qualitative research methods in some depth?
- Can you justify not doing quantitative research?
- Do you know what specific qualitative method to use and why it is appropriate?
- Have you got the personal resources and skills to do qualitative research?
- Have you coded all of your data? If not, can you explain why not?
- Have you spent a great deal of effort refining your codings and categories?
- Precisely what parts of your data are accounted for by your analytic categories?
- How deeply were you engaged in your

FIGURE 25.2 Some quality indicators for novice researchers

- What resources are you devoting to your data collection and analysis? Qualitative data analysis probably requires more personal research skills than much quantitative data analysis. It requires a good interviewing technique, for example, to obtain the richness of data required. Qualitative data require transcription (or quantitative coding), which is time-consuming and exacting. If you do not understand the point of this then your research is almost certainly of dubious quality.

- Have you coded or categorised *all* your data? If not, why not? How do you know that your categories work unless you have tested them thoroughly against the entirety of what you want to understand? If you can only point to instances of categories you wish to use then how do you know that you have a satisfactory fit of your categories with the data?

- Has there been a process of refining your categories? Or have you merely used categories from other research or thought of a few categories without these being worked up through revisions of the data?

- Can you say precisely what parts of your data fit your categories? Phrases such as 'Many participants . . .', 'Frequently . . .' and 'Some . . .' should not be used to cover up woolliness about how your data are coded.

- How deeply engaged were you in the analysis? Did it come easily? If so, have you taken advantage of the special gains which may result from qualitative research?

25.5 Conclusion

Very few of the traditional criteria which we apply to quantitative research apply to qualitative research directly. They simply do not have the same intellectual roots and, to some extent, they are in conflict. There are a number of criteria for evaluating qualitative research, but these largely concentrate on evaluating the quality of the coding or categorisation process (the qualitative analysis). These criteria can be applied but, as yet, there is no way of deciding whether the study is of sufficient quality. They are merely indicators. This contrasts markedly with quantitative and statistical research where there are rules of thumb which may be applied to decide on the worth of the research. Significance testing is one obvious example of this when we apply a test of whether the data are likely to have been obtained simply by sampling fluctuations. Internal consistency measures of reliability such as alpha also have such cut-off rules. This leaves it a little uncertain how inexperienced qualitative researchers can evaluate their research. It is clearly the case that qualitative researchers need to reflect on the value of their analysis as much as any other researcher.

Key points

- Since qualitative research is a reaction to positivism and its influence on research, qualitative research needs to be evaluated in part in its own terms.

- Some criteria apply to both quantitative and qualitative research. The criteria include how the research is located in relation to previously published research, the coherence and persuasiveness of the argument, the strength of the analysis to impose structure on the data, the potential of the research to stimulate further research or the originality and quantity of new insights arising from the research, and the usefulness of applicability of the research.

- Yet other criteria which may be applied are much more specific to qualitative research. These include the correspondence of the analysis with the participant's own understandings, the openness of the report to evaluation, the ability of the analysis to deal with otherwise deviant instances in the data, the richness of detail in the analysis, which is dependent on the richness of the data in part, and how clearly the process of developing the analysis is presented.

- The criteria that novice researchers use to evaluate their own research may be a little more routine. Considerations include factors related to the amount of effort devoted to developing the analysis, the degree to which the analysis embraces the totality of the data, and even questioning whether a quantitative study would have been more appropriate anyway.

ACTIVITIES

1. Could a qualitative researcher simply make up their analysis and get away with it? List the factors that stop this happening.

2. Develop a set of principles by which all research could be evaluated.

Tables

Table A1 - z-scores and the proportion of the standard normal distribution falling above and below each score

z-score	prop. below score	prop. above score	z-score	prop. below score	prop. above score
0.00	0.5000	0.5000	0.49	0.6879	0.3121
0.01	0.5040	0.4960	0.50	0.6915	0.3085
0.02	0.5080	0.4920	0.51	0.6950	0.3050
0.03	0.5120	0.4880	0.52	0.6985	0.3015
0.04	0.5160	0.4840	0.53	0.7019	0.2981
0.05	0.5199	0.4801	0.54	0.7054	0.2946
0.06	0.5239	0.4761	0.55	0.7088	0.2912
0.07	0.5279	0.4721	0.56	0.7123	0.2877
0.08	0.5319	0.4681	0.57	0.7157	0.2843
0.09	0.5359	0.4641	0.58	0.7190	0.2810
0.10	0.5398	0.4602	0.59	0.7224	0.2776
0.11	0.5438	0.4562	0.60	0.7257	0.2743
0.12	0.5478	0.4522	0.61	0.7291	0.2709
0.13	0.5517	0.4483	0.62	0.7324	0.2676
0.14	0.5557	0.4443	0.63	0.7357	0.2643
0.15	0.5596	0.4404	0.64	0.7389	0.2611
0.16	0.5636	0.4364	0.65	0.7422	0.2578
0.17	0.5675	0.4325	0.66	0.7454	0.2546
0.18	0.5714	0.4286	0.67	0.7486	0.2514
0.19	0.5753	0.4247	0.68	0.7517	0.2483
0.20	0.5793	0.4207	0.69	0.7549	0.2451
0.21	0.5832	0.4168	0.70	0.7580	0.2420
0.22	0.5871	0.4129	0.71	0.7611	0.2389
0.23	0.5910	0.4090	0.72	0.7642	0.2358
0.24	0.5948	0.4052	0.73	0.7673	0.2327
0.25	0.5987	0.4013	0.74	0.7704	0.2296
0.26	0.6026	0.3974	0.75	0.7734	0.2266
0.27	0.6064	0.3936	0.76	0.7764	0.2236
0.28	0.6103	0.3897	0.77	0.7794	0.2206
0.29	0.6141	0.3859	0.78	0.7823	0.2177
0.30	0.6179	0.3821	0.79	0.7852	0.2148
0.31	0.6217	0.3783	0.80	0.7881	0.2119
0.32	0.6255	0.3745	0.81	0.7910	0.2090
0.33	0.6293	0.3707	0.82	0.7939	0.2061
0.34	0.6331	0.3669	0.83	0.7967	0.2033
0.35	0.6368	0.3632	0.84	0.7995	0.2005
0.36	0.6406	0.3594	0.85	0.8023	0.1977
0.37	0.6443	0.3557	0.86	0.8051	0.1949
0.38	0.6480	0.3520	0.87	0.8078	0.1922
0.39	0.6517	0.3483	0.88	0.8106	0.1894
0.40	0.6554	0.3446	0.89	0.8133	0.1867
0.41	0.6591	0.3409	0.90	0.8159	0.1841
0.42	0.6628	0.3372	0.91	0.8186	0.1814
0.43	0.6664	0.3336	0.92	0.8212	0.1788
0.44	0.6700	0.3300	0.93	0.8238	0.1762
0.45	0.6736	0.3264	0.94	0.8264	0.1736
0.46	0.6772	0.3228	0.95	0.8289	0.1711
0.47	0.6808	0.3192	0.96	0.8315	0.1685
0.48	0.6844	0.3156	0.97	0.8340	0.1660

Table A1 - (Continued)

z-score	prop. below score	prop. above score	z-score	prop. below score	prop. above score
0.98	0.8365	0.1635	1.47	0.9292	0.0708
0.99	0.8389	0.1611	1.48	0.9306	0.0694
1.00	0.8413	0.1587	1.49	0.9319	0.0681
1.01	0.8438	0.1562	1.50	0.9332	0.0668
1.02	0.8461	0.1539	1.51	0.9345	0.0655
1.03	0.8485	0.1515	1.52	0.9357	0.0643
1.04	0.8508	0.1492	1.53	0.9370	0.0630
1.05	0.8531	0.1469	1.54	0.9382	0.0618
1.06	0.8554	0.1446	1.55	0.9394	0.0606
1.07	0.8577	0.1423	1.56	0.9406	0.0594
1.08	0.8599	0.1401	1.57	0.9418	0.0582
1.09	0.8621	0.1379	1.58	0.9429	0.0571
1.10	0.8643	0.1357	1.59	0.9441	0.0559
1.11	0.8665	0.1335	1.60	0.9452	0.0548
1.12	0.8686	0.1314	1.61	0.9463	0.0537
1.13	0.8708	0.1292	1.62	0.9474	0.0526
1.14	0.8729	0.1271	1.63	0.9484	0.0516
1.15	0.8749	0.1251	1.64	0.9495	0.0505
1.16	0.8770	0.1230	1.65	0.9505	0.0495
1.17	0.8790	0.1210	1.66	0.9515	0.0485
1.18	0.8810	0.1190	1.67	0.9525	0.0475
1.19	0.8830	0.1170	1.68	0.9535	0.0465
1.20	0.8849	0.1151	1.69	0.9545	0.0455
1.21	0.8869	0.1131	1.70	0.9554	0.0446
1.22	0.8888	0.1112	1.71	0.9564	0.0436
1.23	0.8907	0.1093	1.72	0.9573	0.0427
1.24	0.8925	0.1075	1.73	0.9582	0.0418
1.25	0.8944	0.1056	1.74	0.9591	0.0409
1.26	0.8962	0.1038	1.75	0.9599	0.0401
1.27	0.8980	0.1020	1.76	0.9608	0.0392
1.28	0.8997	0.1003	1.77	0.9616	0.0384
1.29	0.9015	0.0985	1.78	0.9625	0.0375
1.30	0.9032	0.0968	1.79	0.9633	0.0367
1.31	0.9049	0.0951	1.80	0.9641	0.0359
1.32	0.9066	0.0934	1.81	0.9649	0.0351
1.33	0.9082	0.0918	1.82	0.9656	0.0344
1.34	0.9099	0.0901	1.83	0.9664	0.0336
1.35	0.9115	0.0885	1.84	0.9671	0.0329
1.36	0.9131	0.0869	1.85	0.9678	0.0322
1.37	0.9147	0.0853	1.86	0.9686	0.0314
1.38	0.9162	0.0838	1.87	0.9693	0.0307
1.39	0.9177	0.0823	1.88	0.9699	0.0301
1.40	0.9192	0.0808	1.89	0.9706	0.0294
1.41	0.9207	0.0793	1.90	0.9713	0.0287
1.42	0.9222	0.0778	1.91	0.9719	0.0281
1.43	0.9236	0.0764	1.92	0.9726	0.0274
1.44	0.9251	0.0749	1.93	0.9732	0.0268
1.45	0.9265	0.0735	1.94	0.9738	0.0262
1.46	0.9279	0.0721	1.95	0.9744	0.0256

Table A1 - (Continued)

z-score	prop. below score	prop. above score	z-score	prop. below score	prop. above score
1.96	0.9750	0.0250	2.45	0.9929	0.0071
1.97	0.9756	0.0244	2.46	0.9931	0.0069
1.98	0.9761	0.0239	2.47	0.9932	0.0068
1.99	0.9767	0.0233	2.48	0.9934	0.0066
2.00	0.9772	0.0228	2.49	0.9936	0.0064
2.01	0.9778	0.0222	2.50	0.9938	0.0062
2.02	0.9783	0.0217	2.51	0.9940	0.0060
2.03	0.9788	0.0212	2.52	0.9941	0.0059
2.04	0.9793	0.0207	2.53	0.9943	0.0057
2.05	0.9798	0.0202	2.54	0.9945	0.0055
2.06	0.9803	0.0197	2.55	0.9946	0.0054
2.07	0.9808	0.0192	2.56	0.9948	0.0052
2.08	0.9812	0.0188	2.57	0.9949	0.0051
2.09	0.9817	0.0183	2.58	0.9951	0.0049
2.10	0.9821	0.0179	2.59	0.9952	0.0048
2.11	0.9826	0.0174	2.60	0.9953	0.0047
2.12	0.9830	0.0170	2.61	0.9955	0.0045
2.13	0.9834	0.0166	2.62	0.9956	0.0044
2.14	0.9838	0.0162	2.63	0.9957	0.0043
2.15	0.9842	0.0158	2.64	0.9959	0.0041
2.16	0.9846	0.0154	2.65	0.9960	0.0040
2.17	0.9850	0.0150	2.66	0.9961	0.0039
2.18	0.9854	0.0146	2.67	0.9962	0.0038
2.19	0.9857	0.0143	2.68	0.9963	0.0037
2.20	0.9861	0.0139	2.69	0.9964	0.0036
2.21	0.9864	0.0136	2.70	0.9965	0.0035
2.22	0.9868	0.0132	2.71	0.9966	0.0034
2.23	0.9871	0.0129	2.72	0.9967	0.0033
2.24	0.9875	0.0125	2.73	0.9968	0.0032
2.25	0.9878	0.0122	2.74	0.9969	0.0031
2.26	0.9881	0.0119	2.75	0.9970	0.0030
2.27	0.9884	0.0116	2.76	0.9971	0.0029
2.28	0.9887	0.0113	2.77	0.9972	0.0028
2.29	0.9890	0.0110	2.78	0.9973	0.0027
2.30	0.9893	0.0107	2.79	0.9974	0.0026
2.31	0.9896	0.0104	2.80	0.9974	0.0026
2.32	0.9898	0.0102	2.81	0.9975	0.0025
2.33	0.9901	0.0099	2.82	0.9976	0.0024
2.34	0.9904	0.0096	2.83	0.9977	0.0023
2.35	0.9906	0.0094	2.84	0.9977	0.0023
2.36	0.9909	0.0091	2.85	0.9978	0.0022
2.37	0.9911	0.0089	2.86	0.9979	0.0021
2.38	0.9913	0.0087	2.87	0.9979	0.0021
2.39	0.9916	0.0084	2.88	0.9980	0.0020
2.40	0.9918	0.0082	2.89	0.9981	0.0019
2.41	0.9920	0.0080	2.90	0.9981	0.0019
2.42	0.9922	0.0078	2.91	0.9982	0.0018
2.43	0.9925	0.0075	2.92	0.9982	0.0018
2.44	0.9927	0.0073	2.93	0.9983	0.0017

Table A1 - (Continued)

z-score	prop. below score	prop. above score
2.94	0.9984	0.0016
2.95	0.9984	0.0016
2.96	0.9985	0.0015
2.97	0.9985	0.0015
2.98	0.9986	0.0014
2.99	0.9986	0.0014
3.00	0.9987	0.0013

Table A2 - r to zr

r	zr	r	zr	r	zr	r	zr	r	zr
0.0000	0.000	0.2000	0.203	0.4000	0.424	0.6000	0.693	0.8000	1.099
0.0050	0.005	0.2050	0.208	0.4050	0.430	0.6050	0.701	0.8050	1.113
0.0100	0.010	0.2100	0.213	0.4100	0.436	0.6100	0.709	0.8100	1.127
0.0150	0.015	0.2150	0.218	0.4150	0.442	0.6150	0.717	0.8150	1.142
0.0200	0.020	0.2200	0.224	0.4200	0.448	0.6200	0.725	0.8200	1.157
0.0250	0.025	0.2250	0.229	0.4250	0.454	0.6250	0.733	0.8250	1.172
0.0300	0.030	0.2300	0.234	0.4300	0.460	0.6300	0.741	0.8300	1.188
0.0350	0.035	0.2350	0.239	0.4350	0.466	0.6350	0.750	0.8350	1.204
0.0400	0.040	0.2400	0.245	0.4400	0.472	0.6400	0.758	0.8400	1.221
0.0450	0.045	0.2450	0.250	0.4450	0.478	0.6450	0.767	0.8450	1.238
0.0500	0.050	0.2500	0.255	0.4500	0.485	0.6500	0.775	0.8500	1.256
0.0550	0.055	0.2550	0.261	0.4550	0.491	0.6550	0.784	0.8550	1.274
0.0600	0.060	0.2600	0.266	0.4600	0.497	0.6600	0.793	0.8600	1.293
0.0650	0.065	0.2650	0.271	0.4650	0.504	0.6650	0.802	0.8650	1.313
0.0700	0.070	0.2700	0.277	0.4700	0.510	0.6700	0.811	0.8700	1.333
0.0750	0.075	0.2750	0.282	0.4750	0.517	0.6750	0.820	0.8750	1.354
0.0800	0.080	0.2800	0.288	0.4800	0.523	0.6800	0.829	0.8800	1.376
0.0850	0.085	0.2850	0.293	0.4850	0.530	0.6850	0.838	0.8850	1.398
0.0900	0.090	0.2900	0.299	0.4900	0.536	0.6900	0.848	0.8900	1.422
0.0950	0.095	0.2950	0.304	0.4950	0.543	0.6950	0.858	0.8950	1.447
0.1000	0.100	0.3000	0.310	0.5000	0.549	0.7000	0.867	0.9000	1.472
0.1050	0.105	0.3050	0.315	0.5050	0.556	0.7050	0.877	0.9050	1.499
0.1100	0.110	0.3100	0.321	0.5100	0.563	0.7100	0.887	0.9100	1.528
0.1150	0.116	0.3150	0.326	0.5150	0.570	0.7150	0.897	0.9150	1.557
0.1200	0.121	0.3200	0.332	0.5200	0.576	0.7200	0.908	0.9200	1.589
0.1250	0.126	0.3250	0.337	0.5250	0.583	0.7250	0.918	0.9250	1.623
0.1300	0.131	0.3300	0.343	0.5300	0.590	0.7300	0.929	0.9300	1.658
0.1350	0.136	0.3350	0.348	0.5350	0.597	0.7350	0.940	0.9350	1.697
0.1400	0.141	0.3400	0.354	0.5400	0.604	0.7400	0.950	0.9400	1.738
0.1450	0.146	0.3450	0.360	0.5450	0.611	0.7450	0.962	0.9450	1.783
0.1500	0.151	0.3500	0.365	0.5500	0.618	0.7500	0.973	0.9500	1.832
0.1550	0.156	0.3550	0.371	0.5550	0.626	0.7550	0.984	0.9550	1.886
0.1600	0.161	0.3600	0.377	0.5600	0.633	0.7600	0.996	0.9600	1.946
0.1650	0.167	0.3650	0.383	0.5650	0.640	0.7650	1.008	0.9650	2.014
0.1700	0.172	0.3700	0.388	0.5700	0.648	0.7700	1.020	0.9700	2.092
0.1750	0.177	0.3750	0.394	0.5750	0.655	0.7750	1.033	0.9750	2.185
0.1800	0.182	0.3800	0.400	0.5800	0.662	0.7800	1.045	0.9800	2.298
0.1850	0.187	0.3850	0.406	0.5850	0.670	0.7850	1.058	0.9850	2.443
0.1900	0.192	0.3900	0.412	0.5900	0.678	0.7900	1.071	0.9900	2.647
0.1950	0.198	0.3950	0.418	0.5950	0.685	0.7950	1.085	0.9950	2.994

Table A3 - Critical values for student's t-distribution

v (= df)	One-tailed Significance			
	0.05	0.025	0.01	0.005
	Two-tailed Significance			
	0.1	0.05	0.02	0.01
2	2.920	4.303	6.965	9.925
3	2.353	3.182	4.541	5.841
4	2.132	2.776	3.747	4.604
5	2.015	2.571	3.365	4.032
6	1.943	2.447	3.143	3.707
7	1.895	2.365	2.998	3.499
8	1.860	2.306	2.896	3.355
9	1.833	2.262	2.821	3.250
10	1.812	2.228	2.764	3.169
11	1.796	2.201	2.718	3.106
12	1.782	2.179	2.681	3.055
13	1.771	2.160	2.650	3.012
14	1.761	2.145	2.624	2.977
15	1.753	2.131	2.602	2.947
16	1.746	2.120	2.583	2.921
17	1.740	2.110	2.567	2.898
18	1.734	2.101	2.552	2.878
19	1.729	2.093	2.539	2.861
20	1.725	2.086	2.528	2.845
21	1.721	2.080	2.518	2.831
22	1.717	2.074	2.508	2.819
23	1.714	2.069	2.500	2.807
24	1.711	2.064	2.492	2.797
25	1.708	2.060	2.485	2.787
26	1.706	2.056	2.479	2.779
27	1.703	2.052	2.473	2.771
28	1.701	2.048	2.467	2.763
29	1.699	2.045	2.462	2.756
30	1.697	2.042	2.457	2.750
35	1.690	2.030	2.438	2.724
40	1.684	2.021	2.423	2.704
45	1.679	2.014	2.412	2.690
50	1.676	2.009	2.403	2.678
55	1.673	2.004	2.396	2.668
60	1.671	2.000	2.390	2.660
65	1.669	1.997	2.385	2.654
70	1.667	1.994	2.381	2.648
75	1.665	1.992	2.377	2.643
80	1.664	1.990	2.374	2.639
85	1.663	1.988	2.371	2.635
90	1.662	1.987	2.368	2.632
95	1.661	1.985	2.366	2.629
100	1.660	1.984	2.364	2.626
200	1.653	1.972	2.345	2.601
300	1.650	1.968	2.339	2.592
400	1.649	1.966	2.336	2.588
500	1.648	1.965	2.334	2.586
1000	1.646	1.962	2.330	2.581
∞	1.645	1.960	2.326	2.576

Table A4 - Critical values for the Pearson correlation coefficient

	One-tailed Significance			
	0.05	0.025	0.01	0.005
	Two-tailed Significance			
N (=df+2)	0.1	0.05	0.02	0.01
4	0.900	0.950	0.980	0.990
5	0.805	0.878	0.934	0.959
6	0.729	0.811	0.882	0.917
7	0.669	0.754	0.833	0.875
8	0.621	0.707	0.789	0.834
9	0.582	0.666	0.750	0.798
10	0.549	0.632	0.715	0.765
11	0.521	0.602	0.685	0.735
12	0.497	0.576	0.658	0.708
13	0.476	0.553	0.634	0.684
14	0.458	0.532	0.612	0.661
15	0.441	0.514	0.592	0.641
16	0.426	0.497	0.574	0.623
17	0.412	0.482	0.558	0.606
18	0.400	0.468	0.543	0.590
19	0.389	0.456	0.529	0.575
20	0.378	0.444	0.516	0.561
21	0.369	0.433	0.503	0.549
22	0.360	0.423	0.492	0.537
23	0.352	0.413	0.482	0.526
24	0.344	0.404	0.472	0.515
25	0.337	0.396	0.462	0.505
26	0.330	0.388	0.453	0.496
27	0.323	0.381	0.445	0.487
28	0.317	0.374	0.437	0.479
29	0.311	0.367	0.430	0.471
30	0.306	0.361	0.423	0.463
35	0.283	0.334	0.392	0.430
40	0.264	0.312	0.367	0.403
45	0.248	0.294	0.346	0.380
50	0.235	0.279	0.328	0.361
55	0.224	0.266	0.313	0.345
60	0.214	0.254	0.300	0.330
65	0.206	0.244	0.288	0.317
70	0.198	0.235	0.278	0.306
75	0.191	0.227	0.268	0.296
80	0.185	0.220	0.260	0.286
85	0.180	0.213	0.252	0.278
90	0.174	0.207	0.245	0.270
95	0.170	0.202	0.238	0.263
100	0.165	0.197	0.232	0.256
200	0.117	0.139	0.164	0.182
300	0.095	0.113	0.134	0.149
400	0.082	0.098	0.116	0.129
500	0.074	0.088	0.104	0.115
1000	0.052	0.062	0.074	0.081

Table A5 - Critical values for the chi-square distribution

df	0.1	0.05	0.025	0.01	0.005
1	2.706	3.841	5.024	6.635	7.879
2	4.605	5.991	7.378	9.210	10.597
3	6.251	7.815	9.348	11.345	12.838
4	7.779	9.488	11.143	13.277	14.860
5	9.236	11.070	12.833	15.086	16.750
6	10.645	12.592	14.449	16.812	18.548
7	12.017	14.067	16.013	18.475	20.278
8	13.362	15.507	17.535	20.090	21.955
9	14.684	16.919	19.023	21.666	23.589
10	15.987	18.307	20.483	23.209	25.188
11	17.275	19.675	21.920	24.725	26.757
12	18.549	21.026	23.337	26.217	28.300
13	19.812	22.362	24.736	27.688	29.819
14	21.064	23.685	26.119	29.141	31.319
15	22.307	24.996	27.488	30.578	32.801
16	23.542	26.296	28.845	32.000	34.267
17	24.769	27.587	30.191	33.409	35.718
18	25.989	28.869	31.526	34.805	37.156
19	27.204	30.144	32.852	36.191	38.582
20	28.412	31.410	34.170	37.566	39.997
21	29.615	32.671	35.479	38.932	41.401
22	30.813	33.924	36.781	40.289	42.796
23	32.007	35.172	38.076	41.638	44.181
24	33.196	36.415	39.364	42.980	45.559
25	34.382	37.652	40.646	44.314	46.928
26	35.563	38.885	41.923	45.642	48.290
27	36.741	40.113	43.195	46.963	49.645
28	37.916	41.337	44.461	48.278	50.993
29	39.087	42.557	45.722	49.588	52.336
30	40.256	43.773	46.979	50.892	53.672
40	51.805	55.758	59.342	63.691	66.766
50	63.167	67.505	71.420	76.154	79.490
60	74.397	79.082	83.298	88.379	91.952
70	85.527	90.531	95.023	100.425	104.215
80	96.578	101.879	106.629	112.329	116.321
90	107.565	113.145	118.136	124.116	128.299
100	118.498	124.342	129.561	135.807	140.169

One-tailed Significance

Table A6 – Critical values for the Mann–Whitney U-test: 5% level of significance

N_B	1	2	3	4	5	6	7	8	9	10	11	12	13	14	15	16	17	18	19	20
N_A																				
1	–	–	–	–	–	–	–	–	–	–	–	–	–	–	–	–	–	–	–	–
2	–	–	–	–	–	–	–	0	0	0	0	1	1	1	1	1	2	2	2	2
3	–	–	–	–	0	1	1	2	2	3	3	4	4	5	5	6	6	7	7	8
4	–	–	–	–	–	–	3	4	4	5	6	7	8	9	10	11	11	12	13	13
5	–	0	1	2	2	3	5	6	7	8	9	10	12	13	14	15	17	18	19	20
6	–	–	–	–	–	5	6	8	10	11	13	14	16	17	19	21	22	24	25	27
7	–	–	–	–	–	–	8	10	12	14	16	18	20	22	24	26	28	30	32	34
8	–	–	–	–	–	–	–	13	15	17	19	22	24	26	29	31	34	36	38	41
9	–	–	–	–	–	–	–	–	17	20	23	26	28	31	34	37	39	42	45	48
10	–	–	–	–	–	–	–	–	–	23	26	29	33	36	39	42	45	48	52	55
11	–	–	–	–	–	–	–	–	–	–	30	33	37	40	44	47	51	55	58	62
12	–	–	–	–	–	–	–	–	–	–	–	37	41	45	49	53	57	61	65	69
13	–	–	–	–	–	–	–	–	–	–	–	–	45	50	54	59	63	67	72	76
14	–	–	–	–	–	–	–	–	–	–	–	–	–	55	59	64	67	74	78	83
15	–	–	–	–	–	–	–	–	–	–	–	–	–	–	64	70	75	80	85	90
16	–	–	–	–	–	–	–	–	–	–	–	–	–	–	–	75	81	86	92	98
17	–	–	–	–	–	–	–	–	–	–	–	–	–	–	–	–	87	93	99	105
18	–	–	–	–	–	–	–	–	–	–	–	–	–	–	–	–	–	99	106	112
19	–	–	–	–	–	–	–	–	–	–	–	–	–	–	–	–	–	–	113	119
20	–	–	–	–	–	–	–	–	–	–	–	–	–	–	–	–	–	–	–	127

Table A7– Critical values of the Spearman correlation coefficient

	One-tailed test			
	0.05	0.025	0.01	0.005
	Two-tailed test			
N	0.1	0.05	0.02	0.01
5	0.900			
6	0.829	0.886	0.943	
7	0.714	0.786	0.893	
8	0.643	0.738	0.833	0.881
9	0.600	0.683	0.783	0.833
10	0.564	0.648	0.745	0.858
11	0.520	0.620	0.737	0.814
12	0.496	0.591	0.703	0.776
13	0.475	0.566	0.673	0.743
14	0.456	0.544	0.646	0.714
15	0.440	0.524	0.623	0.688
16	0.425	0.506	0.602	0.665
17	0.411	0.490	0.583	0.644
18	0.399	0.475	0.565	0.625
19	0.388	0.462	0.549	0.607
20	0.377	0.450	0.535	0.591
21	0.368	0.438	0.521	0.576
22	0.359	0.428	0.508	0.562
23	0.351	0.418	0.497	0.549
24	0.343	0.409	0.486	0.537
25	0.336	0.400	0.476	0.526
26	0.329	0.392	0.466	0.515
27	0.323	0.384	0.457	0.505
28	0.317	0.377	0.448	0.496
29	0.311	0.370	0.440	0.487
30	0.305	0.364	0.433	0.478
35	0.282	0.336	0.400	0.442
40	0.263	0.314	0.373	0.412
45	0.248	0.295	0.351	0.388
50	0.235	0.280	0.333	0.368
60	0.214	0.255	0.303	0.335
70	0.198	0.236	0.280	0.310
80	0.185	0.221	0.262	0.290
90	0.174	0.208	0.247	0.273
100	0.165	0.197	0.234	0.259
200	0.117	0.139	0.165	0.183
300	0.095	0.113	0.135	0.149
400	0.082	0.098	0.117	0.129
500	0.074	0.088	0.104	0.115
1000	0.052	0.062	0.074	0.081

Adapted from Howitt, D. and Cramer, D. (2000). *An Introduction to Statistics in Psychology*, 2nd edn. Harlow, UK: Prentice Hall.

Table A8 – Critical values of the Wilcoxon Signed Rank Test

	One-tailed test		
	0.025	0.01	0.05
	Two-tailed test		
N	0.05	0.02	0.01
6	2	1	
7	4	2	
8	6	4	0
9	8	4	2
10	11	8	3
11	14	11	5
12	17	14	7
13	21	17	10
14	26	21	13
15	31	25	16
16	36	30	20
17	42	35	24
18	47	40	28
19	54	46	33
20	60	52	37
21	68	59	42
22	76	66	47
23	84	74	54
24	92	81	60
25	101	90	67